The Land and People of

THE SOVIET UNION

The Land and People of ®
THE SOVIET UNION

by *William G. Andrews*

HarperCollins*Publishers*

To
THOMAS
Fellow Sufferer
on the
Cross of Knowledge

Country maps by Joe LeMonnier
Suggestions for Further Reading edited by Gilbert McArthur
Adaptations on pages 29, 48–49, 51, 56, 62–63 by Helen Speransky
Every effort has been made to locate the copyright holders of all copyrighted materials and to secure
the necessary permission to reproduce them. In the event of any questions arising as to their use, the
publisher will be glad to make necessary changes in future printings and editions.
Acknowledgments appear on page 294.

THE LAND AND PEOPLE OF
is a registered trademark of
HarperCollins Publishers.

Library of Congress Cataloging-in-Publication Data
Andrews, William George, date
    The land and people of the Soviet Union/by William G. Andrews.
    p.   cm. — (Portraits of the nations series)
    Includes bibliographical references.
    Summary: Introduces the history, geography, people, culture,
government, and economy of the Soviet Union.
    ISBN 0-06-020034-0.—ISBN 0-06-020035-9 (lib. bdg.)
    1. Soviet Union—History—Juvenile literature. 2.Soviet Union—
Geography—Juvenile literature. [1. Soviet Union.] I.Title
II.Series
DK40.A48   1991   90-5746
947—dc20   CIP
                                                               AC

1 2 3 4 5 6 7 8 9 10
First Edition

Contents

IV   From Tsarism to Bolshevism

The Russian Revolutionary Tradition; The Reign of Nicholas II; The Fatal Crisis

V   Bolshevism in Power

Lenin in Power; Stalin's Despotism

VI   Bolshevism in Decline

Khrushchev's Thaw; Brezhnev's Stagnation; Gorbachev's Challenge

VII   A Nation of Nationalities

Population and Demographics; The Peoples of the Soviet Union

Preface

The purpose of this book is to provide a short survey of the Soviet Union for libraries. That apparently simple task is, in fact, very complex. First, of course, the topic is enormous, requiring painful selection and compression of material. Second, the Soviet Union changed with breathtaking speed while the manuscript was being written. The temptation to chase headlines has been tantalizing—but resisted. All material is as current as possible, but unfolding events have not been chronicled.

The frustrations of treating the Soviet Union in such brief compass loom at every turning. Drastic simplification is unavoidable. This is especially true in the historical chapters. The Soviet peoples have immensely long, rich, and varied histories, much of them obscure and subject to heated controversy. The constraints of a survey, however, preclude discussion of the many contending theories and approaches.

Another device to ease those frustrations is the use of themes that weave through the text. These may help the reader find the way and fit the mass of information into a more coherent and understandable pattern. One theme is the recurring paradox of frustrated opportunities that has thwarted Russian and Soviet ambitions so often. Another is the corrosive combination of ideological obsession and inadequate leadership that has plagued the peoples of that great land so relentlessly. Nevertheless, too much should not be made of the themes. They are guides, not scientific theories or laws.

The temptation is great, also, to add cohesion and meaning to Soviet affairs by systematic comparison with the United States. The late, unlamented Cold War generated such a sense of rivalry between the two powers that study of one seemed incomplete without constant reference to the other. Impressions of good and evil in one seemed to require the discovery of comparable amounts of good and evil for the other.

This lure has been resisted also. This book mentions the United States only to give the reader points of reference, not to produce a balanced portrayal of the two countries. This book is not a comparative study. Nor is it intended to enhance the reader's understanding of the strengths and weaknesses of the United States. For that, the reader must turn elsewhere.

Against the frustrations of writing on the Soviet Union today must be set some very exciting opportunities. Chief among them is the sudden availability of information that previously had lain in the realm of speculation and obscurity. Mikhail Gorbachev's *glasnost* has unleashed an avalanche of reliable material on the Soviet Union for the first time. The researcher cannot resist a sense of exhilaration at being able to see Soviet life so clearly after long decades of wading through deceit and disinformation. Unfortunately, the usual space limitations prevent fuller use of the new material.

Readers who think that material unduly harsh may recall that earlier exposés were often considered similarly excessive, but were later seen as far too mild. The truth about the Soviet Union is often difficult to believe, because the system has been so incredibly rotten. If anything, this book is too soft, rather than too hard, on Soviet Communism. For example, the brief mention of Soviet environmental disasters does scant justice to their extent and magnitude.

All authors on the Soviet Union these days owe their first debt of gratitude to Mikhail Gorbachev and his courageous band of reformers. Without them, we would still be shadowboxing with Marxist-Leninist deceit. When I began subscribing to the *Moscow News* in the mid-1950's, it put forth that line unblinkingly. It contained not reliable information, but the official version of Soviet events, deadly dull but essential to understanding the official Soviet mind. Under Gorbachev, it has become a rich and exciting weekly news magazine and my single most important source.

Also, I am grateful to my colleagues, Robert W. Strayer, who read this manuscript with great care and made many useful suggestions and corrections, although his views often differ from mine; Mirko Pylyshenko, who shared with me valuable insights from his long experience living and traveling in the Soviet Union; and Barbara W. Jancar, longtime scholar and perceptive observer of Soviet affairs. The publisher's anonymous reviewer made many constructive comments, 90 percent of which I accepted. The staff of Drake Memorial Library was, as usual, unfailingly patient and helpful.

My editor at HarperCollins, Marc Aronson, has provided loyal and highly professional support and firm, but gentle, guidance. He and his assistant, Catharine K. Rigby, have gone far out of their way to be helpful and to show much more than perfunctory interest in this project, the author, and his family. After five years of collaboration on two major projects, I hope to meet him someday!

This has been my first experience assembling illustrations for a book. I received invaluable help from Vladimir Zaretsky of the Soviet embassy in Washington, the Novosti Press Agency (another practitioner of *glasnost*), the Library of Congress, and the Ukrainian mission to the United Nations. My wife, Monika, lent valuable assistance in the compiling of the index.

Finally, I never would have undertaken this book without the inspiration provided by my fellow social scientist to whom I dedicate it. Indeed, to contribute in some small measure to arousing and satisfying the intellectual curiosity of people like him is the *specific* purpose of this book.

—William G. Andrews
November 1990, Paris

THE WORLD

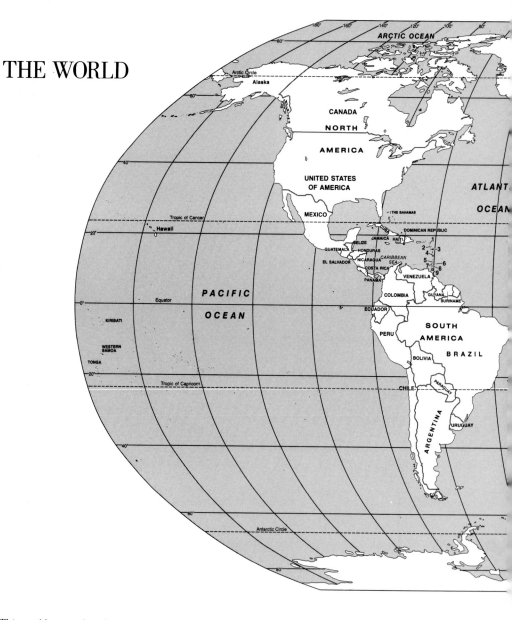

This world map is based on a projection developed by Arthur H. Robinson. The shape of each country and its size, relative to other countries, are more accurately expressed here than in previous maps. The map also gives equal importance to all of the continents, instead of placing North America at the center of the world. *Used by permission of the Foreign Policy Association.*

Legend

—— International boundaries

------- Disputed or undefined boundaries

Projection: Robinson

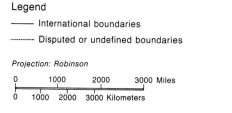

| 0 | 1000 | 2000 | 3000 Miles |

| 0 | 1000 | 2000 | 3000 Kilometers |

Caribbean Nations

1. Anguilla
2. St. Christopher and Nevis
3. Antigua and Barbuda
4. Dominica
5. St. Lucia
6. Barbados
7. St. Vincent
8. Grenada
9. Trinidad and Tobago

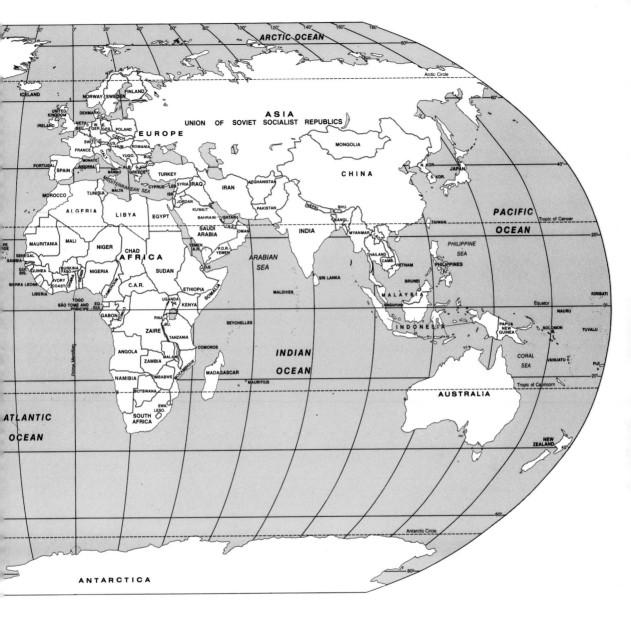

Abbreviations

ALB.	—Albania	C.A.R.	—Central African Republic	LEB.	—Lebanon	RWA.	—Rwanda
AUS.	—Austria	CZECH.	—Czechoslovakia	LESO.	—Lesotho	S. KOR.	—South Korea
BANGL.	—Bangladesh	DJI.	—Djibouti	LIE.	—Liechtenstein	SWA.	—Swaziland
BEL.	—Belgium	E.GER.	—East Germany	LUX.	—Luxemburg	SWITZ.	—Switzerland
BHU.	—Bhutan	EQ. GUI.	—Equatorial Guinea	NETH.	—Netherlands	U.A.E.	—United Arab Emirates
BU.	—Burundi	GUI. BIS.	—Guinea Bissau	N. KOR.	—North Korea	W. GER.	—West Germany
BUL.	—Bulgaria	HUN.	—Hungary	P.D.R.–YEMEN	—People's Democratic	YEMEN A.R.	—Yemen Arab Republic
CAMB.	—Cambodia	ISR.	—Israel		Republic of Yemen	YUGO.	—Yugoslavia

Mini Facts

OFFICIAL NAME: Union of Soviet Socialist Republics

LOCATION: Eastern Europe and North and Central Asia

AREA: 42% of the Eurasian land mass
8.65 million square miles (22.4 million square kilometers)
5,600 miles (10,000 kilometers) east–west; 2,800 miles (4,500 kilometers) north–south

CAPITAL: Moscow

POPULATION: 286,700,000 (1989)
third most populous nation in the world

MAJOR LANGUAGES: Russian, Ukrainian, Georgian

PRINCIPAL RELIGIONS: Russian Orthodox Christianity, Islam, Judaism, Buddhism, Roman Catholicism

TYPE OF GOVERNMENT: Socialist union of fifteen republics

HEAD OF STATE: Mikhail Gorbachev

HEAD OF GOVERNMENT: Mikhail Gorbachev

HEAD OF RULING PARTY: Mikhail Gorbachev

RULING BODY: Council of People's Deputies

ADULT LITERACY: virtually 100%

LIFE EXPECTANCY: 64 (males); 74 (females)

MAIN PRODUCTS: *Agriculture*—grain, cotton, meats, tea, tobacco, wool
Manufacturing—rolled metal, paper and other wood products, cotton cloth, tractors, autos, clocks
Mining—gold, platinum, silver, iron ore, diamonds, phosphate, sulfur, limestone, petroleum, natural gas, coal, lead, zinc, nickel

HIGHEST POINT: Communism Peak, 24,590 feet (7,495 meters)

CURRENCY: ruble

NOTE: As this book goes to press, sweeping constitutional amendments are being enacted. It seems likely that if the reform process proceeds regularly, the relationship between the "all-Union" (national) and "union-republic" (regional) levels of government will be greatly decentralized, and national executive authority will be shared by a popularly elective president and representatives of the union-republics. Even the official name may be changed to "Union of Sovereign Soviet Republics."

Introduction

"A riddle wrapped in a mystery inside an enigma"
—Winston Churchill

That famous description of the Union of Soviet Socialist Republics (the Soviet Union) has been quoted endlessly because it seemed so apt. However, Mikhail Gorbachev's *glasnost* (openness) has cleared the way for fresh study and understanding of the Soviet Union. This book endeavors to use that unprecedented opportunity to describe the great nation and people that were hidden so long. The task is not easy, for the Soviet Union is enormous, much the largest and most diverse country on the face of the globe. It covers almost three times the area of the United States and stretches across eleven time zones. A greater variety of plant and animal life shares its terrain, waters, and climates than is found in any other nation. Its population includes more than a hundred native nationalities, ranging from tall, blond, blue-eyed Scandinavians to short, dark, almond-eyed Orientals. They work and live in an almost infinite variety of ways.

To help sort through and make sense of such a mass of descriptive material, this book develops the theme that the official Soviet philosophy (Chapter 1), the wealth of the land (Chapter 2), the legacies of history (Chapters 3–6), and the rich diversity of the people (Chapters 7–8) have failed to produce satisfactory living conditions (Chapters 9–10), or adequate cultural and scientific accomplishments (Chapter 11).

The Soviet Union as an Ideological State

A major cause of the failures of the Soviet Union may well be relentless pursuit by its forebears, founders, and leaders of the ideas incorporated in the official state philosophy—Marxist-Leninist ideology. Many countries have official beliefs, goals, and ideals. The distinction of the Soviet Union since its birth in 1917 has been its conscious, systematic, even ruthless effort to use its philosophy to transform a backward empire into a model for the world. Inevitably, this has clashed with the desires of many Soviet people to pursue their own private interests and inclinations. Under Gorbachev, ideology has been played down greatly.

Marxism-Leninism is a comprehensive intellectual guide to political, economic, and social action that was elaborated in the nineteenth century and adapted by a succession of Soviet leaders. It began with Karl Marx (1818–1883), a German intellectual and leader of international revolutionary socialism. For more than fifty years, he and his close collaborator, Friedrich Engels (1820–1895), developed doctrines to support and explain their political beliefs and action. They strove with great zeal to understand human nature and society and to make their philosophy scientific.

Their ideology was a remarkable mix of ideas from the main intellectual currents of the nineteenth century and of rational responses to its social problems and ferment. It offered explanations and solutions for such evils as grinding poverty, child labor, and dangerous working conditions.

Later Marxists included a small band of Russian revolutionaries, led by V. I. Ulyanov (Lenin) (1870–1924). These leaders applied Marx's doctrines to Russia. Inspired and guided by Marxism, they seized control of Russia and founded a new state based explicitly on its principles. Their "Russian Revolution" and "Soviet Union" and its policies resulted directly from the efforts to put Marxism-Leninism into practice.

All later Soviet leaders have continued that tradition. From Joseph Stalin (1879–1953) and Leon Trotsky (1879–1940) through Mikhail Gorbachev (1931–   ), all have been Marxist-Leninists and have claimed that their constitutions, laws, policies, and practices applied it. All but Gorbachev have touted their contributions to that ideology.

Mikhail Gorbachev has been eager to court popularity among Soviet citizens, a very new approach for leaders in the Soviet Union.   Novosti.

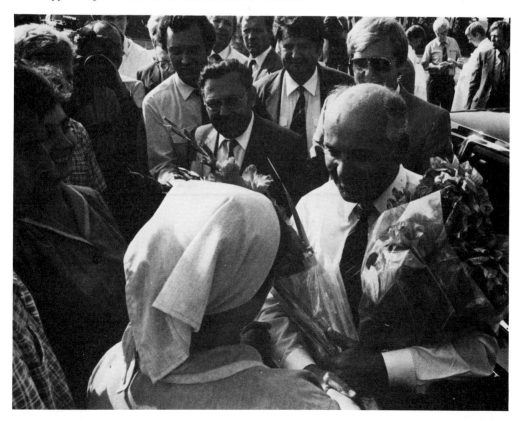

Norilsk

Igarka

East Siberian Sea

Chukchi

Evens

Yakuts

Yakuts

EVENKI NATIONAL OKRUG

Magadan

Kamchatka Peninsula

o Suntar

Sea of Okhotsk

BURYAT
AUTONOMOUS
S.S.R.

Tynda o

Lake Baikal

Sakhalin

Irkutsk
Buryats

Khabarovsk

vin

MONGOLIA

CHINA

JAPAN

Vladivostok

Sea of Japan

POLITICAL MAP OF THE
SOVIET UNION

Soviet Republics

● Capitals

o Other Cities

0   500 Miles

Kirgiz Ethnic Groups

Marxism

Marxism is a very complex and substantial body of philosophical thought. No brief summary can do it justice. What follows is a highly simplified summary of those Marxist concepts that may be most helpful.

Marxism begins with the *historical dialectic*, a "scientific" approach to understanding the development of civilization. It holds that civilization develops inevitably along a route including "thesis," "antithesis," and "synthesis" phases. The characteristics of a society in its initial, (thesis) stage evolve into their opposites in the antithesis stage. Then traits from the thesis and antithesis phases merge in a synthesis. That synthesis becomes a new thesis and the whole process continues. Thus, Marx saw European medieval feudalism as a thesis, modern capitalism as the antithesis of feudalism, and communism as a future synthesis of feudalism and capitalism.

Marx taught that *materialism* drives society along that dialectical course. That is, the economy of a society (its "substructure" or "base") determines the character of all other social institutions and activities (the "superstructure"). Indeed, one characteristic in the economy is determining: the form of ownership of the "dominant means of production." Under feudalism, most people earned their livings at farming. So Marx called agriculture the dominant means of production and claimed that the system of farmland ownership determined the character of all other social institutions and activities such as religion and warfare. In Marx's time, manufacturing dominated the economy and capitalist ownership of factories determined the character of society. Under communism, factories would be owned in common by everyone. Transferring ownership from a few wealthy capitalists to the mass of people would transform society again.

For Marx, the character of society has a key element, the *class structure.* In each type of society, groups of people are classified according to their relationship to the dominant form of property ownership.

"They Have a World to Win"

This paragraph combines key passages in the Communist Manifesto, the key work defining Marx's theories:

The history of all hitherto existing society is the history of class struggles. The modern bourgeois society has not done away with class antagonisms. It has but established new classes, new conditions of oppression, new forms of struggle in place of the old ones. Communists everywhere support every revolutionary movement against the existing social and political order of things. They openly declare that their ends can be attained only by the forcible overthrow of all existing social conditions. Let the ruling classes tremble at a Communistic revolution. The proletarians have nothing to lose but their chains. They have a world to win. WORKERS OF THE WORLD, UNITE!

Karl Marx and Friedrich Engels (1848)

In the Middle Ages, the main classes were the nobility and the serfs in a system of mutual obligation. Now capitalists own the means of production and use the wage system to oppress the propertyless workers, or "proletariat." Under communism, because everyone will have the same relationship to the means of production, social classes will disappear. So will the oppression of nonowners by owners.

Another key Marxist concept is the *state.* In each phase of history, the ruling class forms and controls an organization to impose its will on the other classes. In the medieval period a system of armed knights and vows of service served this purpose. Under capitalism, the nation-state is an "executive committee of the ruling class" to oppress the workers. Communism, without social classes, will need no instrument of oppression. In Engels's phrase, "the government of men will be replaced by the administration of things."

Marx taught that the transition from one dialectical phase to another occurs normally by *revolution*. As society evolves dialectically, the technology of production progresses more rapidly than the social institutions and relationships. This increases tensions, which explode eventually in massive social violence. After the revolution, new, more appropriate social institutions form on the basis of the new dominant means of production. Thus, the French Revolution of 1789 transformed feudalism into capitalism and a future proletarian uprising will usher in socialism, which will develop into communism.

However, Marx foresaw a *dictatorship of the proletariat* during the transition to communism. It would eliminate the remains of capitalism, which was entrenched too deeply to vanish at once. The workers would rule the former capitalists, reeducating them and training them to live in an oppression-free society.

Leninism

The whole thrust of Marxism implied that early-twentieth-century Russia was not ripe for communism. Other European countries, such as Germany and England were more highly industrialized and, therefore, further along the dialectical course of history than Russia. Nevertheless, Lenin and other Russian Marxists refused to despair. Rather, they sought to adapt Marxism to their purposes.

Lenin's earliest major ideological work held that capitalism in Russia was more fully developed than generally believed. Russian Marxists might serve as a spark to ignite revolutions in more advanced capitalist states. Russia's lower level of development could not sustain communism alone. However, if its western neighbors became communist, they could support Russia's revolutionary state until the means of production caught up with its social system. Lenin's view inverted Marx's substruc-

Before Gorbachev, mammoth official portraits of Lenin were found throughout the Soviet Union. David Brown.

ture-superstructure relationship: Now production would follow rather than lead the revolution.

Lenin believed that the possibility of an *alliance of workers and peasants* improved Russian prospects for communism. Most nineteenth-century European farmers owned small amounts of land, whereas Marx expected propertyless proletarians to bring about his revolution. Lenin noted that few Russian peasants owned land individually. Therefore, they were less likely to be infected by capitalism and would naturally join factory workers in a revolution.

Another Leninist concept—*democratic centralism*—enabled him to form an organization capable of overthrowing the regime that ruled Russia. By presenting a dictatorship as the leading edge of a democratic movement, a small, secret, conspiratorial band of terrorists could claim that it had popular support.

Finally, the Leninist doctrine of *national in form, socialist in content* attracted the support of Russia's many minority nationalities, by promising that they could retain their languages and cultures if they accepted the communist political and economic system.

However important Marxism-Leninism may have been in shaping the Soviet Union, other factors played key roles as well. Soviet geography is an exasperating paradox. Its size and wealth of natural resources offer enormous potential, but its northerly location and isolation are obstacles to their development. Soviet history has left a similarly mixed legacy. The Soviet peoples have shown great patience and strength of character through long centuries of adversity, but they benefited only rarely from leadership of comparable quality. This book attempts to show how those factors have shaped today's Soviet Union.

A protester shows his desire for change by tearing apart a photo of Lenin.   AP Wide World Photos.

CHAPTER II

The Land

Nature played a cruel and ironic trick on the Soviet people. With one hand it offered them enormous resources to create an earthly paradise. With the other it raised almost insurmountable obstacles to their exploitation of these assets.

The Soviet Union has greater natural wealth than any other nation, but also more natural barriers to its use. Both resources and difficulties derive mainly from the location, enormous size, and diversity of the country. The paradoxical combination of opportunity and challenge affects the lives of the people in innumerable, important ways.

Territory

Usually, territory is a nation's greatest physical resource. Only people

Winter swimming.　A. Bochinin/VAAP

are more valuable than land. Normally, the more land a country has, the better.

Size

By that measure, the Soviet Union is the most fortunate nation, being by far the largest. The hammer and sickle flies over one sixth of the land surface of the globe (excluding Antartica). Its area of 8.65 million square miles (22.4 million square kilometers) is greater than North America, excluding Greenland. It stretches 5,600 miles (9,000 km.) across eleven time zones from east to west and 2,800 miles (4,500 km.) north to south. To cross it by rail takes seven days.

The Soviet colossus dominates two continents, occupying 42 percent of the vast Eurasian landmass. Soviet Europe is double the size of the other thirty-three European states combined. Soviet Asia exceeds the area of the next five largest Asian countries combined.

Location

The opportunities offered by that huge expanse of real estate are largely frustrated by its inhospitable location. The massive Soviet presence on two continents is on the edge of both. It forms Europe's eastern flank and Asia's northern rim, cut off by its difficult geography from mainstream life on both continents, condemned by nature to be a perpetual outsider.

The frigid northern character of that location accentuates its liabilities. Three fourths of the Soviet Union lie north of the forty-ninth parallel, which forms most of the United States-Canadian boundary. Leningrad has the same latitude as Seward, Alaska, and Moscow is farther north than Goose Bay, Labrador. About 75 percent of the Soviet people live north of the fifty-third parallel, but only 0.5 percent of Americans and Canadians do.

Moreover, despite its great size, Soviet territory is extraordinarily inaccessible. Its coasts are icebound or landlocked. Its longest and most southerly land boundary is blocked by a nearly unbroken barrier of forbidding deserts, rugged uplands, and mountain ranges. The Soviets

Basic Geographical Statistics

AREA: 8.65 million square miles (22.4 million square kilometers); 2.15 million sq. mi. (5.57 sq. km.) in Europe, 6.5 million sq. mi. (16.83 million sq. km.) in Asia

EXPANSE: east–west, 5,600 mi. (9,000 km.); north–south, 2,800 mi. (4,500 km.)

HIGHEST ELEVATION: Communism Peak, 25,738 feet (7,485 meters)

MARSHLANDS: 750,000 sq. mi. (2 million sq. km.)

COASTLINES: 29,200 mi. (47,000 km.)

RIVERS: 45,000 in Europe, 155,000 in Asia
Total length, 2 million mi. (3 million km.)
Navigable length, 300,000 mi. (500,000 km.)
60% flow into the Arctic Sea, 22% into the Pacific, 8% into the Baltic, and 10% into interior lakes

LAKES: 250,000

cannot communicate easily and economically with other countries, except to the west, toward its European neighbors.

Terrain

Soviet terrain seems to offer great opportunities. Its extreme flatness is an asset, making it easier to grow crops, trade over long distances, exploit resources, and move from place to place.

Geologically, the Soviet Union is formed mainly of two mammoth

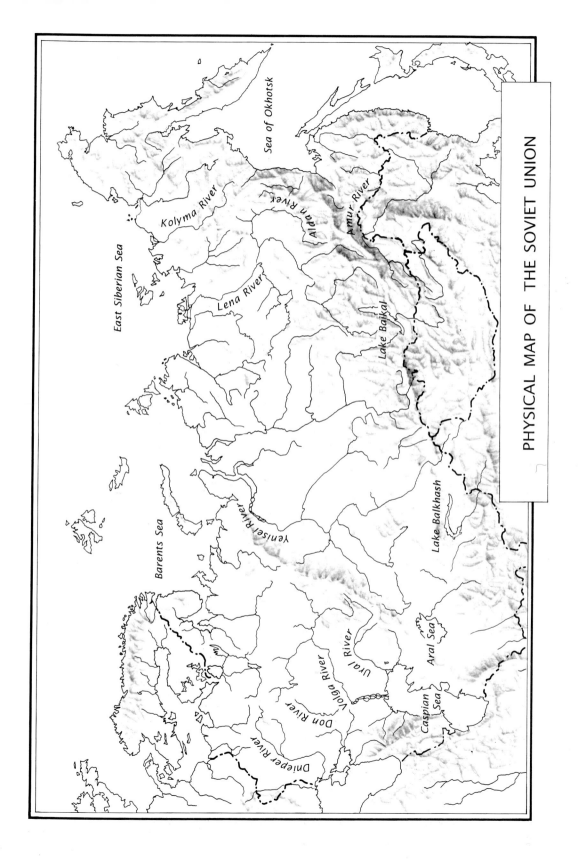

PHYSICAL MAP OF THE SOVIET UNION

Sea of Okhotsk

East Siberian Sea

Kolyma River

Aldan River

Amur River

Lena River

Lake Baikal

Barents Sea

Yenisei River

Lake Balkhash

Aral Sea

Ural River

Volga River

Caspian Sea

Don River

Dnieper River

continental platforms and the mountainous areas between and along them.

The Russian Platform extends 1,500 miles (2,400 km.) from the Polish border to the Ural foothills. It covers some 1.5 million square miles (4 million sq. km.). (The entire United States occupies 3.6 million square miles.) That immense area is so flat that only a few points rise above 1,000 feet (300 meters) in elevation and more than half is below 650 feet (200 m.).

The Siberian Platform begins as a lowland plain 1,250 miles (2,000 km.) wide from the Urals to the Yenisei River. This area of nearly 1 million square miles (2.5 million sq. km.) is even flatter and lower than its Russian counterpart. Nowhere does it rise above 650 feet (200 m.) and about half is below 325 feet (100 m.). Beyond the Yenisei, the platform is broken uplands for another 1,400 miles (2,250 km.) to the Verkhyanski Mountains.

The promise of that world's largest expanse of level land has been largely thwarted. Growing seasons are too short, soil too poor, and moisture too meager and unreliable for most crops. Climate and isolation make most productive activities uneconomical.

The flatness causes serious drainage problems. Enormous areas have little economic value, being marshes or flood plains. Marshlands cover nearly 10 percent of the Soviet territory and some flood plains are more than 60 miles (100 km.) wide.

Mountains   *In Europe.* The Soviet rule of great opportunity and continual frustration is broken by the Urals, which separate the continental platforms. That low, broken string of hills and mountains that forms the boundary between Europe and Asia runs almost north-south from the Arctic Ocean to the deserts near the Caspian Sea, varying in width from 35 to 90 miles (60 to 150 km.). Geologically, the large Arctic island Novaya Zemlya is an extension of the Urals. Their highest point is People's Mountain, and their general elevation is between 750 and

A view of the Firnovoye Plateau, 19,700 feet (5,900 meters) above sea level in the Pamir Mountains, the Soviet Union's highest range. Novosti

3,000 feet (250 and 1,000 meters). (The Appalachians in the United States are about the same length and maximum altitude, but are mostly higher, wider, and more rugged.)

Unlike most mountain ranges, the Urals are more asset than liability economically. They are near heavily populated regions and are so low and crossed by so many valleys that they impede transportation and commerce very little. They are also a veritable treasure house of mineral wealth. As a result, the Urals are one of the country's most important industrial regions.

Soviet Europe has three other notable mountain ranges, all along its southern boundary. In the west is a short slice of the Carpathians and on the Crimean peninsula are two small alpine clusters. The largest,

Principal Mountain Ranges

Ranges	Location	Highest Point
Alai	Central Asia	19,291 ft. (5,880 m.)
Altai	southern Siberia	14,783 ft. (4,506 m.)
Carpathian	Ukraine	6,762 ft. (2,061 m.)
Caucasus	Caucasus	18,510 ft. (5,642 m.)
Cherskogo	northeastern Siberia	10,325 ft. (3,147 m.)
Pamir	Central Asia	24,557 ft. (7,485 m.)
Sredinny Khrebet	Kamchatka	15,584 ft. (4,750 m.)
Tyan Shan	Central Asia	24,406 ft. (7,439 m.)
Ural	Europe/Asia	6,212 ft. (1,893 m.)
Yaila	Crimea	5,069 ft. (1,545 m.)
Rocky Mtns.	United States	20,322 ft. (6,194 m.)

highest, and most rugged European range is the alpine Caucasus Mountains, which stretch from the Black to the Caspian seas and include the highest peak on the continent, Mount Elbrus. The Caucasus Mountains contain important mineral resources, but their greatest value may be that, like the mountains of the Crimea, they shelter a small pocket of mild climate from the harsh weather that prevails elsewhere in the country.

In Asia. The mountain ranges of Soviet Asia are much wilder and more hostile than their European counterparts. They run for thousands of miles along the southern boundary and Pacific coast, interspersed by deserts, rugged uplands, and high, broken plateaus. Their maximum elevations are in the Pamir range on the Afghanistani and Chinese borders, part of the sprawling mountain system that includes the Himalayas. Communism Peak in the Pamirs is the highest point in the Soviet Union.

Other major mountain ranges stretch east from the Pamirs. They include the Tyan Shan, Altai, Sayan, Yablonovy, and Stanovoi systems. The most easterly, the Sikhote-Alin, runs parallel and so close to the Pacific Ocean that it leaves almost no coastal plain. To its north lies the remote, inhospitable northeastern corner of Siberia and the huge Kamchatka Peninsula. Offshore to the east is Sakhalin Island. Mountain ranges, hills, and high plateaus dominate all these areas.

In those inhospitable mountains agriculture, industry, and even life itself are very difficult. Furthermore, by blocking access to southern Asia they reinforce the Soviet sense of isolation. Finally, by hemming in the Asian plains, they worsen the harsh climate, containing the frigid Arctic air and excluding the warming breezes from the south.

Water Resources

The irony of Soviet geography is even more evident in its water resources. The Soviet Union is the world's most richly endowed nation in coastlines, rivers, and lakes. Yet they provide relatively little benefit.

Coastlines
Most coastlines serve nations by providing easy access to oceans and their resources. Moreover, ocean transportation is usually the most convenient and economical means for commerce.

The Soviet coastlines, longest in the world, should be immensely valuable. Two thirds of its 37,000-mile (60,000-km.) boundary is maritime. The Soviets have coasts on three great oceans—Atlantic, Pacific, and Arctic. However, that apparent benefit is a cruel deception. Most of the coastlines are far from major population centers. They border inhospitable seas that are frozen solid much of the year and are littered with dangerous ice floes during even the warmest months.

The only warm-water coasts are on the Black Sea and a short stretch on the Barents Sea near Murmansk. The Black Sea has the serious disadvantage of being separated from open ocean by the Bosporus Straits, the Sea of Marmara, and the Dardanelles, as well as the 2,300-mile (3,700-km.) Mediterranean Sea and the Straits of Gibraltar. The value of the Pacific coast is greatly reduced by being as far from the main cities as Athens is from New York. The Baltic Sea is nearly landlocked and partly frozen in winter.

This lack of ready access to the world's oceans has led to a virtual obsession with securing warm-water ports. For centuries, Russian tsars and Soviet commissars have sought to control the Balkans and, through them, to keep the Black Sea open. In the north they have struggled similarly for space along the Baltic Sea.

Rivers
Rivers are another great asset to most countries through which they flow. Many early civilizations sprang up in the basins of major rivers. Rivers provide convenient and economical transportation for commerce and industry, irrigation for agriculture, drinking water for great population centers, and inexpensive electrical power.

The Soviet Union is uniquely blessed in having more, longer, and larger rivers than any other country. Six are among the twenty longest and nineteen largest in the world. Four Siberian giants—the Ob, Yenisei, Lena, and Amur—drain the runoff from nearly 4 million square miles (10 million sq. km.), an area larger than Canada. Only the Amazon and the Congo carry more water than the Yenisei.

Notable rivers in Soviet Europe are the Volga, Dnieper, and Don. They are smaller and shorter than their Asian cousins, but far more important economically. The Volga drains some 600,000 square miles (1.5 million sq. km.) into the Caspian Sea, and the Dnieper and Don about 350,000 square miles (900,000 sq. km.) into the Black Sea.

So much water in so many rivers provides the greatest amount of potential hydroelectric energy in the world. The official estimate for only the largest rivers is 300 million kilowatts. Such power can be the

Ships moving down Siberia's Lena River, one of the largest in the world.   Novosti

least expensive, least polluting, and most dependable source of energy for industry.

Unfortunately, Soviet rivers provide none of the usual benefits to the extent they should. Most potential hydroelectric energy is in the areas that need it least, as 85 percent of the water flows through the least densely populated part of the country. Similarly, most Soviet rivers flow where there is little agriculture to irrigate. Then, too, many have little navigation value because they freeze over or flood severely much of the year and drain into the Arctic Ocean, which has only 6 percent of Soviet sea traffic.

This perversity of Soviet rivers has provoked strenuous efforts at correction. The Soviets have redirected the Volga to bring some 3 million acres (1.2 million hectares) of agricultural land under irrigation and plan to double that amount of new land. They have diverted two great rivers, the Amu Darya and Syr Darya, to irrigate some 17.2 million acres (7 million ha.) in Uzbekistan.

Principal Rivers and Lakes

River	Location	Length
Amur	Far East	1,786 mi. (2,858 km.)
Dnieper	Byelorussia/Ukraine	1,420 mi. (1,984 km.)
Don	Russia	1,224 mi. (1,958 km.)
Lena	eastern Siberia	2,653 mi. (4,245 km.)
Ob	western Siberia	2,287 mi. (3,659 km.)
Volga	Russia	2,293 mi. (3,669 km.)
Yenisei	central Siberia	2,566 mi. (4,106 km.)
Mississippi	United States	2,348 mi. (3,757 km.)

Lake	Location	Area
Aral Sea	Central Asia	*25,659 sq. mi. (65,687 sq. km.)
Baikal	eastern Siberia	11,780 sq. mi. (30,156 sq. km.)
Balkhash	Central Asia	7,115 sq. mi. (18,300 sq. km.)
Caspian Sea	Caucasus	143,550 sq. mi. (367,488 sq. km.)
Issyk-Kul	Kirghizia	2,355 sq. mi. (6,080 sq. km.)
Ladoga	northern Russia	6,835 sq. mi. (17,700 sq. km.)
Onega	northern Russia	3,710 sq. mi. (9,720 sq. km.)

*Reduced to 15,483 sq. mi. (40,100 sq. km.) by 1989

Superior	United States/Canada	31,800 sq. mi. (81,408 sq. km.)

Some of those efforts have backfired disastrously. The Uzbekistan project has virtually destroyed the Aral Sea, shrinking it 60 percent in volume and 40 percent in area during the past thirty years. Furthermore, the cropland created by that project is ecologically fragile and may be reverting to desert.

The Uzbekistan problem presents a colossal dilemma. The water supply for the Aral Sea can be replenished by reversing part of the flow of the Ob and Irtysh rivers. However, that gargantuan effort might create even greater environmental difficulties. A proposal to divert three European rivers into the Volga poses a similar problem.

Lakes

The Soviet Union is richly endowed with lakes, claiming more than any other country. In part the many lakes result from the numerous depressions in the flat terrain. The same drainage problems that create marshes help to form lakes.

Among these lakes are some of the world's greatest. The saltwater Caspian Sea on the Europe-Asia boundary is the largest inland body of

Beautiful Lake Baikal, one of the largest and deepest in the world. Novosti

water in the world. Four others (Aral Sea, Baikal, Balkhash, Issyk-Kul) are the next largest in Asia, and two (Ladoga and Onega) are the largest in Europe. Baikal is the deepest in the world (5,700 ft., 1,700 m.), holding 20 percent of the world's fresh water—more than all the Great Lakes combined.

The Caspian Sea is one of the richest natural resources of the Soviet Union. However, it loses more moisture by evaporation than it receives from its feeder rivers and is shrinking slowly. Caviar, the eggs of the gigantic sturgeon, are its most famous product, a gourmet delicacy the world over. Many other commercial fish swim its waters. Oil is pumped from its bed, and its surface is a convenient waterway.

Even these rich and beautiful lakes present problems. To keep them alive the Soviets have to limit agricultural and industrial development around them. Pollution in the Caspian Sea has cut caviar production by half since World War II, and irrigation projects have reduced the flow of its feeder rivers. The growth of cities on the shores of Lake Baikal endangers the pristine purity of its waters and their 1,800 species of plant and animal life. Many other lakes are similarly threatened.

Climate

The most demanding fact of nature in the Soviet Union is climate. Virtually every decision must take it into account. It includes all major types, except tropical. About 80 percent of the territory lies in the temperate zone, 16 percent is arctic, and 4 percent is subtropical.

Temperature   The "temperate" designation for most of the Soviet Union requires qualification. Because of its great size, much of the land is remote from the moderating effects of the oceans. This makes summers warmer and the winters much colder than in other parts of the temperate zone. Everywhere but on the arctic islands and its most northerly peninsula, temperatures may reach 85°F (30°C) in

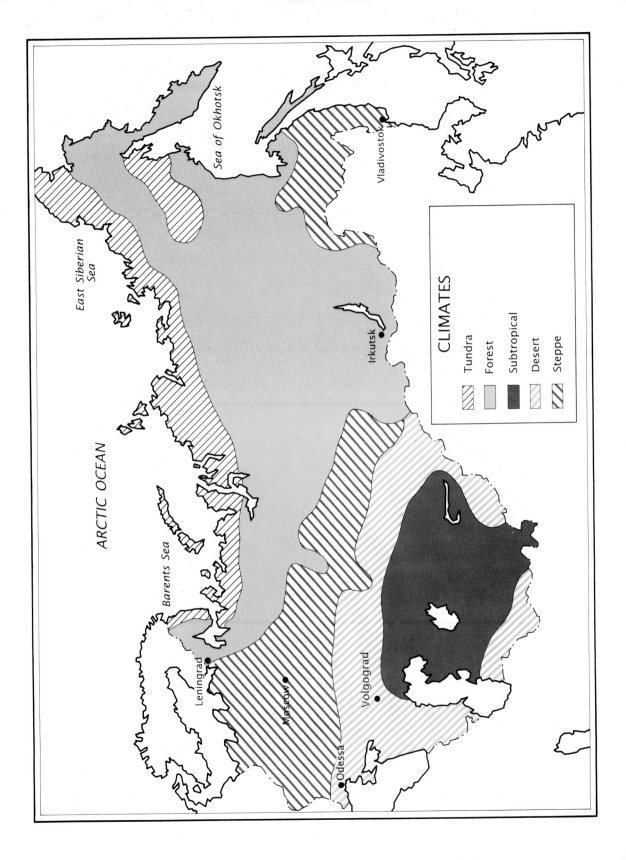

ARCTIC OCEAN

East Siberian
Sea

Sea of Okhotsk

Vladivostok

Irkutsk

Barents Sea

Leningrad

Moscow

Volgograd

Odessa

CLIMATES

Tundra

Forest

Subtropical

Desert

Steppe

the summer, and everywhere but the Crimea and the Caucasus they may fall to −20°F (−30°C) in winter. Average temperature ranges between January and July are very great. In some parts of Siberia they reach 150°F (83°C).

Summers are short but hot. Only about one fourth of the territory has temperatures above 67°F (19°C) more than sixty days per year. Yet, even in the heart of Siberia, highs of 100°F (38°C) are not unusual.

Winters are long and cold. Snow covers nearly the entire country at least one hundred days each year and over half the land for six months. In about four fifths of the territory, the temperature falls below freezing more than ninety days a year. The average January temperature is above freezing only in small areas along the Black Sea.

Siberia has the harshest winters of any inhabited area on the globe. Temperatures of −60°F (−51°C) are common, and the coldest temperature ever recorded in a settled place was −90.04°F (−67.8°C.) in Verkhoyansk. (The United States record low of −80°F [−62.22°C] was in Prospect Creek, Alaska.)

When nature turns the thermostat so low, unusual things happen. Human breath crystalizes and hangs in the air. Rubber tires shatter like glass. Kerosene congeals and cannot be poured. Snow pops like fire-crackers underfoot. Deep rivers freeze to the bottom. Ordinary activities require great effort. Engines must be left running continuously. Several additional layers of clothing are needed. Huge amounts of fuel must be consumed to heat homes.

That hostile climate produces permafrost, a condition that affects about half the Soviet soil by freezing it to a depth of several hundred feet. In summer the top 6 feet (2 m.) or so dissolve into quagmires. This causes severe difficulties for construction, transportation, agriculture, industry, and almost all forms of human activity. Houses sink into the mud, roads become impassable, railway rails bend and ties buckle, fields are untillable. Only extraordinary effort, expense, and imagination can overcome permafrost.

Precipitátion   Dryness, another typical characteristic of continental climates, affects the Soviet Union. About 90 percent of the territory receives less than 24 inches (600 millimeters) of precipitation annually. Some desert spots near the Iranian border get only 1.2 inches (30 mm.) of moisture annually. At the other extreme, Achishko in the Caucasus Mountains has received 157.5 inches (4,000 mm.) in a year.

The moisture shortage is especially evident on land that is otherwise suitable for agriculture. Only one percent of the land that can be cultivated receives 27.5 inches (700 mm.) of rainfall annually (in the United States, 60 percent). Where the amount of precipitation is adequate, it may come when least helpful for growing crops. In most of the country, snow accounts for 25 to 30 percent of total precipitation. Even in those few areas where moisture and warm weather coincide, scorching winds often reduce its value.

Natural Resources

The Soviet Union exceeds all other countries in the range and value of its natural resources. It has more than 17,000 plant varieties, more than half the world total. Its animal species number 100,000 to 150,000. However, this is only 8 to 9 percent of the world total for about 15 percent of the land area. Among larger animals, the Soviet Union contains 300 species of mammals, 702 of birds, 128 of reptiles, 33 of amphibians, and about 1,500 of fish. Beneath Soviet soils lie the greatest mineral deposits on the globe. Yet much of that great natural wealth cannot be exploited fully because of its inhospitable location.

Five Ecological Regions   Five distinct zones of vegetation, soil, and animal life can be identified:

1. *The tundra.* This bleak, treeless "cold desert" covers the northernmost reaches of the country. The surface layer of its thin, infertile soil is largely peat—partially carbonized vegetation—and the decomposed

remains of scrubby plants. Beneath that is waterlogged clay, resting on permafrost.

Tundra plants are hardy, stunted perennial herbs, dwarfed woody shrubs, mosses, and lichens. They have adapted to severe weather, poor soil, and long, dark winters.

This arctic area is surprisingly rich in animal life. Many migratory birds and mammals live there in summer. Year-round residents include lemmings, wolves, arctic foxes, ermine, snowy owls, and ptarmigans. Some 2.5 million domesticated reindeer graze on the tundra.

A tiger from the Amur Valley in the Soviet Far East.   Novosti

2. *Forests.* The southern tundra gives way gradually to seemingly endless forested plains. With the adjacent forested hills and mountains, they cover half the Soviet territory. They are by far the largest forests in the world, one fourth of the total. Soviet timber resources are estimated at 2.8 trillion cubic feet (79.3 billion cu. m.).

Forests have played such a major role in the lives of the Soviet peoples that several trees have symbolic meaning in folklore and poetry: oak is a symbol of male strength and courage; birch, which itself symbolizes Russia, is traditionally associated with female beauty; willow is tied to sorrow and mourning; cedar to old age; and poplar symbolizes gracefulness.

Over 80 percent of Soviet forests are evergreens, especially pines, but also spruces, firs, and cedars. They are concentrated in the taiga zone, which includes the northern 40 percent of European Russia and almost all of Siberia. The taiga spans some 3,000 miles (5,000 km.) east to west and 600 miles (1,000 km.) north to south. The broad-leafed hardwood forests (oak, birch, maple) are found mainly in Byelorussia, Ukraine, and the Far East. Upland areas in Central Asia have extensive mixed forests of evergreens and hardwoods.

The thick taiga forests produce a peculiar kind of soil that resembles ashes and is acidic, infertile, waterlogged, and bleached. About 10 percent of the taiga is bogs, which have organic matter in the surface layer and clay below.

Soviet forests shelter more fur-bearing animals than any other area on the globe. They include foxes, martens, ermine, beavers, sable, mink, squirrels, otter, and muskrats. Furs were the original lure for Russians venturing into Siberia. Many wild animals are still hunted for

The taiga forest near Lake Baikal.   Novosti

their pelts, but fur farming has become increasingly important. Furs remain a major Soviet product, some $100 million worth reaching the official market each year, about half of which are exported.

Other forest animals are brown and black bears, elk, reindeer, and several varieties of deer and rodents. Tigers and leopards prowl the Far East. Typical birds are owls, woodpeckers, jays, and nutcrackers.

Some bogs cover 4,000 square miles (10,000 sq. km.) or more. Vasyuganye is the largest in the world at 20,500 square miles (53,000 sq. km.) (twice the size of Maryland). Bogs also cover some 25 percent of such western areas as the Baltic states, Byelorussia, and northern Ukraine. Bog vegetation consists of reeds, sedges, and mosses. They decompose gradually into peat, which is used for fuel and fertilizer.

3. *Steppes.* The southerly forests thin out gradually into the vast, treeless plateaus called steppes, similar to the American Great Plains.

Because of the persistently dry climate, vegetation is dominated by drought-resistant grasses. For centuries, the steppes' productivity was limited to grazing, but under Khrushchev in the 1950's, some 100 million acres (40.5 million ha.) in Kazakhstan and Siberia were planted in grains. About half of that land was too dry to be productive, but the rest is still being cultivated.

About three quarters of the steppes are covered by a rich, fertile "black earth" soil as much as 39 inches (1 m.) thick. Grasses as tall as a man grow naturally on it. Elsewhere, shallower, less fertile "chestnut" soils predominate. Everywhere on the steppes, natural fertility is diminished by the strong prevailing winds.

Chernoziòm

The Russians have an expression, chernoziòm—*the black earth, mold. They mean by it the broad and deep belt of fertile humus that extends from Podolia to Kazan and even across the Urals into Siberia. The wonderful fertility of this soil is ascribed to the slow decay of the grass of the steppes, which has been going on for centuries.*

This belt of rich soil reminds us of the richest and broadest Russian natures—open, rich, luxurious, receptive, warm without glow or heat, but which give the impression of inexhaustible exuberance. Even the circumstance that the Russian nature has been lying fallow for hundreds of years increases its wealth.

—Adapted from Georg Brandes, *Impressions of Russia* (1889)

Chernoziòm is found far away from large cities—so saying "he's got *chernoziòm* under his nails" or just *"chernoziòm"* also means rural common people with simple tastes, something very close to "rednecks."

Before the steppes were plowed, antelope, wild horses, deer, and wolves roamed there in abundance. Farming has restricted their range and forced many of them into the adjacent forests. Ground-nesting birds have been affected similarly. Rodents are now the principal fauna.

4. *Deserts.* Nearly 10 percent of Soviet territory, especially south of the steppes between the Caspian Sea and the Himalayas, is desolate desert or semidesert. The extreme temperatures; perennial drought; and sandy, stony, salty, and clayey soil provide very inhospitable growing conditions. Vegetation is limited to wormwoods, hardy and meadow grasses, brush, and scrubby, gnarled salt bushes.

Antelope, gazelle, cheetahs, and the wild ass were once common in desert areas, but their numbers have been much reduced by hunting and other human inroads. Foxes, hares, and wildcats are still found. So are lizards, tortoises, and snakes. Birds are scarce, except at oases. Some river and oasis areas have wild boars, jackals, and even tigers.

5. *Subtropical.* The Soviet subtropics are the southern coast of Crimea, the Transcaucasian lowlands, and along the easternmost Manchurian border. The yellow and reddish clay soil is several feet thick and rich in organic material and volcanic ash. The natural vegetation is luxuriant, including dense broad-leafed forests (oak, hornbeam, beech, poplar), evergreen bushes, ferns, fruit trees, and such climbing plants as ivy and grapevine. The fauna include deer, bears, panthers, hyenas, tigers, jungle cats, and porcupines.

Subsoil Resources

The mineral wealth of the Soviet Union is a prime example of its frustrating irony. The country is far richer than any other in such resources. Yet much of it is so difficult to extract or so distant from industrial areas as to lose much of its worth.

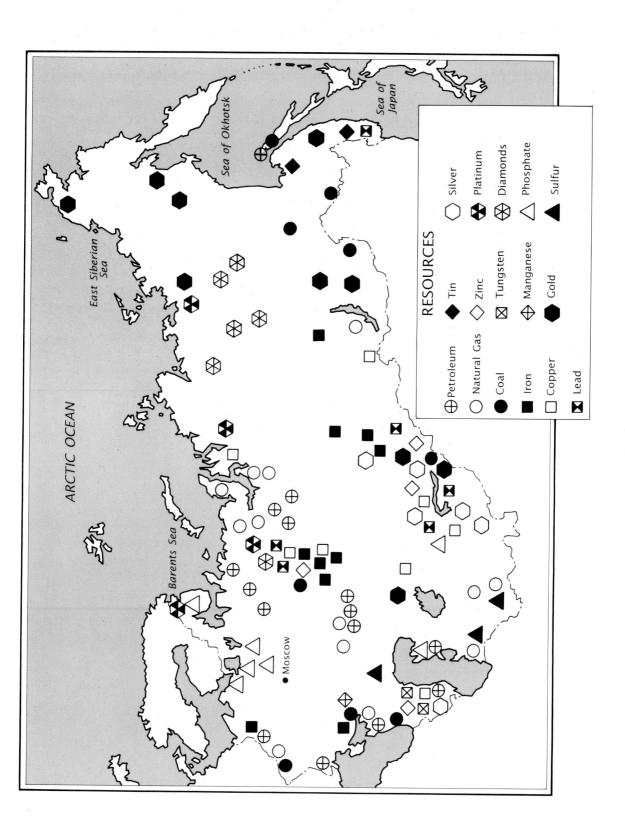

ARCTIC OCEAN

East Siberian Sea

Sea of Okhotsk

Sea of Japan

Barents Sea

• Moscow

RESOURCES

		Silver	Platinum	Diamonds	Phosphate
	Tin	Zinc	Tungsten	Manganese	Gold
Petroleum	Natural Gas	Coal	Iron	Copper	Lead

Sulfur

Subsoil Resources

Mineral	Main Location of Deposits	Annual Production	
		World Rank	Percentage of World Output
Asbestos	Urals	1	40
Bauxite	various places	4	6
Chromite	Kazakhstan	1	34
Coal	various places	2 or 3	
Copper	Central Asia/Caucasus	3	17
Diamonds	eastern Siberia	1	25
Gold	various places	2	20
Iron	Europe	1	
Lead	Kazakhstan	2	
Limestone	various places	1	17–20
Magnesium	Carpathians/Amu Darya	2	33
Manganese	Caucasus/Ukraine	1	20
Mercury	Kirghizia/Ukraine	1	30
Natural gas	various places	1	

Metals   The Soviet Union is the world's largest metal producer. Its production consistently places it among the top two or three countries for most major industrial metals. It is also a world leader in precious metals, ranking second to South Africa in gold production and first in platinum and silver. Important new discoveries of gold deposits in Armenia and Kazakhstan promise to hold that ranking.

The Soviets have half the world's reserves of iron ore (11 billion

Mineral	Main Location of Deposits	World Rank	Annual Production Percentage of World Output
Nickel	various places	1	28
Peat	various places	1	
Petroleum	western Siberia	1	
Phosphate	Kola Peninsula	2	21
Platinum	Siberia/Far East	1	54
Potash	Urals/Byelorussia	1	35
Silver	Siberia/Far East	1	14
Salt	Donets/Urals/Crimea	2 or 3	
Sulfur	Carpathians/Amu Darya	1	20
Tin	Siberia/Far East	2	15
Tungsten	eastern Siberia	2	28
Uranium		3	12
Vanadium	Urals	2	
Zinc	Kazakhstan	2	14

tons), the most basic industrial product, and three fourths are found in conveniently accessible European regions. Yet the richest deposits are deep in the earth, beneath thick, water-bearing rock and, thus, very difficult to exploit.

The Soviets have already mined most of the high-grade iron ore and must rely increasingly on lower-grade deposits. And the coal needed for smelting (refining) iron ore is either remote geographically or is nearby but costly to mine. Despite that, the Soviet Union has been the world's leading iron-ore producer in recent years.

Marxist-Leninist ideology contributes to Soviet frustrations. Marxist thought dictates that industry should be developed rapidly to lay the "substructure" for communism. As a result, *quantity* is the basic measure of performance, to the exclusion of profitability, efficiency, economy, and quality. According to this belief, it is more important that industries exist than how well they perform. The consequence is an enormous waste of raw materials. For instance, the Soviets use far more metal to manufacture the same amount of machinery than do their foreign counterparts.

Nonmetal Minerals

The Soviet Union is very well endowed in nonmetallic minerals. It mines about 40 percent of the world's asbestos and more diamonds and mineral fertilizers—especially potash and phosphate—than any other country. It vies with the United States for tops in sulfur production, has inexhaustible deposits of salt, and is the largest producer of limestone, which is mainly used to make cement.

Hydrocarbons

Perhaps the most important subsoil resources in today's industrial society are petroleum and its hydrocarbon relatives. The Soviet Union ranks third in oil reserves and is much the largest petroleum producer, pumping about half again as much as second-place United States. But the more accessible and easily exploited Soviet reserves have been depleted, and production is three times as expensive as it was in the mid-1970's.

The Soviet Union is a world leader in producing natural gas and coal, claiming greater coal reserves than the entire rest of the world. The bogs of Soviet Asia contain enormous amounts of peat, by far the largest in the world. However, its extraction has been inhibited in recent years by fears of environmental damage, and its economic importance has been declining.

The seemingly inexhaustible natural resources described above have tempted Soviet leaders to pursue the production obsession of Marxism to its extreme. They have spared no effort to extract everything from the land that might possibly help them to build the industrial and agricultural might of the country. Unfortunately, in all too many cases the result has been disastrous for the environment. Farm fields have

The nuclear power plant at Chernobyl after the explosion of 1986.   Novosti

become so saturated with chemicals that they can no longer be worked. Factories spew forth 60 million tons of pollutants a year, far more than the much larger American industry. Lakes and rivers have shrunk or become too polluted to support fish or plant life. An estimated 60 percent of the Soviet people live in "ecological disaster zones" or "ecologically unfavorable conditions," according to Alexei Yablokov, head of the biology institute of the U.S.S.R. Academy of Sciences. This helps explain the poor state of Soviet health.

Under Gorbachev, the truth of the unhappy situation has finally been admitted—and some steps are being taken to change it. A small, but growing, environmentalist movement is pushing in the same direction. However, the task is enormous and the character of the Soviet system and its ideological basis make such changes slow, difficult, and uncertain.

That great land, polluted or not, has provided a magnificent stage for one of the great dramas of history, the story of the Russians and the other peoples of the Russian empire and the Soviet Union. The next chapters will portray that rousing pageant with its glories and miseries. As the land supplies the physical context, history has given the human background for the contemporary life of the Soviet Union.

The Rise of Tsarist Russia

The Soviet Union inherited an immense, diverse, wealthy, and frustrating land from the Russian empire. For a thousand years successive rulers had formed and reigned over that domain before the Communists seized power in 1917. As the ruling dynasty passed on that geography they also bequeathed a rich and troubled history.

The Themes of Russian History

At least six distinct themes stand out in the complex pattern of Russian history. One is the development of an autocratic tradition. Over the centuries, political and governmental power and authority became concentrated almost completely in the hands of a single ruler. The will of that monarch came to overrule all other institutions. Nothing remotely like a parliament existed before the Council of State was created in

Chronology

400,000 B.C.	First human habitation of present Soviet Union
4,000 B.C.	Last Ice Age begins to end
800 B.C.	Scythians invade
329–328 B.C.	Alexander the Great conquers Central Asia
A.D. 552–88	Turkic khanate flourishes
Late ninth century	Kievan state founded
988	Vladimir I adopts Christianity
1237	Tatars invade
1252	Alexander Nevsky becomes Grand Prince
1302–1521	Expansion of Muscovy principality
1380	Russians defeat Tatar Golden Horde at Kulikovo
1533	Ivan IV, "the Terrible," becomes Grand Prince
1547	Ivan IV crowned Tsar
1584	Fedor I becomes Tsar

1810, and even the Duma (parliament), after 1905, had far less authority than most western legislatures. The emperors—called tsars—wielded absolute executive power and served as the highest court of appeal. Neither laws nor civil liberties restrained the tsars; their will was absolute. That autocratic tradition provided a convenient base on which the Bolsheviks could plant their own dictatorship.

A second theme in Russian history concerns the link between the autocracy and the Russian Orthodox church. That alliance gave to the state a holiness that raised it above earthly criticism or opposition. The doctrines of the church made the tsar or tsarina a kind of demigod and they in turn intervened freely in church affairs to ensure that it would conform to their will in secular matters. After 1917, and especially after

1598	Boris Godunov becomes Tsar; "Time of Troubles" begins
1613	Mikhail Romanov becomes Tsar, founds dynasty
1667–1671	Stenka Razin revolt
1682	Ivan V, Peter I become Tsars; Sophia is regent
1703	St. Petersburg (Leningrad) founded
1725	Death of Peter I
1762	Catherine II, "the Great," becomes Tsarina
1773–1775	Pugachev revolt
1805	Russia joins war against Napoleon's France
1815	Russia joins Holy Alliance
1854–1856	Crimean War
1861	Decree issued abolishing serfdom
1881	Alexander II assassinated; Alexander III becomes Tsar
1894	Nicholas II becomes Tsar

1924, the Bolsheviks converted that mystical aura into worshipful cults for the successive leaders of the Soviet state.

A third theme holds that the greatest success of that sanctified autocracy has been the expansion of its realm from a small principality on the banks of the Volga River to an enormous empire that spans two continents. Although much of Russia's history concerns its efforts to protect itself from foreign invaders, it has nevertheless managed somehow to increase the size of its territory during most of those struggles.

Fourth, the greatest failure of the Russian empire and the Soviet Union has been an inability to modernize, to transform itself into a democratic and constitutional state capable of realizing the full potential of its geography and population. Toward the end of tsarism, Russia seemed to be making great strides economically, at least in terms of industrial development. Yet the antiquated legal and governmental institutions responded little to reform efforts. That resistance eased the path for the Communists, who were uncompromising in their pursuit of modernization. However, they have failed to bring about many of the improvements they sought.

Fifth, a crucial and ongoing problem in the nation's history has been the lack of leaders possessing the combination of intellectual and personal qualities required by the tasks they faced. When Russia has been ruled by men or women of great ability, they have exhibited catastrophic defects of personality and character. When they have been relatively normal in those latter respects, they have lacked the drive or competence for effective leadership. Mikhail Gorbachev may, at last, be the great exception to that rule.

Sixth, that failure of leadership has been caused at least partly by the dilemma of whether to turn east or west, toward Asia or toward Europe.

Before Russia

Prehistory   The harsh land known now as the Soviet Union discouraged early habitation. Although humans inhabited Africa some 4 million years ago, they reached present Soviet territory only about 400,000 years ago. They remained there only intermittently until the glaciers of the last Ice Age began to recede about 6,000 years ago.

During ice-free intervals 40,000 to 100,000 years ago, Neanderthal-type humans settled on the lower Volga, in the central Urals, and in Siberia. About 3,000 B.C. Neolithic (polished-stone-tools culture) settlements appeared in parts of Russia, Ukraine, Siberia, and the Caucasus.

Before the Slavs   The earliest known organized human societies in the present Soviet territory were in Central Asia sometime between 3,000 and 1,000 B.C. About 1,000 B.C. Transcaucasian tribes

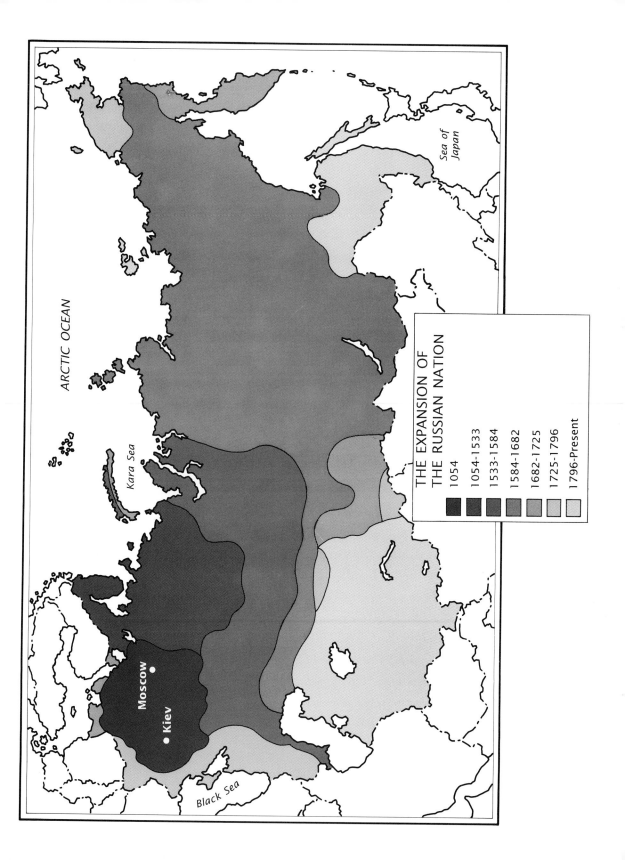

THE EXPANSION OF
THE RUSSIAN NATION

1054
1054-1533
1533-1584
1584-1682
1682-1725
1725-1796
1796-Present

ARCTIC OCEAN

Sea of
Japan

Kara Sea

Black Sea

● Moscow

● Kiev

formed a "kingdom" and flourished as powerful rivals of the Hittites and Assyrians of the Middle East. By 500 B.C. Persians had conquered them and, later, Armenians displaced them. During that early period, successive waves of Asian nomads invaded and occupied the territory of present-day Russia. The first of them known to history were the Scythians. They conquered the prehistoric Cimmerians about 800 B.C. and settled near the Black Sea.

The Scythians were also the first predecessors of the Soviets who are known to have confronted the dilemma posed by contact with the west. Greek colonies in the area offered cultural enrichment from the most highly developed civilization of the day. However, they were also a military danger to the Scythians. By 200 B.C., the Scythians yielded to the Sarmatians, other Asian nomads, who faced the Greeks' successors, the Romans, in another bout of east-west conflict. The western cultures that had the most to offer culturally were also the greatest military threats.

From the fourth century A.D. until the founding of the Kievan state late in the ninth century, a bewildering array of marauders swept across the Russian steppes. They invaded mainly from Asia (Huns, Khazars, Avars, Bulgars, Mongols, Turks, Alans), but also from the Baltic-Scandinavian region (Goths, Finns, Lithuanians, Vikings).

Throughout that period, pressure from east and north ground the local people against the firm resistance of the Byzantines, who ruled remnants of the former Roman empire in the eastern Mediterranean. This often sent the locals squirting westward across central Europe. The Byzantine capital was Constantinople (now Istanbul, in Turkey), which had been the capital of the Roman empire since A.D. 330. Over time Byzantine Christianity differed from that of Rome. And in 1054 the two branches split apart. The eastern, or Orthodox, church has dominated in Russia. (For more on Byzantium see *The Land and People of Turkey.*)

Another east-west conflict confronted the remaining steppes dwellers.

The Europe-oriented Byzantines were sophisticated—artistically, culturally, politically, diplomatically, religiously, commercially, and financially. The Arabs burst out of the peninsula now occupied by Saudi Arabia to overrun them in the seventh century. They were rustic, nomadic, boisterous, energetic, and powerful militarily.

The Slavs

Out of that raging caldron of conflict and conquest emerged the Slavic people. Their origins are lost in the confusion of the time. They seem to have formed gradually from the swirling mix of peoples in the Carpathian Mountain area. For centuries they were the underclasses—even slaves—for successive conquerors, as battles for domination raged overhead.

Slavic groups were identified as early as the Scythian period. By the fifth century A.D. they had grown enough to trouble the Byzantines. Mainly, however, they expanded peacefully north, east, and south, gradually infiltrating and imprinting their character (language, customs, etc.) on their oppressors.

That harsh forge of history shaped a distinctive character that many observers have noted in the majority peoples of the Soviet Union. Its traits are said to include a long-suffering patience; a tendency to evade, rather than resist, the grinding force of authority; a preference for communal, rather than individual, effort and achievement; and a stubborn hardiness toward both oppressive rulers and the cruelty inflicted by the natural elements.

In the sixth century the Antes people founded the first Slavic state in Bessarabia and Ukraine. About the same time, the Rukhs-As emerged as the most prominent Slavs. Eventually, they gave their name to the largest of the modern Slavic nationalities, the Russians. The stimulus for that—and for the founding of the Russian state—is often seen as invasion from the north by Vikings.

Russia Before 1800:
The Rulers and the Ruled

Origins   Historians disagree about the origins of the Russian state. One common interpretation sees its founding in a Viking principality of the late ninth century. The Norsemen had been raiding and trading in eastern Europe since the middle of the eighth century. Many

Uncovering Novgorod

Archaeologists have been able to learn quite a lot about life in ancient Novgorod. The clay soil on which the city was built preserved the wooden planks that lined city streets and the foundations of houses. These have enabled scientists to define much of what the city looked like. According to one Soviet archaeologist, Valentin Yanin, the jewelry, combs, swords, and other artifacts also found in the city almost make it

possible to imagine the merchants concluding contracts with Swedes and Karelians, peasants selling wares at the market, innumerable sailing ships coming in along the Volkhov laden with expensive foreign wine, the smell of fish, shoemakers stitching sandals, women adorning themselves with furs and jewelry, street musicians plucking their psalteries.

This picture is even more complete because over 700 birchbark letters, or *beresty*, have also been unearthed. These include schoolbooks in which young children practiced writing, letters between family members, and information on legal and political affairs. Archaeologist Yanin quotes some as reading:

had settled in what is now northern Russia, adopting the local language and culture and dominating the leadership. They were called "Russians," the first use of the name.

In the mid ninth century, Viking leaders extended their rule over the Turkic Khazars and Magyars to their south and moved their capital from Novgorod to Kiev. This was the most extensive unification that territory had known.

Greetings from the priest to Grechin. Paint me two six-winged seraphim on two icons for the top of the iconostasis. I kiss you. God will reward you or we'll make a deal. . . .
From Nikita to Ulyanitsa. Marry me. I want you and you
me. . . .
From Boris to Nastasya. As soon as you receive this letter send me a man on horseback, since I have a lot to do here. Oh yes, send a shirt. I forgot one.

Since there may be many more of these letters buried in Novgorod, it may turn out to be one of the richest sources of information about the history of the Russian people.

Adapted from Valentin L. Yanin, "The Archaeology of Novgorod," *Scientific American* Volume 262, Number 2 (February 1990) pp. 84–91.

The Kiev state expanded until, by A.D. 1054, it covered most of modern Russia, Byelorussia, and Ukraine. A crucial event in Russian history occurred when Prince Vladimir I (980–1015) converted to Christianity and imposed his new faith on his people.

Christianity: The Baptism of Russia

Ancient Slavs believed in spirits—forces of nature such as the sun and the wind, but also the shades of their ancestors. Many of their rites and rituals were designed to ensure the goodwill of the dead. Gifts such as meat, honey, drinks, and special breads were brought to graves as offerings.

In the tenth century after some Slavic princes had visited Byzantium and studied Christianity, Prince Vladimir became a Christian and married the Byzantine princess Anna. But Christianity remained unpopular. In 988 Prince Vladimir changed that by ordering everyone to become a Christian. He sent for priests from Byzantium to baptize the whole population of Russia. Wooden images of pagan gods were burned or thrown into the rivers. This mass conversion was not easily accomplished, however. Many Slavs did not want to part with their gods. They cried, refused to be baptized, and beat and killed the priests. But willing or unwilling, they were all driven into rivers and baptized. After that, for many years, there were still "magicians" who wandered from village to village calling to the peasants to keep their old rituals; when found, they were cruelly killed. Gradually, the Slavs got used to their new religion, but their old pagan beliefs did not disappear altogether. For example, even now the Russians have great festivities dedicated to the end of winter and the beginning of spring, which is called *Maslyennitsa* ("butter time"). They dance and sing, burn the straw image of winter, and build an image of the sun in the center of a

His decision to adopt Byzantium's Greek Orthodox version had far-reaching consequences. Some scholars believe that the emphasis in the Byzantine church on strict adherence to official doctrine discouraged political dissent.

dancing crowd. They cook special *blini* (which are very large round and thin pancakes that symbolize the sun and invite the spring to come). All these rituals date back to pagan times.

But Christianity did change Russia in fundamental ways. As a Christian country, Russia grew closer to Byzantium, and to other countries of western Europe. Beautiful cathedrals and monasteries were erected, as were schools. Two Bulgarian monks—Cyril and Methodius—invented an alphabet based on Greek to be used for Slavic languages. In a modern form it is still used today, and is called Cyrillic, after the monk. Christianity brought to the Slavs a new conception of marriage: two people united for life in a church in the presence of a priest and with the help of a religious ritual. Christian ideals such as mercy, kindness, and forgiveness took hold among many peasants and princes. Prince Vladimir, who had forced the nation to accept Christianity, was lovingly named "Vladimir the Beautiful Sun," and his name is repeated in folk songs and poems. Christian religion also centralized the power of princes and *boyars* (aristocrats) over the rest of the people. The priests in the churches declared everywhere that "The Prince rules his people by the will of God; as their Father is in Heaven, so is the Prince [and later the tsar] on Earth." The Russians accepted this idea immediately. The tsar (as God himself) was very frequently called "Father" and even "Daddy" by the common people. Their faith in the tsar was boundless; he could never be wrong.

Adapted from *Pages from History* by S. Syrov (Moscow: Russian Language Publishers, 1975).

Велнкій кнзь Влаоймеръ Свдтосодвічь

Portrait of Prince Vladimir.   Novosti

Icons

After the conversions, icons—large pictures of Christ, the saints, and the events of their lives—were prominently placed in cathedrals and churches. Gradually they became part of people's homes and lives. Small-size icons (called "images") were always given a place of honor in homes. A close friend was always seated "under the images." Icons started and ended a Russian life. When a baby was born, he or she was given a tiny icon on a chain. When somebody died, the icon was put into his or her hands. A young couple on their way to church for a wedding always came to the parents' house for the blessing. The father took his best icon off the wall and blessed the young couple with it. Going to war, a young man would always wear a tiny "image" given to him by his mother to protect him from death. Certain icons belonged to families for centuries and, in addition to their religious and artistic value, served as reminders of countless births, weddings, wars, and burials.

Victor Solovyov, artist and restorer, working on the restoration of the thirteenth-century Danilov Monastery, Moscow. This kind of work is one sign of Gorbachev's liberalized policies toward religion. APN Photo/Novosti

From Tatars to Muscovy

For two hundred years, the Kievans divided their energies between internal squabbling and resisting raiders from the east. Ultimately, that latter effort failed disastrously when the Mongolian Tatars utterly destroyed that kingdom in 1237–1242 and founded their own. Known to history as "the Golden Horde," the Tatars killed or captured more than half the population, and many of the rest fled.

Unlike most of their predecessors, the Tatars were not merely marauders. They settled permanently, establishing their capital on the banks of the Volga and ruling with epic ruthlessness, cruelty, ruinous taxation, and periodic massacres. During their rule Russia suffered 133 foreign invasions and 90 domestic clashes. This devastation struck when the other great peoples of Europe were undertaking the monumental tasks of nation and state building. It delayed Russian emergence from the medieval period by several centuries.

The calamitous Tatar occupation continued until the late fifteenth century, though the firmness of their control varied considerably by region and relaxed toward the end. As it declined, the princely state of Muscovy emerged gradually as an organized center of resistance. A Russian army drove out the Golden Horde in 1480, and dissident Crimean Tatars destroyed it in 1502. As the Tatars waned, the grand duchy of Muscovy waxed. Its territory grew from about 15,000 square miles (39,000 sq. km.) in 1425 to 55,000 square miles (142,000 sq. km.) in 1533, becoming one of the largest states in Europe. (For more on the Tatars see *The Land and People of Mongolia.*)

The long Tatar occupation left an indelible stamp on the Russian political temperament. Perhaps most striking was the acceptance of the absolute political authority of the ruler. As warrior tribes, the Tatars were organized along military lines that concentrated power in their chiefs. While kings were also warriors in other countries throughout the world, competing forces—such as the nobility or the church—diminished their powers. The tradition of Tatar leadership may help to explain Russian, and later Soviet, submission to tsarist and Stalinist tyranny and the hesitant response to Gorbachev's liberalism.

Daily Life in Early Russia: Peasantry

The ongoing warfare before and during the Tatar occupation necessarily affected the daily lives of all Russians profoundly, leaving traces to the present day. The leaders who emerged were primarily soldiers without fixed residence. They moved about, following the fortunes of struggle. That mobility, and the availability of plunder from their raids, led them naturally to engage in trade.

Despite the power and wealth that came from trade and conquest, even the greatest leaders had precious little comfort or ease. Because of the dangers of soldiering, their lodgings were designed mainly for protection from hostile armed forces and were cold, dark, and damp. Being mobile, they accumulated few material possessions, so their quarters were very sparsely furnished. In later centuries, as the warfare abated somewhat, the nobility became more settled and land emerged as the main basis of fortune and status.

The peasants (some 95 percent of the population) and the common townspeople were often the principal victims of the fighting among their rulers. The men were drafted into the rival armies or were attacked by them. Their homes were plundered and burned, their crops destroyed, and their wives and children carried away. The peasants made their living mainly by hunting, trapping, beekeeping, and farming. Townspeople were largely artisans (shoemakers, carpenters, bakers, etc.) and small traders.

Peasant homes in the early period were little more than caves or dugouts roofed with earth-covered logs. Later, small, rude log cabins became common in the forested regions and timber-framed clay in the grasslands of the south. The typical dwelling was virtually bare of furnishings, except for a large clay or brick fireplace or stove built into the structure and occupying much of the meager floor space. It provided

Serfs

Until about the end of the sixteenth century, most Russian peasants were relatively free. Then, as serfdom was disappearing in western Europe, it became the dominant form of life in the Russian countryside. About 95 percent of Russians were peasants, and after serfdom developed, about 95 percent of the peasants were serfs. About half of the serfs were owned as state property on crown lands. The others belonged to private landowners.

State serfs paid a heavy tax for the privilege of working the land and met certain other obligations as well. About one third of the private serfs paid a similar rent to their landlords, and the others met their commitment by laboring on the owners' land, usually for three workdays a week. Often the landlords abused their power by requiring additional days of work to which they were not entitled.

heat and a place for cooking, and its top served as the family bed. Domestic animals shared those quarters.

If commoners were captured by enemy forces, whether serving in the army or not, they were enslaved. Others sold themselves into slavery or fell into that state through indebtedness. Slaves had no civil rights and were bought and sold freely. They usually worked at the most menial and dangerous tasks.

Summer clothing for men was linen shirts and trousers and for women linen shirts and woolen skirts or sleeveless dresses. In winter, they wore woolen robes and sheepskin coats. Their diet consisted of bread, game, beef, mutton, pork, fish, vegetables, fruit, and dairy products. Food, clothing, and most of their other daily needs were produced at home.

Quite apart from the armed violence that was so common, life was full of peril. Neither noble nor commoner was protected against epidem-

The average tax levy was so high that most peasants could survive only by hiring themselves out beyond the requirements of the rent payment. Usually, they could save so little that bad weather or crop failure would drive them into debt to their landlords, enabling the landowners to extract still more labor from the peasants.

Serfs could be bought, sold, or bequeathed. Families could be dispersed by the owner. They could be punished for laziness, insubordination, or other offenses by whipping, fines, imprisonment, or exile.

Most serfs belonged to communal villages, called *mirs*. In theory the *mirs* were self-governing associations. They assigned land for cultivation among the villagers and regulated the use of common meadows, woodlots, and pastures. In practice, the landlords intervened actively in their affairs.

ics, common diseases, famine, natural disasters, harsh winters, fires, and accidents, or had adequate means to recover from them.

Ivan the Terrible
The effects of the Orthodox and Tatar legacies can be seen especially vividly in the reign of Ivan the Terrible, who came to the throne at the age of three in 1533. He joined the Tatar concept of political absolutism to the Byzantine practice of a union of church and state. On them he laid the foundations for the modern Russian state and society.

Ivan's application of the principle of political absolutism brought autocracy to full flower in Russia. Until then, the power of the rulers had been curbed somewhat by an entrenched landed nobility (the *boyars*). Ivan distrusted these nobles deeply and, beginning in 1564, waged a bloody and vicious campaign against them. So autocratic was his power that Ivan carried out a political, economic, social, and governmental revolution entirely on his own authority, without the advice or agreement of anyone not totally dependent on him personally.

Ivan created a new class of nobles (*oprichniks*), numbering about one thousand at the outset, many of whom had had no previous standing. They formed a kind of courtly brotherhood whose principal pastimes were pious worship and drunken orgies. Using them as an imperial guard, he drove the *boyars* from their estates, wiped out their economic base, and exiled them to the Siberian frontier. He installed the *oprichniks* in their stead, but controlled them so tightly that they never could challenge him or his successors. Ivan also reduced the church to complete subservience. When its leader showed some glimmer of independence, Ivan had him murdered.

Oprichniks

Oprichniks might be seen as the great-great-grandfathers of the modern-day KGB (secret police). They had a special uniform, and a dog's head and a broom were tied to the saddle of their horses. These were emblems of their mission. They had to sniff out, follow, and sweep away treason, and to bite and kill all their enemies. Oprichniks had to wear all-black clothes from head to toe, ride only on black horses, and saddle them in black. Contemporaries called them "pitch-black darkness" or "dark as night."

Something of a monk and a villain at the same time, Ivan the Terrible gathered in the *oprichnik* "order" people "mean and in every sense evil"; and, just like monks, they had to kiss the cross and swear allegiance to it.

Nor were ordinary people spared Ivan's autocratic ruthlessness. In the process of destroying the *boyars*, he impoverished almost the whole population. His mere suspicion that some residents of Novgorod were conspiring against him resulted in the destruction of the city and the slaughter of sixty thousand men, women, and children. He imposed serfdom on a peasantry that had been free until then and that has in many ways not yet recovered its freedom after more than four hundred years.

To symbolize his assumption of autocratic authority, Ivan took the title of "tsar" a form of the word "caesar," which had been used for the rulers of ancient Rome. Yet, paradoxically, in 1566 he also took the first step toward a Russian parliament by founding the appointive, consultative Zemsky Sobor.

Ivan waged war incessantly to protect and expand his realm. By conquest and annexation, he extended it to the Caucasus Mountains in the south and across the Urals into western Siberia. However, he failed to gain access to the Baltic, to recover historic Slavic lands in the west, or to end the pillaging expeditions of the Crimean Tatars from the south.

The Time of Troubles

After Ivan's death in 1584, social disorder degenerated rapidly into utter chaos, known as "the time of troubles." In a fit of rage Ivan had murdered with his own hands his eldest son and heir. The throne went to his next son, the feebleminded Fedor.

Russia's real ruler during Fedor's fourteen-year reign was his brother-in-law, Boris Godunov, who became tsar himself when Fedor died in 1598. After Godunov's death in 1605, six tsars paraded across the throne in six years. Then a two-year gap preceded the 1613 coronation of Mikhail Romanov, founder of the dynasty that ruled until 1917. The first four Romanovs were weak children. The court intrigues continued.

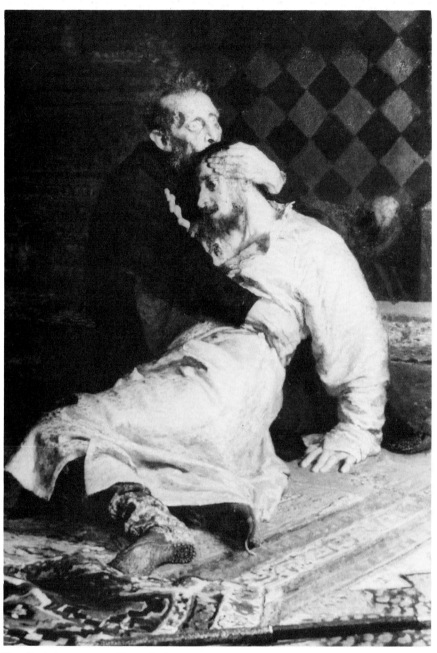

Ilya Repin's painting of Ivan the Terrible and his son Ivan, whom he murdered in a mad rage. Novosti

The dynastic confusion reflected the social situation. Famine, foreign invasions, economic collapse, mass executions, pillaging, civil war, and peasant uprisings were all part of the picture. At the same time, paradoxically, the state grew ever more oppressive, centralized, and bureaucratized. The institutions that would otherwise check a ruler's power, such as independent courts or an assembly, could not take shape under these extreme and chaotic conditions. Instead, successive autocrats and rapacious courtiers vied for power.

Ivan's successors strengthened the close alliance of church and state. During the seventeenth century the state gained clear control over the church, largely because the church adopted a modernized Greek ritual. This infuriated many worshippers and clergy, who regarded Moscow as the only true seat of Christian orthodoxy. The quarrel concerned such seemingly trivial matters as whether to make the sign of the cross with two or three fingers. The dissenters broke away as an "Old Believers" sect that clung with incredible fervency to the traditional rites.

Orthodoxy

Orthodoxy gained ground in the Russian nation, and at last grew to be a part of its very flesh and bones. For six centuries orthodoxy was identified with its very life. In the most solemn and tragic moments of its history—when struggling desperately with the sword and by statecraft against the overwhelming power of the Tatars for the right of calling their bodies and goods their own, or when defending the state and the integrity of the empire against the Poles and Swedes—the Russians always had to face enemies of another faith as well as another nationality. Whenever they met on a peaceful footing with aliens, they found them different—save a mere handful of Greeks—in religion as well as in speech and race. Orthodoxy became linked with the idea of nationality. It was felt to be an attribute of the whole nation. Even minor deviations from strictest adherence to its customs so affronted the patriotism of ordinary Russians on occasion that they triggered riots and insurrections.

Yet those same Russians who exhibited that striking readiness to stand by their religion to the last drop of their blood showed complete indifference to religion in their everyday lives and utter carelessness in fulfilling their religious duties. They did not observe the rites of the church, ignored its teachings, and rarely attended its services. Only the ever-present icon in the corner of even the most humble cottage served as a daily reminder of their religion. The clergy were addicted to riotous drinking and immoral lives. For long periods little preaching was done and services were conducted in great disorder.

Adapted from Stepniak, *The Russian Peasantry*, 1888

A Russian Orthodox priest performing Easter services in a church near Moscow.
Novosti

Meanwhile, Russian-ruled territory continued to expand. Trappers, merchants, soldiers, and colonizers spread gradually eastward across Siberia, reaching the Bering and Okhotsk seas by 1676. To the west, Ukraine was annexed in 1654.

That territorial growth sharpened the gap between Russia's size and its power. Russia was the largest and most populous European country, but trailed its western neighbors militarily, politically, and economically. Poor leadership and location thwarted the centuries-old yearning to escape international weakness.

One reaction to that situation was to send emissaries to the west to learn its ways and to bring westerners to Russia. However, those aliens tended to be greedy adventurers, more interested in lining their own pockets than in serving their adoptive land loyally. Therefore, their expertise was a mixed blessing.

Peter the Great: The Westernizer

Peter I, the Great, the fifth Romanov, came to the throne in 1682 at age ten. However, he differed from the four previous child tsars, for his monumental eccentricities were combined with greatness.

Peter was precocious physically and mentally, but he remained an adolescent emotionally throughout his life. He particularly enjoyed things military, mechanical, and western. The main activities of his youth were religious rituals, elaborate war games, and drunken orgies.

Peter's behavior changed little in adulthood—at enormous cost to his family and the Russian people. He imprisoned his first wife for decades in a remote convent and tortured and executed his son and heir on trumped-up charges of treason. He imposed ruinous financial and human burdens in pursuit of his military ambitions, devastated the economy, and caused a spreading deterioration of the social order.

Peter had spent his teenage years much in the company of foreigners and toured Europe for fifteen months in 1697–1698, studying western culture, science, and technology. Upon returning, he set about to modernize Russia along western lines by imposing revolutionary reforms with demonic haste and fury. He outlawed traditional beards and dress, shaving the nobles himself. He founded the Russian navy and modernized the army; established technical schools, the Academy of Science,

Splendor

The pomp and glitter of the Russian tsar's court life can be seen in this menu of one of the wedding lunches served to the Tsar Alexei Michailovich and his newlywed wife—Natalie Naryshkina—in the first half of the seventeenth century:

Served to the Tsar Alexei . . . during his wedding with Natalie Naryshkina:
two pairs of swans
sautéed in saffron
hazel hens in lemon sauce
fried geese and
goose's stomach pâté

and personally served to Her Majesty, The Empress:
piglet steak
chicken steamed with lemons
chicken with noodles
chicken in cabbage soup
rich with different fillings

Also to both Their Majesties the Tsar and the Tsarina were additionally served:
a dish of oatmeal bread
a chicken pie with eggs

and state-owned factories and mines; reformed and strengthened the state financial system; revised the calendar and alphabet; reorganized the church to bring it firmly under his control; changed the governmental and administrative system drastically; proclaimed himself emperor;

a lamb pie
a dish of sour pies with cheese
a dish of fried larks
a dish of thin pancakes with caviar
a dish of egg pies
a dish of curd pancakes
a dish of crucians with lamb

Also:
10 soups
12 salads
8 sauces

And:
turtles
little pigeons with crabs
deer's lips
herrings' cheeks
 (1,000 herrings were needed to cook one plate of this)
steak of lynx
salted peaches
pineapple in vinegar, etc.

Adapted from Peter Veil and Alexander Guenis, *Russian Cuisine in Exile* (Moscow, Almanach, 1987).

and restructured and rigidified the system of social classes. He built St. Petersburg on the swampy shores of the Baltic at horrendous human cost and moved his capital there from tradition-bound Moscow.

The herculean effort to build a new capital had military motivation. Peter sought an adequate base for the wars he waged ceaselessly against all his neighbors, pursuing—as always—the Russian dream of securing easily accessible warm-water ports. The results were mixed. He established a permanent Russian presence on the Baltic and in the great power politics of Europe, but could not break the Turkish stranglehold on the Black Sea. Russian control of Siberia was solidified, but China blocked his drive to the Pacific.

Excerpt from *The Bronze Horseman*

Here is how Alexander Pushkin, Russia's most famous poet, describes Peter's ambitions and the founding of St. Petersburg (now Leningrad), in his *The Bronze Horseman*:

On a deserted, wave-swept shore, he stood filled with his lofty thoughts and gazed into the distance. Before him the river sped on its wide course; a humble, lonely skiff moved fast on its surface. On the mossy and swampy banks, black huts were dotted here and there—the homes of miserable Finns; and the forest . . . roared all around. And thus he thought: "From here we shall threaten the Swede, here a city shall be founded to spite our arrogant neighbor. Here we are destined by Nature to cut a window into Europe. . . . Ships of every flag will come to visit us." A hundred years passed, and the young city, the ornament and marvel of its dark neighbors, rose resplendent and stately from forests and swamps, and old Moscow has paled before the young capital like a widow mother before a new empress.

The Reign of Mediocrity
Peter's death from venereal disease in 1725 opened sixteen years of reign by four successive mediocre rulers chosen by makeshift councils of officials in the ominous presence of palace guards. They were Catherine I (1725–1727), the illiterate Livonian peasant girl who became Peter's mistress and, later, his wife and empress; Peter's eleven-year-old grandson, Peter II (1727–1730); Anne (1730–1740); and Ivan VI (1740–1741), who succeeded to the throne when he was two months old and was deposed thirteen months later. The real rulers of Russia were a swirling band of foreign adventurers who manipulated the various strands of the Romanov dynasty and the palace guards.

That period of mediocrity was followed by two more long reigns of powerful, but perverted, rulers. Elizabeth I (1741–1761) and Catherine II, the Great (1762–1796), became empresses by palace coup. During the six-month interim, the weak-minded Peter III, who was Elizabeth's nephew and Catherine's husband, reigned. He was deposed and assassinated in a plot engineered by Catherine, a German princess reared by French Protestants.

Catherine the Great wanted to be known as an enlightened ruler and cultivated the acquaintance of such western philosophers as Voltaire and Diderot. In practice, however, she hardened the lot of the serfs, especially by making them clearly the property of the landowners. She increased the privileges and governmental functions of the nobility, widening still further the gap between it and the serfs. Those measures precipitated the bloodiest peasant revolt, under Yemelyan Pugachov in 1773–1775.

Territorially, the eighteenth century was one of great expansion. By its end, Russia had shared in the partition of Poland, driven the Turks from the northern coast of the Black Sea, and conquered Crimea and Georgia. Its domain covered Siberia, the Kamchatka Peninsula, and the Kurile Islands, and extended to Alaska and northern California. However, that expansion cost enormously in money, lives, and social disruption.

None of those monarchs provided effective leadership for the evolution into modernity that Russia's western neighbors were undergoing. Nor were there laws, legislatures, or courts as alternatives to and restraints on the tsars. Instead, rulers and court favorites tended to be immigrant westerners. Their origins conditioned them to understand modernization, but denied them the devotion and loyalty of true Russians.

Russia, 1800–1917: Romanovs and Revolutionaries

Paul I Nineteenth-century Russia was divided politically between tsarist autocrats and revolutionaries. Both of those groups were themselves split between slavophiles and westernizers. The former believed that the solution to Russia's problems lay in typically slavic traditions or social sources, such as the peasantry, the Orthodox Church, or the tsar. The latter thought that western-type modernization held the answers. Slavophile tsars tended to be conservative and westernizer tsars leaned toward reform. However, nothing was clearcut. Leaders often shifted back and forth from one position to another.

Paul I, the first nineteenth-century monarch, wavered between the two approaches. He admired all things Prussian and sent his armies deep into western Europe, exposing them to western ideas and practices. But he was slavophile in clinging to extreme views on autocracy and in ambivalence toward reform. Above all, he was erratic, quite incapable of leading Russia consistently in any direction.

Paul's reckless plunge into European politics first engaged Russia in a military coalition that sought to destroy the French Revolution. Then he undertook to switch alliances when Napoleon came to power in France. Before he could complete that reversal, he was assassinated in a March 1801 palace coup.

Alexander I
Paul's son and heir, Alexander I, was similarly ambivalent. He had a liberal intellect, but conservative instincts. Early in his reign he was as liberal as any tsar. He ordered Michael Speransky to plan a sweeping reform of the administrative and governmental structure. It would have established the first genuinely representative assemblies.

In his last few years, however, Alexander became increasingly conservative. The only parts of his governmental reform that were put into practice created the appointive and consultative Council of State and reorganized the ministries. Perhaps more importantly, he introduced principles of legality and regularity that went as far toward governmental modernization as any in prerevolutionary Russia.

Under Alexander, Russian expansion continued. He annexed Georgia, Finland, Bessarabia, and Azerbaijan. Alexander's vacillation toward France led Napoleon to invade Russia in 1812. The French captured Moscow, but their victory was hollow. The Russians had burned the city and refused to talk peace. The French withdrew in disorder in the dead of a fierce Russian winter.

That Napoleonic episode impressed Russian minds deeply. The mighty western military force, rolling across the steppes, drilled into the Russians a sharp sense of their technological inferiority. At the same time, French notions of nationalism infected the Russians. All previous wars had been tsarist; this one was Russian. The hostile reaction of the Russian people arose at least partly because the tsar's enemies were foreign nationalists.

Russia's membership in the victorious alliance launched it definitively into the ranks of the Great Powers. It had become the most powerful force on the European continent and Britain's principal rival.

Excerpt from *War and Peace*

This is how Leo Tolstoy describes Alexander, and the feelings evoked by the tsar in general, in his book *War and Peace*:

Standing in the foremost ranks of Kutuzov's army, which was the first the Tsar approached, Rostov experienced the same feeling as every other man in that army: a feeling of self-oblivion, a proud consciousness of might, and a passionate devotion to him who was the cause of that triumphant occasion. One word from that man, he felt, and this huge mass (including the insignificant grain that was himself) would go through fire and water, commit crimes, die, or perform deeds of the greatest heroism, and he could not but tremble, and his heart stood still, at the imminency of that word.

"Hurrah! Hurrah! Hurrah!" thundered from all sides, as one regiment after another greeted the Tsar with the strains of the general's march; and again "Hurrah!" and again the march, and "Hurrah! Hurrah!" the sound increasing and swelling into a deafening roar. Each regiment in its silent immobility was like a lifeless body till the Tsar reached it, but the instant he came level with it, it came to life, its thunder joining the roar of the line along which he had already passed. Through the terrible, deafening sound of those voices, amid the mass of troops standing motionless in their squares as if turned to stone, the hundreds of officers composing the suites rode casually, but symmetrically and above all freely, and in front of them, two men—Emperors. And upon these two men the undivided, rapt, and passionate attention of that mass of men was concentrated.

That handsome young Emperor Alexander wearing the uniform of the Horse Guards and a cocked hat, with his pleasant face and resonant though subdued voice, attracted the full force of their attention.

Rostov stood not far from the buglers, and with his keen sight had recognized the Tsar from a distance and watched his approach. When he was within twenty paces and Nikolai could clearly distinguish every feature of that handsome, happy, youthful face, he experienced a feeling of tenderness and ecstasy such as he had never before known. Everything about the Tsar—every feature, every gesture, seemed to him entrancing.

Stopping in front of the Pavlograd regiment, the Tsar said something in French to the Austrian Emperor and smiled.

Seeing that smile, Rostov involuntarily smiled himself and felt an even stronger access of love for his sovereign. He longed to express his love in some way, and knowing that this was impossible, he was ready to weep. The Tsar called the regimental commander and said a few words to him.

"Oh, God, what would happen if the Tsar were to speak to me?" thought Rostov. "I should die of happiness!"

The Tsar also addressed the officers.

"I thank you all, gentlemen" (to Rostov every word was like a voice from heaven), "I thank you with all my heart."

How gladly would Rostov have died then and there for his Tsar!

"You have won the St. George standards, and I know you will be worthy of them."

"Oh, to die, to die for him!" thought Rostov.

The Tsar said something more, which Rostov did not hear, and the soldiers, straining their lungs, shouted, "Hurrah!"

This resulted largely from Alexander's personal leadership in international politics, especially his initiative for the formation of the "Holy Alliance" and the Quadruple Alliance (Britain, Russia, Prussia, Austria-Hungary).

The Decembrist Revolt

Another by-product of 1812 was the modern Russian revolutionary tradition. After Napoleon's defeat thirty thousand tsarist troops helped occupy Paris. Some officers were greatly impressed by the advanced technology of the west and wanted something similar for their homeland. They believed this required overthrow of the antiquated tsarist system.

Upon returning to Russia, these officers promoted their cause through secret political societies. When Alexander died suddenly (November 19, 1825) and his eldest brother, Constantine, refused the throne, they organized uprisings on December 14 and 28 to exploit the confusion.

The Decembrists' ill-prepared and poorly executed revolt was put down quickly but had enduring results. The rulers concluded that serious reform was unacceptably dangerous and that unrelenting political repression was essential for their survival. In turn, the tsarist reaction convinced the opposition that legal, gradual, and peaceful change was impossible, that only violent revolution could succeed. The Decembrist revolt became the specter that haunted Russian political life for the next century.

Nicholas I

The Decembrist revolt impressed no one more deeply than the new monarch, Nicholas I, Alexander's second brother. The uprising so frightened him that its immediate effect was tragically counterproductive.

At last Russia had a competent, reasonably intelligent, sane ruler. But his reaction against the abortive revolt was so enduring that he did

The Decembrists

This is how one of the Decembrists' leaders, Kakhovsky, explained the rebellion in a letter to the Tsar Nicholas I:

The beginning of the reign of Emperor Alexander was marked with bright hopes for Russia's prosperity. The gentry had recuperated, the merchant class did not object to giving credit, the army served without making trouble, scholars studied what they wished, all spoke what they thought, and everyone expected better days. Unfortunately, circumstances prevented the realization of these hopes, which passed without their fulfillment. The unsuccessful, expensive war of 1770 and others disorganized our finances, though we had not yet realized it when preparing for the national war of 1812. Finally, Napoleon invaded Russia and then only, for the first time, did the Russian people become aware of their power; only then awakened in all our hearts a feeling of independence, at first political and finally national. That is the beginning of free thinking in Russia. The government itself spoke such words as "Liberty, Emancipation." It had itself sown the idea of abuses resulting from the unlimited power of Napoleon, and the appeal of the Russian Monarch resounded on the banks of the Rhine and Seine. The war was still on when the soldiers, upon their return home, for the first time disseminated grumbling among the masses. "We shed blood," they would say, "and then we are again forced to sweat under feudal obligations. We freed the Fatherland from the tyrant, and now we ourselves are tyrannized by the ruling class." The army, from generals to privates, upon its return, did nothing but discuss how good it is in foreign lands. A comparison with their own country naturally brought up the question, Why should it not be so in our own land?

almost nothing to drag his backward realm into the modern world—even though he fully recognized the necessity to do so. His primary policy was to ensure that no later imitators of the Decembrists would succeed. Revolutions in western Europe, in 1830 and 1848, reinforced his resolve.

Nicholas ruled as well as reigned. No Russian monarch was more personally, directly, and actively involved in formulating and implementing state policy than Nicholas. The slogan "Orthodoxy, autocracy, nationality" expressed his basic goals perfectly.

Nicholas realized that pursuit of those conservative objectives sometimes required reform. He began to systematize and perfect the various measures to control the Russian people that his predecessors had introduced piecemeal. For one thing, the Russian legal system had developed as a hodgepodge of local, regional, and national practices, customs, and decrees. He organized it into a single, uniform code, and removed the worst excesses of serfdom, though he considered emancipation premature.

But these reforms had nothing to do with liberalism. Nicholas was a rigid disciplinarian and authoritarian. His professed desire to rule as a benevolent dictator led only to arbitrary despotism in a police state. The tsar's long reign produced no significant modernization of Russian social, political, or governmental institutions.

This was also true for the economy. Serfdom had become increasingly counterproductive. The system's built-in inefficiencies left Russia's enormous agricultural potential largely unrealized. Prohibitive tariff legislation, the use of serfs as workers, and stifling bureaucratic controls inhibited domestic industry and foreign trade. Nevertheless, during Nicholas's reign, the Russian economy grew modestly and evolved from subsistence, in which crops are mainly grown for use by the producer, to market, in which products are raised for sale.

Nicholas's conservatism was nowhere more evident than in diplomacy. He articulated and pursued consistently a policy of intervening

The Russian peasants see the tsar as the common father of the country, its protector, and the supreme dispenser of impartial justice to all, defending the weaker members of the community from the stronger. The tsar is duty bound to step in and redistribute equitably the natural riches of the country whenever this is needed in the common interest. The people repose implicit confidence in the tsar's wisdom and justice. He is absolute master of the life and property of every man within his dominions, and no exception may be taken to his orders. The occasional blunders of the tsar, however heavy they may be, must be borne with patience, as they can be only temporary; the tsar will redress the evil as soon as he is better informed on the matter.

Adapted from Stepniak, *The Russian Peasantry*, 1888.

wherever possible to protect dynastic legitimacy, suppress liberalism, and prevent revolution. He repressed the Polish insurrection of 1830–1831, advocated an international military crusade to undo the 1830 revolutions in France and Belgium, shored up the tottering Ottoman (Turkish) regime in 1833, and joined in reviving the Holy Alliance expressly to preserve the European status quo. In 1848 he massed four hundred thousand troops on Russia's western border in readiness to attack the revolution in France and assisted the Austro-Hungarian empire to repress similar revolts.

However, Nicholas's conservatism faded when he had opportunities to continue Russian expansion. In 1828–1829 he conquered and annexed two Persian provinces, seized Turkish territory along the Black Sea, secured the right of free passage through the Bosporus, and established a protectorate over the Ottoman provinces of Moldava and Wallachia in the Balkans (now provinces of Romania). Later, he absorbed the Polish province of Krac\u00f3w, expanded Russian Central Asia, and occupied the Amur River basin and Sakhalin Island in the Far East. By the close of his reign, the Russian empire had virtually reached its maximum extent.

In the end Nicholas's expansionism led to disaster in the Crimean War of 1854–1856, when Russia fought Turkey, France, Britain, and Austria-Hungary. Nicholas died in February 1855 (perhaps a suicide), before the hostilities ended, but after his catastrophic failure had become evident. The resulting treaty required that Russia demilitarize the Black Sea and cede Moldava, Wallachia, and part of Bessarabia.

Alexander II   The Crimean War made clear to everyone the dire need for reform. Alexander II, Nicholas's eldest son and successor, recognized this early in his reign through several very important steps. The most dramatic and significant was the abolition of serfdom.

This last real opportunity for reform was largely frustrated by ambivalences in Alexander's character. He was tsar for six years before issuing the emancipation edict—on February 19, 1861—which, even then, was partial and defective. (By comparison, Lincoln issued the Emancipation Proclamation on September 22, 1862, eighteen and a half months after becoming president.) Indeed, its imperfections outlasted both the tsar and tsardom. Alexander's decree initiated a long process not scheduled to end until the 1950's. It pleased neither landowners nor serfs and never really solved the problem of serfdom.

Serfdom was so closely intertwined with local government that liquidation of the former required a sweeping reform of the latter. An 1864 law revived and reorganized the *zemstvos* (county and provincial assemblies) as the basic units of local rural administration. A similar system for towns and cities was introduced in 1870.

These reforms were not very liberal. The nobility remained dominant and the serfs benefitted little. The financial resources and authority of the local councils were grossly insufficient for the areas they governed.

Not surprisingly, the new system never functioned very well. True reformers considered it inadequate. The upper classes feared it would encourage liberal and radical agitation. The bureaucrats resented its intrusion. Consequently, subsequent laws curtailed the meager role of the *zemstvo* still further. Nevertheless, the *zemstvo* gave Russia its first real taste of representative government.

Judicial reform ran a similar course. Alexander inherited an incredibly complex, corrupt, and vicious system. The abolition of serfdom rendered it hopelessly and obviously inappropriate. In 1864 he introduced western principles and partially relaxed Nicholas's police-state measures. Reactionary officials prevented the reforms from taking full effect, created many exceptions, and subverted its objectives. Nevertheless, the surviving changes modernized and humanized the system dramatically.

Emancipation of the serfs and the catastrophic inefficiency of the army in the Crimean War necessitated fundamental military reforms. Alexander extended compulsory military service to all classes, rather than only peasants, and reduced the term of active duty from twenty-five years to six. He ended the use of the army as a form of imprisonment and abolished the harshest punishments. Once again, practice fell far short of principle. Numerous exceptions remained and old habits died hard. Still, the reforms gave the army a giant push toward the modern world.

Constitutional reform made little progress under Alexander. His attempt to liberalize Polish government was aborted when the Poles revolted in 1863. He established a Council of Ministers, but it never really functioned. Only in Finland, where he revived the diet (parliament) of 1809 and permitted wide autonomy, did his constitutional measures have any significant effect.

Economically, Alexander's record was mixed. Emancipation failed to produce the expected economic benefits, and agriculture languished. Trade, communications, transportation, and manufacturing grew rapidly, though unevenly. However, the state and foreigners provided most

Peasants

All peasants, rich or poor, live in the same sort of narrow dwelling, fifteen to twenty feet square, with one or two rooms. Children and adults are all huddled together. The amount of air space is so puzzlingly small that only the draftiness of the walls prevents their suffocation.

Most peasants possess no furniture beyond a big unpolished table of the simplest pattern, which stands in the place of honor in a corner under the icons, and some long wooden benches, about two feet deep, running along the walls. These benches are used for sitting in the daytime and for sleeping at night. Some of the members of large families sleep on shelves, which line the wall, like hammocks on a ship. The only coverings for benches and floor are a few worn-out rugs. Coats serve as blankets. In winter the large top of the stone oven is the favorite sleeping place and is generally reserved for the elderly.

of the financial and managerial leadership. Private business enterprise of the sort that gave backbone to modern economic development in the west played only a minor role in Russia.

After the middle 1860's Alexander lost much of his commitment to reform. He undertook no major new initiatives, and some of his earlier measures were diluted or sabotaged.

In foreign affairs, Alexander followed his father's policies closely. He supported monarchy and conservatism whenever that did not endanger Russian territorial aspirations. However, he was less inclined toward foreign military intervention, perhaps having learned from the Crimean lesson. Territorially, Alexander's reign was a close standoff. He sold Alaska to the United States, but consolidated Russian control of Central

Peasant dress is extremely simple: no underwear, a homespun shirt and light cotton or linen trousers. The richer wear boots. Shoes made from hemplike fibers, a type that has not been worn elsewhere since the Middle Ages, are common in the summer and homemade woolen boots in winter. Coats are long woolen homespun or sheepskin. They seldom change their clothes, but keep their bodies very clean.

Food is their chief item of expense. The rich or well-to-do eat wholemeal bread and gruel year round. The diet of the average peasant is chiefly vegetarian and extremely simple. They eat meat on Sundays and occasionally on a weekday, but never every day. If they can help it, they spend nothing on themselves, using only what is homemade, homegrown, or raised on the premises.

Adapted from Stepniak, *The Russian Peasantry*, 1888.

Asia and of the Amur region and Sakhalin Island in the Far East.

The pan-Slavic movement brought Alexander's support for legitimacy into conflict with his pursuit of territorial security. The pan-Slavs were a small group of intellectuals who argued that Russia had a mission to liberate other Slavic peoples from non-Slavic states, especially the Austro-Hungarian and Ottoman empires, and to unify them under Russian political and religious leadership. The pan-Slavs reinforced the traditional Russian yearning for free access to the Mediterranean and overrode Alexander's reluctance to threaten anyone else's throne. The result was Russian involvement in the Balkan wars of the late 1870's and some increased influence there at the expense of the collapsing Ottoman Empire.

Alexander III   The assassination of Alexander II in March 1881 brought his son to the throne as Alexander III. The new tsar was physically powerful but mentally weak and prided himself on being "The Peasant Tsar." He was conservative, autocratic, and pan-Slavic—by natural inclination and through the influence of his tutor and chief advisor, the conservative jurist and philosopher Constantine Pobedonostsev.

Alexander III undertook to undo many of his predecessor's reforms. He vetoed or rescinded various measures that introduced western-type institutions or freedoms. On the other hand, he catered to the peasants by easing the terms of their emancipation, reducing their taxes, relaxing restrictions on their migration, and establishing banks for them. He also enacted important laws protecting labor.

Despite Alexander III's reactionary constitutional and political policies, Russian economic development progressed greatly during his reign. Industrialization proceeded more rapidly than ever before or since. The number of factory workers doubled. So did the production of iron, the basic industrial commodity. Production increased by half for coal and sevenfold for oil. Railroad trackage rose from 15,000 miles (24,000 km.) in 1881 to 24,000 miles (39,000 km.) in 1895, and planning for the great Trans-Siberian Railway was begun in 1891. Farming continued to languish, however, and a terrible famine swept the country in 1891.

In foreign affairs, Alexander's reign was characterized by an almost unprecedented period of peace. His most notable policy was to reverse alliances from Germany to France. He expanded Russian holdings in Central Asia, especially along the Afghan border, and continued efforts for more Russian influence in the Balkans.

Unlike most of his predecessors, Alexander died peacefully of natural causes on November 1, 1894. This ended a reign that seemed highly successful. Yet the stability, tranquility, growth, and progress

A cotton-cleaning plant in Tashkent early in the twentieth century. Novosti

concealed a fundamental problem and a new, hostile political movement.

That fundamental problem was the virtual absence of modern economy, government, or society. That hostile movement was the Russian version of Marxist socialism. The ability of the movement to exploit the problem brought the entire overblown tsarist structure crashing into oblivion less than a quarter century later. In the final, supreme irony of tsarism, its ruins served as the foundation of a new regime that incorporated, in fresh guise, most of the characteristics of the old autocracy; many of the evils the Marxists had so hated lived on in their new Soviet state.

From Tsarism to Bolshevism

As the twentieth century began, tsarist Russia seemed like one of the great certainties on the Eurasian map. Romanov after Romanov had succeeded to the imperial throne for nearly three centuries. Despite their monumental defects, their territory grew ever larger and their rule ever tighter. Yet in less than twenty years all was swept away. This chapter tells of those dramatic decades. It recounts the rise of the revolutionaries, the waning years of the regime they overthrew, and the events through which Russia's great transformation into the Soviet Union took place.

The Russian Revolutionary Tradition

Immediately after the abortive Decembrist revolt, the Russian revolutionary movement seemed to disappear completely. However, through the long, repressive winter of Nicholas I, it lay dormant in the minds of a few intellectuals. Their memories of those bold, quixotic rebels inspired a handful of semisecret literary-political study groups. Late in the century, that seedbed germinated the organizations that formed the regimes that replaced tsarism.

Socialists and Narodniks

The early successors of the Decembrists tended to follow them in the westernizer tradition. The most notable was the founder of Russian socialism, Alexander Herzen (1812–1870), illegitimate son of a wealthy nobleman and a disciple of the French experimental socialist Count Saint-Simon. In Russia until 1847 and then abroad, Herzen worked tirelessly for socialist revolution in Russia.

Another early westernizer was M. V. Butashevich-Petrashevsky (1821–1866), a nobleman, minor bureaucrat, and follower of another French experimental socialist, Charles Fourier. His discussion circle included novelist Feodor Dostoyevski, the most eloquent slavophile after 1860.

In the 1860's, the slavophile *narodniks* emerged as a major revolutionary movement. They believed that the *mir*, which was the most common type of village organization, would be the means to bring socialism to Russia. Being a form of property in which a whole village owned and used land jointly, it seemed more socialist than capitalist. The *narodniks* expected peasants, rather than industrial workers, to overthrow tsarism.

Narodnik study groups formed after Alexander II turned away from his early reformism. They included the "Circle of Chaikovsky" after 1869. Among its members were anarchist Prince Peter Kropotkin and Ekaterina Konstantinova Breshko-Breshkovskaya, daughter of a wealthy landowner, who later became a founder of the Socialist Revolutionary Party.

Chronology

1845–1849	Petrashevsky Circle revolutionaries meet
April 10, 1870	Lenin (Vladimir Ilyich Ulyanov) born in Simbirsk
1873	*Narodnik* agitation of peasants begins
December 12, 1879	Stalin (Joseph Vissarionovich Dzhugashvili) born in Gori
1883	Plekhanov forms Marxist Liberation of Labor Party
1895	Union of Struggle for Emancipation of Workers formed
1898	First Congress, Russian Social Democratic Workers Party
1901	Socialist Revolutionary Party formed
1903	Second Congress, RSDWP. Bolshevik faction formed
1904–1905	Russo-Japanese War
1905	Revolution; tsarist reforms; S. Y. Witte is prime minister

Assassinations, Attempted Assassinations, and Trials

The early revolutionaries encountered many frustrations, largely because they were isolated from the masses they expected to lead. Tsarist repression drove most Russian revolutionary leaders abroad. Revolutionaries were mainly from the middle and upper classes and had little real contact with peasants.

In 1873 they tried to mobilize industrial workers. When that failed, they went into the countryside disguised as common workers during the summer of 1874 to stir up the peasants. This was a fiasco. The people

1906	First Duma meets; P. A. Stolypin is prime minister
1907	Second and Third Dumas meet
1911	Stolypin assassinated
1914	World War I begins; Germany attacks Russia
December 1916	Rasputin murdered
March 8, 1917	"February" Revolution begins
March 12, 1917	Petrograd Soviet of Workers' Deputies formed
March 15, 1917	Nicholas II abdicates; provisional government formed
April 16, 1917	Lenin arrives in Petrograd from exile abroad
June 3, 1917	All-Russian Congress of Soviets meets
July 24, 1917	Kerensky becomes prime minister
August 25, 1917	Kornilov affair begins
November 6–7, 1917	Bolsheviks seize power
December 20, 1917	Cheka (secret police) organized
January 18, 1918	Constituent Assembly meets; is dispersed January 19

failed utterly to respond, and hundreds of agitators were arrested and imprisoned. An attempt to infiltrate the peasantry in 1877–1878 by masquerading as the type of leaders it respected failed in the same way.

An 1876 effort to organize a mass demonstration in St. Petersburg was another disappointment, but it had far-reaching consequences. Vera Zasulich, a seasoned revolutionary and daughter of a minor nobleman, shot and seriously wounded the St. Petersburg military governor to avenge the punishment inflicted on one of the demonstrators. Her trial and acquittal lent credibility to terrorism.

The resulting assassination campaign slew several important tsarist officials, but Alexander II was the main target. The peasants' traditional reverence for the tsar had hindered the revolutionaries greatly; they made at least eight attempts on his life between 1879 and 1881 before killing him. However, even then, no popular uprising ensued.

The first of a new type of radical political party was the short-lived *Zemlya i Volya* (Land and Liberty) Party (1861–1864). *Narodniks* revived that name in 1876, but split in 1879 over the question of terrorism. After 1901 the branches evolved into the legal Socialist Revolutionary Party and its illegal, terrorist wing.

By then some discouraged narodniks were turning to Marxism. Georgy Plekhanov organized the first Russian Marxist party, Liberation of Labor, in Geneva in 1883. This group never developed much of a following inside Russia and remained mainly a discussion and propaganda circle for exiles. Marxist groups formed within Russia during the following decade, but did not become significant in the revolutionary movement until 1895, the year after Alexander III died.

The Reign of Nicholas II

Alexander III was succeeded by his eldest son, Nicholas, a weak, dull, incompetent ruler, totally incapable of dealing with the successive crises that swept over his realm. His reign was a disaster from beginning to end. Even his devoted but sickly wife undermined his reputation and ability to govern credibly by her mysticism and her association with the evil monk Grigory Rasputin.

Famine wracked the land in the first years of Nicholas's reign. Then his expansionist policies in the Far East led to the disastrous war with Japan (1904–1905), which cost Russia four hundred thousand casualties. The assassination in 1904 of Vyacheslav Konstaninovich Plehve, the reactionary but competent interior minister, weakened the regime further.

Industrialization and Social Change

Dramatic changes swept Russian economic and social life during the late nineteenth and early twentieth centuries. Suddenly Russia became the most rapidly modernizing major country in the world. The total population increased 260 percent and the urban population 875 percent from 1851 to 1914.

The pace of industrialization was even more dramatic, though uneven. From 1877 to 1913, industrial production increased 954 percent and railroad mileage 347 percent. The most spectacular feat was the construction of the $200-million, 5,542-mile (8,917 km.) Trans-Siberian Railroad between 1892 and 1905.

Russian industrialization was characterized by extreme centralization. Typically, industries were controlled by monopolies rather than competing firms. Factories with over a thousand workers employed 35 percent of industrial laborers (U.S. 17%). Cartels, groups of companies that cooperated to set prices, controlled 70 percent of the coal and 80 percent of the gasoline industries, and the state monopolized the alcohol and banking industries and owned 60 percent of the rail lines and many factories.

Social changes were similarly great. The peasant reforms and industrialization gave new significance to social class. The *mirs*, whose members differed little in status, were yielding to a system of farm owners and laborers. Factory workers, managers, and owners became important elements in society. Elementary and secondary schools increased from 1,621 in 1850 to 122,000 in 1915, and their enrollment grew from 10.4 per 1,000 population in 1868 to 43.5 in 1913. Public medical care and sanitation improved greatly.

Bloody Sunday: The Revolution of 1905

What a terrible day. . . . Troops had to open shooting in some parts of the city. There are many victims. What pain. Oh Lord! How unhappy I am!

Diary entry, Nicholas II, January 9, 1905, from *Soviet Life*

Political and governmental modernization lagged far behind those social and economic improvements. General discontent filled Russia. There were political and economic strikes by industrial workers, peasant riots, reform agitation by liberal landowners and intellectuals, and military and naval mutinies. The unrest culminated in a mass procession to the Winter Palace in St. Petersburg on January 9, 1905. A priest, Father George Gapon, led 140,000 peaceful petitioners, carrying icons and portraits of the tsar. Forty thousand soldiers responded with bloody brutality. Estimates of the dead range from 150 to 1,000, with 200 to 3,000 wounded.

"Bloody Sunday" sent a wave of uprisings sweeping across the country. Troops from the Far East and reform promises by the tsar saved the regime, but widespread unrest continued throughout the year. In the autumn, revolutionaries attempted to seize power through industrial strikes and a council of socialists and workers—called a "Soviet of Workers' Deputies" ("soviet" means "council")—that became a model for their successors in the Bolshevik Revolution of 1917.

The Twilight of Tsarism
The most important tsarist institutional reform was the creation of an assembly, the Duma, which had some of the powers held by western legislatures. The Duma brought Russia closer to parliamentary democracy than ever before or since, but lacked the key parliamentary powers to overthrow a government or control the budget. Further, a system of weighted voting distorted its representativeness. Either the appointive Council of State or the tsar could veto its actions, and the tsar could dissolve it at will and could enact laws by himself between Dumas.

Another major reform granted broad civil liberties, including freedom of thought, speech, assembly, and association and a ban on unlawful imprisonment. Count S. Y. Witte, first prime minister in the new system, proposed sweeping land reforms that the large estate owners blocked. Instead, much more modest reforms were made.

The Duma became the focus of the liveliest political activity Russia has known, at least until Gorbachev. Extremists of left and right boycotted it, but liberals, moderates, conservatives, and moderate *narodniks* participated. Indeed, the opposition parties won two-thirds majorities in the 1906 and March 1907 Dumas. Debates were animated and the deputies tackled legislative tasks vigorously.

Russia now had a golden opportunity to channel the process of change into a modern, moderate, democratic, constitutional monarchy. If the Duma had evolved like similar early parliaments in western Europe, modern politics and government might have emerged in Russia. Instead, the tsarists harassed and corrupted it into subservience.

Nevertheless, the Duma enacted some significant legislation. The most important granted the peasantry full legal equality. Other major laws modernized the judicial and educational systems and permitted the first labor unions.

The government's corruption of the Duma coincided with brutal repression of revolutionaries. Persons accused of political crimes faced court-martials. Some fourteen thousand were executed after the 1905 revolution and another three thousand during the prime ministership of conservative P. A. Stolypin (1906–1911). Mass revolutionary zeal receded during that period, but terrorism continued.

Nicholas's foreign policies were dictated largely by Russia's weakness in Europe and its relative strength in Asia. In the west he organized alliances and called peace conferences to neutralize potential aggressors. His pursuit of a close alliance with France forced him to abandon a short-lived secret agreement with Germany and his enmity toward Great Britain. In the east, he consolidated the Russian empire further by nibbling at Chinese territory—until Japan called an abrupt halt with the 1904–1905 war—and expanding his influence in Persia. The Balkans trapped Nicholas in an increasingly tense and difficult situation.

The Revolutionary Movement   Behind the facade of official politics seethed the murky world of the revolutionaries. The most extreme factions joined the most reactionary tsarists to block the feeble steps toward modern democracy. Their success in destroying tsarist rule ensured the rise of the even more tyrannical Soviet dictatorship.

Early in the reign of Nicholas II, various *narodnik* factions gradually came together to form the Socialist Revolutionary Party (SRP), much the strongest branch of the revolutionary movement. In March 1905 the SRP could mobilize ten thousand workers for an uprising, while the Marxist Social Democrats claimed no more than a few hundred.

After 1905 the SRP became a legal political party with a platform advocating democracy, republicanism, federalism, and the "socialization" of land. It appealed broadly to peasants, industrial workers, and intellectuals who supported radical reform through constitutional, nonviolent means. The SRP and its *Trudoviki* (Labor) allies won 26 percent of the Duma seats in 1906 and 20 percent in March 1907. After the tsarist electoral machinations, however, they won only 3 percent in November 1907 and 2 percent in 1912.

Soon after its first congress (1905), the SRP split over policy objectives and methods. An underground terrorist branch carried out numerous assassinations and bombings until its leader was exposed in 1908 as a police spy. That scandal virtually destroyed the SRP and gave the tsarists a pretext for the electoral manipulation that eliminated the opposition from the last two Dumas. Not until 1917 did the SRP reemerge as a significant political organization.

During the reign of Nicholas II, the westernizers were dominated by Marxists. Their first important organization was the St. Petersburg Union of Struggle for the Emancipation of the Working Class, founded in 1895 by Vladimir Ilyich Lenin and Julius Martov. In 1897 Jewish Marxist groups in several Russian cities formed a national *bund* that merged in 1898 with the St. Petersburg Union and with other Marxist groups as the Russian Social Democratic Workers Party (RSDWP), the first national Russian Marxist party.

The first RSDWP congress had only nine members and very little practical consequence. All or almost all the delegates were arrested immediately after the meeting. Its only real accomplishment was to recognize Lenin as a leader by appointing him editor of a pamphlet series.

Lenin's role in Russian history is fitting, for his life reflected many of his country's ambivalences and ironies. He was born Vladimir Ilyich Ulyanov in Simbirsk, a provincial capital on the Volga. His birthplace was on the Asian flank of European Russia, and his ancestry was both Asian and European. His maternal grandfather was a titled doctor and landowner and his father a titled administrator and teacher. Yet all five Ulyanov children became active revolutionaries.

Lenin began law studies at Kazan, but was expelled because of his brother's revolutionary activities. After he was allowed to complete his degree in St. Petersburg, he became a professional revolutionary himself. He began as a *narodnik,* but converted to Marxism.

For his part in organizing the St. Petersburg Union, Lenin was arrested and exiled to Siberia until January 1900. Six months later he left for western Europe. He did not return until the Germans shipped him back in a sealed railroad car in April 1917 in the hope that he would disrupt the Russian war effort. Throughout that long period, Lenin labored unceasingly for a Marxist revolution in his homeland.

Lenin's ideas mainly adapted Marxism to Russia. First, he argued that a Marxist revolution *was* possible in Russia, thereby justifying revolutionary effort by Marxists. Second, he showed how Marxism could be applied to the Russian peasantry, thereby bridging the slavophile focus on the peasantry and the westernizer's interest in specific programs. Third, he presented in Marxist terms the organizational forms and behavior required by the unique political conditions of Russia.

More important than Lenin's ideas was his ability to organize Marxists into a party of full-time, disciplined, dedicated, professional revolutionaries. Almost irresistibly persuasive in small group discussions, he was also a brilliant stump speaker and pamphleteer, especially as editor of the newspaper *Iskra* (*Spark*). At the second SD congress in 1903, Lenin's insistence on unswerving obedience split the party definitively between his Bolsheviks (meaning "majority") and Julius Martov's Mensheviks ("minority"). The division was mainly a power rivalry between the two factional leaders, but also reflected the more extreme radicalism of the Bolsheviks.

Despite Lenin's long years of work and planning, the Bolsheviks did not initiate the 1905 or February 1917 revolutions. Instead, Lenin's eventual triumph resulted from his success at filling the vacuum left by the collapse of the old regime. That collapse had not resulted in any way from Lenin's actions. Rather, it almost inevitably followed the defeat of the Russian army by Germany in World War I. Indeed, wartime defeats destroyed the governmental systems of all four conquered powers (Russia, Germany, Austria-Hungary, and Turkey).

The Fatal Crisis

The spark that set off that fatal conflagration was the assassination of the Austro-Hungarian crown prince by a Serbian nationalist on June 28, 1914. In reprisal, Austria-Hungary declared war on the tiny Slavic country. Russia's alliances obliged it to aid Serbia. Russian mobilization on July 30 led to a cascade of declarations of war. Within a week, all the major powers of Europe fell on each other's throats.

A collage of paintings and photographs of Lenin as Soviet ruler, showing him meeting with common people in his Kremlin office, relaxing outdoors with his wife and two children (not his), chatting with Stalin, holding a cat, helping workers at physical labor.

Library of Congress

The Ulyanov family in Lenin's childhood. Lenin is seated at the lower right. Library of Congress

В. И. Ленин беседует с крестьянами
С картины художника М. Соколова

В. И. Ленин на Всероссийском субботнике
С картины художника М. Соколова

В. И. Ленин и Н. К. Крупская с племянником и
дочерью рабочего в Горках. 1922 г.

В. И. Ленин и И. В. Сталин в Горках
С картины художника В. Сварога

В. И. Ленин в Горках

Лист 14 Фотовыставка № 12

Russia was ill prepared for that conflict. Its principal military asset was the naïve zeal of the soldiers. Their patriotism came partly from loyalty to the tsar. Many pan-Slavic nationalists saw the war as a mission to rescue Slavic peoples from alien oppressors. However, the enormous army—15.5 million men—was poorly trained, organized, and led. Moreover, Russia lacked adequate means to produce and transport arms, ammunition, and supplies to its soldiers.

Disaster followed inevitably. The Russians occasionally succeeded against the Austrians, but were hopelessly outfought by the German army and the Turkish navy. By early 1917 they had suffered some 8 million casualties, including 1.3 million killed. Moreover, the Germans occupied large parts of Russian territory. Mutinies and desertions spread like wildfire.

The military and economic catastrophes were compounded by the tragic situation in the royal household. The tsar's incompetence became ever more evident. He repeatedly exercised abominable judgment in the most important affairs of state. The German-born tsarina was widely, but unfairly, suspected of treason. Rasputin's influence intruded increasingly into governmental matters—until his murder in December 1916.

By early 1917 Russia's social fabric was weakening rapidly. Food shortages and riots, monetary inflation, a record number of industrial strikes, and general economic disruption battered civilian morale. Duma deputies and other political and governmental leaders talked openly of a coup d'état. Russia was ripe for revolution.

Nevertheless, tsarism collapsed with unexpected swiftness. On March 8, 1917, an unplanned combination of events brought tens of thousands of workers and housewives into the streets of Petrograd (the new name for St. Petersburg), striking and clamoring for bread. The next day they numbered hundreds of thousands, and on March 10 the strike became general.

So far, the demonstrations had been spontaneous and peaceful. Nei-

Rasputin

Rasputin.   Michael Gofman.

Rasputin, a vile and dissolute Siberian peasant-turned-unordained-
holy-man, was the most influential personal and political advisor to
the tsarina after November 1905. Because she dominated the
weak-willed tsar, this made him the most powerful person in the
empire. Rasputin was the early nickname for Grigory Yefimovich
Novykh. It means "licentious" and identifies the most striking of
his many distinctive personal characteristics. He had wild, piercing
eyes and was towering in stature, coarse and disheveled in
appearance, and foul of body and mouth. He associated with a cult
that believed that eternal salvation resulted from humility, which
came, in turn, from sinfulness. This led to gross excesses of

religious fervor and sexual orgies involving members of the imperial entourage. Rasputin owed his initial hold on the tsarina to his seemingly supernatural ability to stop the hemophilic bleeding of Alexius, the baby heir to the throne. This led the rather simpleminded tsarina to regard him as divinely endowed. Rasputin exploited that faith to interfere in governmental affairs. In particular, he forced the replacement of all liberal and moderate ministers by reactionaries. His control of the government became so notorious, entrenched, and harmful that in December 1916, several highly placed members of the imperial family and nobility undertook to assassinate him. They fed him enough poison to kill an elephant, with no apparent effect. They fired five shots into him, but still he lived. They clubbed him, to no avail. Finally, they threw him into the Neva River, where he drowned. True to one of Rasputin's prophecies, within two months of his death the Romanov dynasty fell.

ther revolutionary organizations nor prominent leaders were involved. The forces of order seemed well prepared and loyal. They handled the crowds without serious incident.

That situation changed dramatically on March 11. Troops fired on the crowds, killing people. The next morning the soldiers refused orders and joined the rioters. By late afternoon, governmental authority had collapsed and revolutionaries held the capital. When that news reached other parts of the country, they followed suit.

For three days Nicholas struggled to recover control before abdicating in favor of his brother, the Grand Duke Mikhail. He refused the throne, ending tsarism. About 1,300 persons, on both sides, died in the insurrection. On July 16, 1918, the Bolsheviks killed Nicholas and his entire family.

The strikes and disturbances in the city are more than impudent. . . . This is a hooligan campaign, with boys and girls running about shouting that they have no bread—merely to create unrest; there are also workers who prevent others from working. Had the weather been colder, they would all most likely have stayed at home. All this will surely pass off and calm down provided the Duma behaves itself.

Letter, Tsarina Alexandra to Nicholas II, February 25, 1917, reprinted in Albert Nenarokov's *An Illustrated History of the Great October Socialist Revolution*, Progress Publishers, Moscow, 1987

Crises: The Provisional Government

Three forces rushed to fill the void created by the collapse of the old regime: 1) a "provisional committee" of liberals, moderates, and some radical deputies from the Fourth Duma; 2) a "Soviet of Workers' and Soldiers' Deputies" convened by other radical deputies, Mensheviks, and Socialist Revolutionaries—emulating 1905. The provisional committee and the soviet collaborated to form and support a "provisional government"; 3) the Bolsheviks, who floundered in uncertainty until Lenin reached Petrograd on April 16. Thereafter, they denounced the provisional government and called for a republic ruled by "Soviets of Workers', Farmhands', and Peasants' Deputies."

The provisional government was headed initially by Prince George Lvov, a landowning reformer and head of the Union of Zemstvos. However, the great energy and oratory of Alexander Kerensky, minister of justice and vice-president of the soviet, soon brought him to the fore. By May he held the key post of minister of war and navy and in July became prime minister.

Like Lenin, Kerensky had been born in Simbirsk, his father had been a petty nobleman and a school official, and he had studied law in St. Petersburg before entering revolutionary politics. Unlike Lenin, he had

Врем. Испол. Комитеть Государственной. Думы 352

The Provisional Government of 1917, which replaced the tsar and was overthrown by the Bolsheviks. Alexander Kerensky, who emerged as its strongest leader, is standing second from the right.   Library of Congress

remained an SRP slavophile. He was their leader in the Fourth Duma.

The early provisional government was liberal and reformist. It sought to: 1) establish a constitutional, limited monarchy or republic through a democratic constituent assembly; 2) grant political amnesty and broad civil liberties; 3) democratize local government; 4) effect a legal, orderly land reform; 5) accord autonomy or independence to such subject peoples as the Finns and Poles; and 6) continue Russian participation in the war.

The government was reorganized in May, July, and September. Each time, it became more leftist in composition and policies. By September, socialists dominated. That shift was caused partly by the Petrograd soviet. This body both competed with and supported the government.

A cumbersome, amorphous, chaotic assembly, it numbered as many as three thousand "representatives" of factory workers and soldiers.

The soviet took radical steps to retain its popularity. A prime example was the order of its military committee on March 14. By effectively revoking the authority of the military leaders, that decree virtually destroyed army discipline and deprived the government of its means to maintain order.

The Petrograd Soviet's claim to the right to govern Russia was reinforced by the spread of the soviet movement. In April the Petrograd group added representatives of provincial assemblies to its executive committee, and in June it held an All-Russian Congress of Soviets. However, the elections for the congress were not really free, and its executive committee was dominated by Petrograd members. Nevertheless, the revolutionaries in the capital could claim that theirs was a national, democratic institution.

As the soviet undermined the provisional government, the Bolsheviks chipped away at the soviet. They were a minority but the best organized and most outspoken and extreme. With Lenin leading, they criticized every hint of moderation, compromise, or weakness as betraying the revolution. They outbid the SRP and Mensheviks for popular support by insisting on immediate peace and land reform.

In late August the power struggle was complicated further. General Lavr Georgiyevich Kornilov, the supreme military commander, ordered troop movements that Kerensky interpreted as preparations for a counterrevolutionary, perhaps tsarist, coup. Kerensky removed and imprisoned Kornilov, but the affair gave credibility to Bolshevik warnings of counterrevolutionary dangers.

The Kerensky government was hampered fatally by the general deterioration of civil order. Through the summer a spontaneous mass upheaval against all established institutions swept the country. Military discipline evaporated and the army disintegrated. Peasants scrambled frantically to grab land. Revolutionary workers destroyed the industrial economy with strikes and plant seizures. Minority nationalities clamored for independence. Ironically, the anger vented against centuries of tsarist oppression destroyed the only liberal government Russia ever had and opened the gates to its harshest tyrants.

Bolshevik strength grew dramatically after the Kornilov affair. By September 19 they held a majority in the Petrograd soviet, and on October 8 elected Leon Trotsky as its president. Next, they set about to transfer to the soviet the remaining power and authority of the provisional government.

They began that effort by establishing, on October 22, a Bolshevik-dominated "Military Revolutionary Committee" of the Petrograd soviet headed by Trotsky. That group gradually gained control over the major military units in the Petrograd area, while it trained and armed the Red Guard, a militia of factory workers.

The Fall of the Winter Palace

On November 3 the Bolsheviks began to mobilize. Their mass demonstration the following day manifested their strength impressively. On November 5 the strategically placed Peter and Paul Fortress became the last important garrison in the capital to fall under Bolshevik control.

The provisional government fell in less than twenty-four hours on November 6 and 7. Beginning late at night on the sixth, Bolshevik soldiers occupied, one by one, the principal vantage points in the capital: railroad stations, bridges, banks, telephone switchboards, etc. The few remaining provisional government troops gave only token resistance. Kerensky, disguised as a woman, fled in a diplomat's car flying an American flag to seek reinforcements.

The last bastion to fall was the Winter Palace, where the provisional government was meeting. That enormous building and the government were captured on the evening of the seventh. The final struggle cost the lives of only six revolutionaries and no defenders.

Ten Days That Shook The World

John Reed was an American reporter sympathetic to the Bolsheviks who wrote a first person account of the events of November 1917. *Ten Days That Shook The World* is a partisan and not always accurate description of the revolution, but it captures the drama, hope, and passion of the times. Here is an excerpt:

Suddenly, by common impulse, we found ourselves on our feet, mumbling together into the smooth lifting unison of the Internationale.* *A grizzled old soldier was sobbing like a child. Alexandra Kollontai rapidly winked the tears back. The immense sound rolled through the hall, burst windows and doors and seared into the quiet sky. "The war is ended! The war is ended" said a young workman near me, his face shining. And when it was over, as we stood there in a kind of awkward hush, some one in the back of the room shouted, "Comrades! Let us remember those who have died for liberty!" So we began to sing the Funeral March, that slow, melancholy and yet triumphant chant, so Russian and so moving. The* Internationale *is an alien air, after all. The Funeral March seemed the very soul of those dark masses whose delegates sat in this hall, building from their obscure visions a new Russia—and perhaps more.*

*The *Internationale* is the anthem of international socialism.

John Reed, *Ten Days That Shook The World* (New York: Vintage Press, 1960) pp. 177–78.

The Bolshevik coup coincided with the opening of the second All-Russian Congress of Soviets of Workers' and Soldiers' Deputies. Its large Bolshevik majority moved swiftly to enact decrees calling for immediate peace and abolishing private ownership of land and other natural resources. An all-Bolshevik fifteen-member "Council of People's Commissars" was now installed as Russia's new government. Lenin was its head, Leon Trotsky foreign minister, and Joseph Stalin minister for nationality affairs.

Trotsky

Lenin's closest collaborator in the Bolshevik coup was Trotsky. Lenin was the strategist; Trotsky was the tactician and principal organizer. He had been born Lev Davidovich Bronstein in 1879 to a prosperous Ukrainian Jewish farm family. He had left college after a few months to become a professional revolutionary in St. Petersburg in 1898.

Initially he allied himself with Lenin, but was too proud and strong-willed to accept Lenin's dictatorial control. After 1903 he usually was aligned with the Mensheviks, although he always exhibited great independence of mind and behavior. He had played a prominent role in the 1905 Revolution, heading the short-lived Soviet of Workers' Deputies. In July 1917, soon after returning from exile, he switched to the Bolsheviks and was elected to their central committee.

Trotsky was brilliant, arrogant, and boundlessly energetic. He contributed importantly to Russian Marxist ideology with his "permanent revolution" doctrine. It held that even though Russia was largely "precapitalist," proletarian revolutionaries could drive it rapidly toward communism without a long capitalist stage. They could "deepen" the revolutionary process and gain support and protection from revolutions in more advanced industrial countries inspired by their example.

A major problem confronted the new government. Constituent Assembly elections—scheduled for November 25—were unlikely to produce a Bolshevik majority and thus would be embarrassing. So many Russians had placed so much hope in a Constituent Assembly for so long that its cancelation might bring about a mass uprising. A representative body to reform the Russian state had long been demanded by most revolutionaries, including the Bolsheviks, and the provisional government had promised elections since February.

The Dictatorship of the Proletariat
The Bolsheviks resolved the problem typically. They allowed the elections, winning only 25 percent of the vote, compared to 58 percent for the Socialist Revolutionaries. When the Assembly met on January 18, they demanded that it endorse their program wholesale. When it refused, Bolshevik soldiers drove the deputies from the chamber.

In its sole, seventeen-hour session, the Assembly endorsed the Bolsheviks' land decree, passed an ambiguous call for peace negotiations, and declared Russia to be a democratic, federated republic. Those three items are the total legislative output of genuinely democratic national institutions in Russia's entire history so far.

With their legislative and executive institutions formally in place, the Bolsheviks began the long, difficult, and bloody task of establishing their hold over the whole country. By the end of 1917 they had secured an armistice with Germany, gained control over the key parts of the territory, socialized much of the economy, and replaced most tsarist institutions with their own police state. Nevertheless, they had solved none of the problems that had plagued the provisional government. The next chapter describes their successful efforts to overcome those obstacles and to establish their system firmly. It also portrays the eventual results of Bolshevik rule in Stalin's totalitarianism.

Bolshevism in Power

Lenin in Power

War Communism   As 1918 began, the appearance of power in the Bolsheviks' hands concealed quite a different reality. The armistice with Germany was not a peace treaty. The Communists' domestic foes had been routed but not eliminated. Their revolutionary decrees had been issued but not implemented. At least three years passed before those illusions were converted into substance.

The first major problem to be resolved was the war. The harsh Brest-Litovsk Treaty was signed March 3, 1918, with Germany and its allies. Finland, Estonia, Latvia, Lithuania, Poland, and Ukraine became independent; Bessarabia became Rumanian; and Kars, Batum, and Ardagan became Turkish. Russia lost 1.3 million square miles (3.4 million sq. km.) of territory (half again as much area as the United

Chronology

November 1917	Bolshevik government issues first revolutionary decrees
January 19, 1918	Constituent Assembly meets and is dissolved
March 3, 1918	Brest-Litovsk Treaty signed
April 5, 1918	Japanese begin foreign intervention
July 10, 1918	First Soviet constitution adopted
July 17, 1918	Tsar Nicholas II and family shot
March 2, 1919	First Comintern Congress begins
February 28, 1921	Kronstadt revolt begins
March 21, 1921	New Economic Policy begins
May 26 and December 22, 1922	Lenin suffers first two strokes
March 9, 1923	Lenin suffers third stroke
January 21, 1924	Lenin dies
January 31, 1924	Second Soviet constitution adopted
April 1925 to October 1926	Stalin defeats Trotsky, Kamenev, Zinoviev
December 1927	Collectivization of agriculture campaign begins
May 28, 1928	First five-year economic plan adopted
December 5, 1936	Third Soviet Constitution adopted
January 1935 to March 1938	Four Great Purge trials held
August 23, 1939	Molotov-Ribbentrop treaty signed
September 17, 1939	Red Army invades Poland
June 22, 1941	German army invades Soviet Union
May 8, 1945	Germany surrenders
September 1947	Cominform established
January 25, 1949	Comecon established
October 1952	Nineteenth CPSU Congress
March 5, 1953	Stalin dies

States east of the Mississippi) and was assessed 300 million gold rubles in reparations.

The Brest-Litovsk settlement worsened the civil war that had erupted in December 1917. Russia's allies, including the United States, denounced the separate peace treaty, imposed a blockade, and sent a relief and military expedition to shore up the anti-Bolshevik forces and return Russia to the war. The Allied intervention was halfhearted and ended in early 1919, but the blockade lasted until January 1920.

Early in the civil war, the Bolshevik Red Army controlled barely one fourth of the nation's territory. However, the armies of their opponents—called the "Whites"—were widely dispersed and poorly coordinated. The White Army fell short of the Red Army in leadership, discipline, training, and morale. By late 1920 the Red Army defeated the main White forces and in March 1921 made peace with its Polish allies.

Next, the Bolsheviks set about to reconquer parts of the Russian empire that had defected during the civil war. They retook Ukraine, Azerbaijan, Georgia, and Armenia in 1921, eastern Siberia in 1922, and Central Asia in 1926. Bessarabia remained Romanian and the Baltic states stayed independent until World War II. A small part of Finland and about half of Poland were retaken then, too. Those two countries survived as separate states, though the Red Army occupied Poland after World War II. Thus, Finland is the only province of the old Russian empire that made good its escape.

As the Bolsheviks were retaking territory, they were also transforming society and the economy. They decreed radical measures, called "War Communism," to eliminate all "capitalist" practices and operate all economic enterprises through a centralized Supreme Economic Council. They took control of all banks, shipping, cooperatives, libraries, large homes, precious objects, foreign and domestic trade, and industries, and outlawed the market economy, money, interest, inequalities of wealth and income, and social distinctions.

This poster reads, "Comrade Muslims! Under the green banner of the Prophet, you went and conquered your steppes, your villages. The enemies of the people took from you your native fields. Now under the red banner of the Workers' and Peasants' Revolution and under the celestial army of all the oppressed and the working people, gather together from east to west, from north to south. In the saddle, comrades! All in regiments, universal military training for all!" It was used to rally Central Asians to support the revolutionary forces.

War Communism was supposed to produce complete social and economic equality by abolishing private property. Industrial workers would take over and manage the factories and peasants would do the same to the land. The mansions of the wealthy would be carved up into apartments for as many as a dozen families. The economy would function on the basis of barter. For instance, a dairy farmer would exchange a pail of milk with a fruit farmer for a bushel of apples, and a cobbler would pay a physician's fee with a pair of shoes.

Governmental reforms were similarly drastic. They swept away the Duma and Council of State, the judicial system, and the local government system and changed the legal system radically. In July 1918 the All-Russian Congress of Soviets adopted the first Soviet constitution.

That constitution sanctioned the institutions that had developed pragmatically since October. The Congress of Soviets, elected mainly by urban workers, was supreme—but was never more than a mass ratifying rally without real power. A two-hundred-member committee acted for the Congress between sessions and appointed an eighteen-member council to head the executive branch. The national minorities were recognized and the local government system reformed. Only the working class enjoyed such civil liberties as the rights to bear arms and to vote, and the freedoms of religion, expression, assembly, and association. Church and state were separated. The Bolshevik party (renamed Communist) was not mentioned, though it monopolized legal political power.

Chaos   Revolution, foreign and civil wars, foreign intervention, and radical transformation of social and economic institutions inevitably produced chaos. In response, the Bolsheviks became increasingly repressive. By December 1917 they had created a secret police force and drumhead revolutionary tribunals. They outlawed opposition political parties and controlled the press and associations. As the economic situation worsened, they established forced-labor armies. They requisitioned and rationed food through a system that favored workers over the middle and upper classes. Finally, they encouraged terrorism to intimidate the people.

As War Communism dragged on, it became tragically clear that autocratic rulers had yielded to fanatically autocratic rulers and inefficiency to catastrophic inefficiency. Lawlessness, tyranny, epidemics, and starvation swept the country. Millions died. Similar numbers were homeless, suffering, and diseased. The production, transportation, communication, monetary, and distribution systems collapsed. Human misery was more widespread than in any European country of modern times. Whether War Communism was cause, effect, or failed solution mattered little. All who would see realized that survival required abandonment of its bizarre combination of naïve ideological idealism and thundering greed for power.

The New Economic Policy

At long last, the hopelessness of War Communism became clear even to Lenin, who had clung stubbornly to his Marxist beliefs. The blinding flash that finally illuminated the truth was the mutiny of the fifteen-thousand-man garrison of the Kronstadt naval base and fortress in the Gulf of Finland near Petrograd on March 7 to 18, 1921. Kronstadt had been one of the staunchest Bolshevik bastions during the October Revolution. Now it turned against the Communists.

The Kronstadt dissidents expressed the feelings of most Russians in wanting the extreme dictatorial measures rescinded, but not a counter-revolution. The Bolsheviks responded with a harsh ultimatum and ten days of siege and assault. When loyal troops reconquered the stronghold, they slaughtered thousands of surviving defenders. Nevertheless, the Communist Tenth Party Congress, meeting in Moscow at the time, accepted some demands by relaxing the severe economic measures.

That dramatic reversal, the New Economic Policy (NEP), administered a moderate dose of economic freedom and small-scale capitalism to revive the economy. But it kept state ownership of what Lenin termed the "commanding heights" of the economy and tightened Communist political control. The government collected a tax of a fixed amount instead of requisitioning grain, and the peasants could sell any surplus. Small private trade and industry were allowed. Compulsory labor was abolished and money was issued again, to replace the barter system.

The effect was dramatic. Industrial production leaped from 13.8 percent of the prewar level in 1920 to 31 percent in 1921. Private enterprise accounted for 75.2 percent of all retail trade by 1922–1923. Land under cultivation grew from 132.3 million acres in 1922 to 159.3 million acres a year later.

NEP was temporary. Already in October 1921, Lenin was anticipating its early end, and in March 1922 he said, "We must call a halt." Probably only his failing health prevented him from ending NEP, and it continued, in much-diminished form, until replaced by the five-year-plan system in 1928.

The Comintern

Because Marxist-Leninist ideology held that socialism could not survive in Russia without support from similar regimes in the west, the Bolsheviks' prime foreign-policy goal immediately after taking power was to promote Marxist revolutions elsewhere. Practically, however, the hostile intervention by the west required conciliation. Foreign governments were more likely to leave Russia if they felt less threatened.

The Bolsheviks solved that dilemma by pursuing both goals at once. They dealt with the practical problem by seeking treaties or trade agreements with their foreign enemies. Meanwhile, they pursued their ideological goal by founding the Communist International (Comintern) and aiding revolutionaries in capitalist countries. The second Comintern congress in July–August 1920 adopted Lenin's "21 Points." Essentially, those principles required that all member parties pledge unquestioning support for Soviet Russia in international affairs and accept Soviet leadership on ideology, strategy, tactics, and organization.

Lenin's Death

As Soviet Russia was emerging from the most desperate phase of its crisis, tragedy struck. On May 26, 1922, Lenin suffered a partially disabling stroke after a failed assassination attempt. He returned to work October 2, but was bedridden permanently by two more strokes on December 16, 1922, and March 9, 1923.

The magnitude of the difficulty this situation posed for the other Soviet leaders can be easily imagined. Lenin had dominated decision making so thoroughly that no alternative was readily available. For twenty months, public business slowed drastically while he and his

Crowds in Red Square, mourning the death of Lenin in January 1924.   Novosti

collaborators wrestled with the insoluble problem of governance by an incapacitated dictator. Finally, after a fourth stroke on January 21, 1924, Lenin died.

Stalin's Despotism

The Succession Crisis
The Bolshevik system was so much the lengthened shadow of one man that it lacked a succession procedure. Moreover, Lenin did nothing effective during his twenty-month illness to prepare for his death, except to dictate an ambiguous "secret testament." However, it identified no one clearly as his preferred successor. Thus, when he died, neither the constitutional successor of a republic nor the heir designate of a monarchy could fill the gaping vacancy. The result was a free-for-all bare-knuckles political brawl, with neither rules nor mercy.

Several of Lenin's associates were credible contenders for his mantle because he had entrusted important positions to them. They were the principal actors in the great succession drama, whose outcome affected the lives of hundreds of millions of people for decades. Trotsky, Zinoviev, and Kamenev were Stalin's main rivals. Other major participants in the power struggle were Alexei I. Rykov, who had succeeded Lenin as Prime Minister; Nikolai I. Bukharin, the leading ideologue; and Mikhail P. Tomsky, trade union leader.

Stalin Means "Steel"
The eventual winner was Joseph Vissarionovich Dzhugashvili, who had taken the revolutionary alias of "Stalin," Russian for "steel," perhaps to indicate how tough he was. He had humble and entirely non-Russian origins, having been born in Gori, Georgia, in 1879, the only surviving child of an impoverished cobbler. His father, an abusive drunkard, died when Joseph was ten. Probably one of his beatings crippled his son's arm for life. Tens of millions of Soviet people paid with their lives for that savage cruelty,

Rivals

Trotsky. Leon Trotsky was far and away the surviving leader best known among the general public and the most accomplished writer and orator. He had headed the Petrograd soviet in 1905 and 1917, led the Red Army throughout the civil war, and been foreign minister. At Lenin's death, he was minister of war and a Politburo member.

Zinoviev. Grigory Yevseyevich (Radomylsky) Zinoviev had been born into a middle-class Jewish family in 1883. He had led the Bolsheviks in Petrograd since 1917 and the Communist International since its founding in 1919 and was a Politburo member. Zinoviev ranked next to Trotsky in public popularity and prominence.

Kamenev. Lev Borisovich (Rosenfeld) Kamenev was the same age as Zinoviev, had the same middle-class Jewish background, and had been associated closely with him at every step in his career. He had been editor of *Pravda*, the party newspaper; chaired the first Congress of Soviets; and was head of the Moscow organization, deputy prime minister, and a Politburo member.

for Stalin's wretched childhood left his heart and soul as twisted and broken as his withered limb.

Joseph's mother was a seamstress, verging on madness but passionately devoted to the Greek Orthodox religion and to her son. She enrolled Joseph in the Tiflis Theological Seminary in 1894. He completed its course of study in May 1899, but was expelled for refusing to take the final exams. As late as 1936, when Stalin was the mightiest tyrant in history, his mother expressed public regret that he had not become a priest.

While in seminary, Stalin had joined the Social Democratic Party. He became one of Lenin's most loyal supporters, a Central Committee member, and *Pravda* editor. During the civil war he was a troubleshooter and head of the inspectorate general of the Council of Defense.

Although Stalin was little known to the general public, he accumulated an impressive array of party and government positions. Those jobs made him responsible for the party organization, for policy on the minority nationalities, and for ensuring that decisions at the top were implemented.

Stalin's climb to the top lasted for years. He was clearly the primary leader by the late 1920's, although some of his collaborators continued to show independent thinking until the great purges ended in 1938. At one level the battle was a series of factional disputes within the leadership. Stalin joined Kamenev and Zinoviev to beat down Trotsky. Then he supported Bukharin, Rykov, and Tomsky against Kamenev and Zinoviev. In each case, Stalin occupied the moderate center, while portraying his adversaries as extremists, first of the right and then of the left.

The general public and rank-and-file party workers found Stalin's ideas, policies, and organizational plans more attractive than those of his opponents. Meanwhile, Stalin used his control of strategic party jobs to infiltrate his supporters into key posts. He also promoted a quasireligious cult of Leninism and preempted the role of high priest, a part he had learned well in seminary.

Unbridled Tyranny

By 1928 Stalin was so well entrenched that he could begin to show his true colors. He replaced the last rem-

Stalin delivering his funeral oration for Lenin, the first step in the development of his "cult of personality." Lenin in his casket. Library of Congress

nants of the NEP with undiluted state control over all aspects of economic life. A series of five-year plans set detailed production goals for all economic activities and mandatory priorities for the use of resources. The overall objective was forced industrialization, as dictated by the Marxist-Leninist doctrine that requires an advanced industrial substructure for a communist society. That industrialization drive conformed to an age-old Russian yearning to overcome its technological inferiority to the West. Now, finally, it seemed, the vast nation would modernize and take its place as a world leader. But to accomplish this, a nation of peasants had to be transformed into a nation of factory workers.

To build and run factories requires a very large, available work force. Because the overwhelming majority of Soviet people worked the land, Stalin undertook an enormous, brutal campaign to collectivize agriculture. He banned private farming and forced all peasants to leave the land or join state-owned farms or state-controlled cooperatives. This served another Marxist-Leninist goal by converting capitalist property to socialist ownership.

Harvesttime on the Lenin kolkhoz *in Zhazhkovsky District of Russia in 1933, the height of Stalin's collectivization campaign.*   Novosti

Those policies frustrated the profound land hunger of the peasants, and they resisted fiercely. Stalin struck back with the full fury of the army and police. Ten million peasants were slaughtered or died in the resulting famine that Stalin deliberately caused. By 1936 90 percent of the remaining peasants worked state or collective farms.

Stalin claimed impressive industrialization results. By 1940 official statistics showed an 8.5-fold increase in industrial production over 1913. The manufacture of capital goods had increased 15.5 times and consumer goods 5 times. The Soviet Union had modernized its industries, but at what cost?

Along with the economic measures came stringent controls over all aspects of social life. The state monopolized all cultural, educational,

The Glories of Stalinism

Alexander Avdeyenko recounts a trip by 120 Soviet writers along the Stalin Canal in the 1930's, after which they reported on the glories of Stalinism:

We eat and drink according to the requirements and do not pay for anything. Smoked sausages. Cheeses. Caviar. Fruit. Chocolate. Wines. Cognac. And all of this in a hungry year! . . .

All along the track stood ragged, barefooted, emaciated children and old people. Skin and bones—living mummies. And all of them with their hands outstretched toward the cars passing by. On the lips of everyone there was the one easily discernible word: bread, bread, bread.

Writers wander about the cars. Corks pop and glasses clink. Laughter and noisy conversation on and on. . . .

Moscow News, No. 10, March 5–12, 1989

and informational activities and required them to serve its interests as defined by Stalin. Stalin expanded Lenin's secret police force and increased its powers greatly. He banned emigration and travel abroad, except by diplomats, and closely restricted visits by foreigners to the Soviet Union.

"The Kremlin Mountaineer"

This poem was composed by Osip Mandelstam in 1934 about Stalin, the "Kremlin mountaineer." It circulated by word of mouth, becoming very popular, and is thought to have been the reason Stalin had Mandelstam thrown in prison, where he died:

We no longer feel the land under our feet,
you can't hear us ten steps away,
but when anyone starts a conversation
they mention the Kremlin mountaineer.
His thick fingers are like worms,
his words ring as heavy weights.
His cockroach moustache laughs, perching on his top lip,
and the tops of his boots shine.
He is surrounded by his scrawny-necked henchmen,
and amuses himself with their services.
One whistles, one meows and another whimpers,
he alone points at us and thunders.
He throws order after order like horseshoes,
hurling them at the groin, the forehead, the brow, the eyes.
Every execution spurts on his tongue like the juice of a raspberry,
he wishes he could embrace like old friends back home.

Translated by Richard and Elizabeth McKane and reprinted from *Moscow News*, No. 15, April 9–16, 1989

The blood purges of 1935–1939 completed the establishment of Stalin's tyranny. They resulted in the deaths of all of Lenin's surviving comrades, except Stalin himself; most top political and military leaders, including 60 percent of the officer corps; almost all active party members; and millions of other officials and private citizens. The purges culminated in three show trials of fifty-four of Stalin's closest former collaborators who were forced into abject and patently false confessions and were convicted and executed.

One of those who was forced to confess and then was executed in the purges was Nikolai Bukharin, who had been a close associate of both Lenin and Stalin. Arthur Koestler's powerful novel *Darkness at Noon* is a fictionalized reconstruction of the psychological pressures that might have led him to make a false confession. In 1988 when Bukharin was officially rehabilitated, his wife released a secret last testament in which he finally cleared his name: "I am absolutely confident that better times will come in Russia. People will then understand that we were not guilty of any crimes. Only then should you take out my 'will' to prove: we knew it."

Scene at a meeting of Memorial, a group organized to remind the Soviet people of Stalinist tyranny. S. Tytov/VAAP

Thus, Stalin prolonged the cruel irony of leadership in Russian history. No ruler of that great land had ever undertaken more monumental efforts at modernization. Yet his methods and attitudes resembled the worst excesses of the distant past, light-years removed from modern norms.

The Structure of Power

Stalin followed Lenin in cloaking traditional Russian authoritarian and autocratic contents in modern western democratic and constitutionalist forms. Ten days after Lenin's death, a new constitution was issued, drafted by Stalin but endorsed by Lenin. It introduced federalism, which gave "union republics"—based on the homelands of the main minority nationalities—formal constitutional equality with the national government.

In 1936 Stalin issued a third constitution. It reduced the authority of the union republics and introduced direct parliamentary elections with universal adult suffrage. Parliament was now called the Supreme Soviet, consisting of a Soviet of the Union and a Soviet of Nationalities. The constitution specified fundamental citizens' rights and duties, but subordinated them to the interests of the state as determined by the rulers.

The democratic, constitutionalist appearance of both documents was utterly counterfeit. Elections were meaningless, because the voters had no choice. The parliaments never exercised real legislative or oversight power.

Behind that phony governmental facade, but unmentioned in either constitution, lurked the real ruler, the Communist Party of the Soviet Union (CPSU). In practice, the CPSU made all public policy and oversaw its implementation. The governmental system merely executed those orders under close supervision.

The CPSU membership included only a small percentage (never more than 10 percent) of the population, supposedly the elite of society—the "vanguard of the working class" in Marxist-Leninist terms. Each neighborhood or workplace "cell" had about fifteen members. The party structure rose from that base as a pyramid of territorially defined committees.

Formally, the party's ruling body was the Congress, a cumbersome convention of thousands of delegates from the membership units that met at increasingly long intervals. Each Congress chose a Central Committee (CC) of two hundred to three hundred members to act for it between sessions. The CC elected a Politburo (policy-making office) of nine to twelve members and a smaller number of candidate members. They met more or less weekly as the ruling oligarchy. A Secretariat of six to eight Politburo members administered the daily party operations under Politburo instructions.

Those institutions functioned in an atmosphere of terror and suspicion that prevented effective resistance to Stalin's will. As his power grew, the state and party structures and the distinctions between them became increasingly irrelevant. Furthermore, Stalin used the various agencies—secret police, armed forces, control commissions, inspectorates—against one another.

Stalin drove Lenin's "democratic centralism" to its ultimate extreme by concentrating all power in himself and making the government and CPSU instruments of personal despotism. The power structure became virtually identical with his person. More truly than any previous tsar, more than France's Louis XIV, Stalin could have said, *"L'etat c'est moi"* ("I am the state"). Yet he exercised that most ancient autocracy in the name of the most visionary future, the Marxist-Leninist world of communism.

Fortress Russia

A key ideological concept in Stalin's drive for power was "socialism in one country." This challenged the orthodox Bolshevik view that their rule could survive only if world revolution followed quickly. Instead, he argued for a "Fortress Russia" whose people would strengthen their socialist state, defend it vigorously

A Soviet propaganda poster during the height of Stalinism, portraying an enormous crowd of smiling people paying homage to a genial dictator.   Library of Congress

against all enemies, and wait patiently for the inevitable collapse of capitalism. This shifted attention from high-risk international ambitions to domestic affairs. Nevertheless, Stalin maintained Lenin's Comintern to encourage and support Marxist-Leninist parties abroad.

By the mid-1930's Nazi Germany and Fascist Italy had become more serious and immediate threats than the western democracies. Stalin now cultivated better relations with the democracies by downplaying the Comintern. Nevertheless, he signed a pact (the Molotov-Ribbentrop treaty) with Nazi Germany in 1939 that enabled him to recover parts of the old Russian empire from Poland, the Baltic states, Romania, and Finland.

That treaty did not prevent Germany from invading the Soviet Union two years later. The German army drove to the outskirts of Moscow, besieged Leningrad (the renamed Petrograd) for nine hundred days, and nearly reached the Caucasus oilfields. It occupied large areas of the country for two years and killed or captured millions of Soviet troops and civilians.

Stalin fought back. He courted the Orthodox church, dissolved the Comintern, and appealed to the people with Russian nationalism rather than Soviet communism. German atrocities inspired Soviets to defend their homeland. The Soviet people rallied behind their despot, mounted a heroic resistance, and drove out the invader by mid-1944.

World War II inflicted staggering losses on the Soviet Union. It cost 20 million deaths, including civilians, left another 25 million homeless, and caused a shortfall of about 15 million births. By comparison, the United States suffered 400,000 deaths in the war. Official property damage estimates are 679 billion rubles ($1.1 trillion). Some 70,000 towns and villages, 32,000 industrial enterprises, 100,000 farms, and 40,000 miles of railroad trackage were damaged or destroyed.

As a result of the war, the Soviet Union acquired an empire of satellite states in eastern Europe and Asia. The Red Army occupied and installed Communist governments in Poland, eastern Germany, Czechoslovakia, Hungary, Romania, Bulgaria, Albania, and North Korea. Those governments imitated the Soviet Union closely and followed its lead slavishly in international affairs.

That expansion and other belligerent acts inaugurated a period of great tension—the Cold War—between the Soviet bloc and the West. In some parts of the world Soviet interests coincided with those of nationalist movements by colonial peoples. Major Cold War events included the Czechoslovakian coup (1948), the Berlin blockade (1948–1949), the Chinese civil war (1945–1949), Communist insurrections in Greece and Indochina (1947), Soviet threats against Turkey and Iran (1947), and North Korea's invasion of South Korea (1950).

Stalin's Death   During the twilight of Stalin's rule, recovery from World War II dominated Soviet life. In 1945 industrial production was 92 percent and consumer-goods production 59 percent of 1940 levels. By 1950 they had risen to 173 and 123 percent.

Agricultural recovery was slower. Fewer than half of the farm tractors, 28 percent of the horses, and 40 percent of the cattle survived the war. A terrible drought in 1946 was a further setback. Despite the postwar territorial acquisitions, Soviet crop area in 1950 was 2.7 pecent below 1940 and agricultural production was characterized officially as "inadequate."

The recovery effort was accompanied by brutal measures of social control. Stalin tightened labor discipline and imposed production quotas with great ferocity. He imprisoned millions of Soviet citizens and foreigners and shipped millions of others to Siberia and Central Asia. He defined social and political orthodoxy ever more narrowly, punished deviations harshly, and waged campaigns against foreigners and Jews. In all, some 20–40 million of his countrymen died from his tyranny.

Stalin's "cult of personality" reached a deafening crescendo during his last years. All Soviet achievements were credited to his vision and genius. His name, portrait, and statues were omnipresent. Nauseatingly effusive praise of him was obligatory in every public speech and publication, no matter what the topic. The battered and belittled boy from Gori had become the ultimate megalomaniac.

In his last months, Stalin became increasingly paranoiac. Two Politboro members once overheard him say to himself, "No, I'm finished. I trust no one, not even myself." These fears turned him again on his closest associates. In August 1952 he transformed the nine-member Politburo into a twenty-five-member Presidium, seemingly to train new men so that he could replace the old.

In January 1953 in Kremlin meetings, he accused three Presidium members of treason and proposed to ship to the far north all Soviet Jews and their relatives—categories that included half of the people at his table. The same month *Pravda* announced that certain Kremlin doctors—mostly Jews—had confessed to murdering or attempting to murder Soviet leaders. Nikita Khrushchev said later that these and similar incidents had been intended to set off a new round of blood purges.

Before that plan went into effect, the Great Dictator died on March 6, 1953, of a cerebral hemorrhage.

Immediately after Stalin's death, mass hysteria and grief swept Moscow and other cities. Many Soviet citizens had been led by the long propaganda campaign to believe that Stalin had been a great and benevolent ruler. His funeral and entombment in Lenin's mausoleum was a final flicker of his cult. His former associates outdid each other in fulsome homage. Stalin seemed destined to be enshrined in the pantheon of Soviet heroes only slightly below Lenin.

That destiny was not fulfilled. Soviet history since Stalin's death has been largely a tale of frustrating efforts to free the country from his death grip. Stalin fell from his pedestal in a few years, but his system was imbedded in so intricate a web of power, privilege, fear, and ideology that a full generation passed before any real headway was made in dislodging it—an effort that, even now, is not at all sure of success. The following chapter recounts the main events in that endeavor.

Bolshevism in Decline

The long, agonizing, halting struggle to dismantle the Leninist-Stalinist system has dominated Soviet history since 1953, impeded by the rationalizations of Marxism-Leninism, which wired it together and bound the minds of Stalin's successors. The confused efforts of Khrushchev and the "stagnation" of Brezhnev have given way to the resourceful and pragmatic determination of Mikhail Gorbachev. Since his accession in 1985, the age-old blights of faulty leadership and ideological tyranny may, at last, be fading from the Soviet landscape.

Khrushchev's Thaw

The Succession Crisis

Stalin's abrupt departure left a gigantic void that his former lieutenants struggled for several years to fill. They unceremoniously returned most of the 1952 Presidium newcomers to the obscurity from which Stalin had dragged them. Next, they announced that they would form a "collective leadership." Then they engaged in the same dog-eat-dog factional maneuvers that had marked the Lenin succession. However, no clear victor ever emerged, despite Khrushchev's fragile ascendancy, for several years.

As in the 1920's, the contenders' official positions influenced the struggle significantly. Policy stands played major roles as well. Each rival adopted a political platform that affected his success. The contenders, their places in the hierarchy, and their principal platform planks were:

Georgy Maksimilianovich *Malenkov* had been born near the Urals of Cossack-Bashkir descent, the son of a government official or small landowner. His fleshy, easygoing, cultured appearance concealed an inner ruthlessness. He had risen through the ranks by doing Stalin's bidding—including murders and massacres—with utmost fidelity. He was a vice-prime minister and a party secretary at Stalin's death. He emerged in the last months of Stalin's life as his chosen successor and delivered the main speech at the nineteenth party congress. His main power base was the governmental structure and its technocrats, and his platform was broadly reformist, a shift from heavy industry to consumer goods at home and peaceful coexistence abroad.

Lavrenty Pavlovich *Beria* had been born in 1899 in Georgia, the son of a middle-class peasant. He was obsequious, vain, sexually depraved, and an unscrupulous intriguer. His service in the secret police since 1921 had included purging the purgers after the show trials. He was a vice-prime minister and head of the secret police, which was his main power base. His principal platform planks were to relax international tensions by concessions in Germany and Korea, improve conditions in the slave-labor camps, and grant more autonomy to the minority nationalities.

Vyacheslav Mikhailovich Scriabin *Molotov* had been born in 1890 in eastern Russia, the son of a prosperous small-town merchant and

Chronology

1894	Khrushchev born in Kalinovka
1906	Brezhnev born in Kamenskoye (later renamed Dneprodzerzhinsk)
1931	Gorbachev born in Stavropol
March 6, 1953	"Collective Leadership" succeeds Stalin
June 1953	Beria executed
September 1953	Khrushchev becomes CPSU First Secretary
1953	Soviet interventions in East Germany and Czechoslovakia
February 1956	Khrushchev secret speech attacks Stalin
October 1956	Soviet interventions in Poland and Hungary
July 1957	"Anti-Party group" tries to remove Khrushchev
March 1958	Khrushchev becomes prime minister
August 1961	Berlin Wall built
October 1962	Cuban missile crisis
1963	Nuclear test ban treaty signed
October 15, 1964	Khrushchev removed, retires; succeeded by Brezhnev and Kosygin
August 1968	Soviet intervention in Czechoslovakia
September 1971	Khrushchev dies

nephew of the composer Alexander Scriabin. Later he adopted the name Molotov, or "hammer." His square face and steely blue eyes reflected an implacable, tightly disciplined personality. He had participated in the 1905 revolution, joined the Bolsheviks in 1906, and been Politburo member since 1926 and a high-ranking government leader since 1928. At Stalin's death, he was deputy prime minister. His principal support lay among the "old Bolsheviks" and conservatives. His platform was

1977	Fourth Soviet constitution adopted
November 1979	Soviet intervention in Afghanistan
November 1982	Brezhnev dies; succeeded by Andropov
February 1984	Andropov dies; succeeded by Chernenko
March 1985	Chernenko dies; succeeded by Gorbachev
1987	Intermediate Nuclear Forces treaty signed
June 1988	Nineteenth CPSU Conference approves Gorbachev reform program
March–May 1989	Elections for First Congress of People's Deputies
May 25, 1989	Congress of People's Deputies elects Gorbachev president of Soviet Union
August 4, 1989	First meeting of new Supreme Soviet
November 9, 1989	Berlin Wall opened
December 1989	Lithuania declares its independence
January 7, 1990	Bells of St. Basil cathedral in Red Square peal for Christmas after seventy years of silence
May 1990	Supreme Soviet of Russian Republic first meets and elects Boris Yeltsin president
July 1990	Twenty-third CPSU Congress meets Yeltsin resigns from CPSU
November 1990	Gorbachev reorganizes governmental structure

hard-line conservative—priority for heavy industry, no concessions to the West, no relaxation of domestic social controls.

Nikita Sergeyevich *Khrushchev* had been born in 1894 near Ukraine to a Russian coalminer. His first wife died in the famine of 1921, leaving two small children, and he remarried in 1924. He was short, portly, coarse in appearance and manner, always affecting the behavior of the stereotypical Russian peasant. He remained an obscure Bolshevik

Nikita Khrushchev at the height of his power in 1962. Library of Congress

from 1918 until appointed Moscow party leader in 1935. Then he worked up through the ranks rapidly, being Moscow party leader, agricultural tsar, and a senior party secretary at Stalin's death. His main power bases were the party bureaucracy and Ukraine. His platform emphasized party preeminence and agricultural development.

Immediately after Stalin's death, Malenkov seemed to secure his place as heir with the most prominent role at the funeral and by becoming the top official in both the government and party hierarchies. Within days, however he relinquished his party post. Then, briefly, he and Beria were allies.

In June Beria was removed and executed. His policies had gone sour. Labor-camp prisoners had gone on strike, "bourgeois-nationalist" sentiment had appeared, and concessions in Korea and Germany had boomeranged. Moreover, his rivals suspected him of plotting to seize power.

For more than two years the surviving contenders jockeyed back and forth. Their struggle centered on the de-Stalinization issue. Immediately after the dictator's funeral, his heirs began to tone down his cult and rehabilitated—or restored the reputations of—7,379 of his victims, but they continued to honor him in more subtle ways.

De-Stalinization—The "Secret Speech"

The twentieth party congress in February 1956 changed that dramatically. To a closed session, Khrushchev delivered a speech that criticized Stalin squarely, though not sweepingly. This was the first time any Soviet official had acknowledged publicly that their great leader was less than perfect. The "secret speech" had an electrifying impact when it leaked out in Eastern Europe and in the West, but it was not published in the Soviet Union for thirty-three years.

Khrushchev's speech complained about Stalin terrorizing party members and the army and his one-man rule, but praised his industrialization and collectivization policies. Nearly six years later Stalin's corpse was quietly removed from the Lenin mausoleum and reburied near the Kremlin wall. In June 1970 his bust was placed above it—with the eyes carved carefully to look away from the nearby Lenin tomb.

While Khrushchev denounced Stalin's "cult of personality," he was building his own. Well before the congress, he had emerged as much the most active and prominent leader. He went everywhere—at home and abroad—making speeches, attending to every sort of business, incessantly proposing and promoting innovative policies.

However, Khrushchev's real power declined during the eighteen months after his speech. Some of his policies failed, and his associates grew increasingly apprehensive about his "reckless and adventuresome" programs and power grabs. By June 18, 1957, his opponents, the "Anti-Party group," formed a majority of the Presidium and attempted to force him out. Despite being outnumbered, Khrushchev fought back and won his case before a special, free-swinging, week-long Central Committee meeting.

After the dust had settled, at least six of the fifteen Presidium members were not his protégés. His struggle for control continued for the remaining seven years of his tenure. The Presidium was now too much a "band of brothers" to be manipulated and intimidated as Stalin had done.

Finally, in October 1964, Khrushchev's comrades tired of his game and removed him. Ostensibly, Khrushchev resigned voluntarily; in fact, his opponents had plenty of grievances. They objected to his capricious, willful policy-making, his attacks on the governmental administration, his uncouth public behavior, especially abroad, some monumental policy failures such as his ill-conceived efforts to improve agriculture, and his policy clashes with the armed forces and heavy industry.

Khrushchev retired quietly. He was not punished further but became a nonperson, his name disappearing from all public mention in the Soviet Union. He died of natural causes in September 1971.

Domestic Affairs

During the Khrushchev years, Soviet society underwent sweeping, but not revolutionary, change. The oligarchs abandoned the blood terrorism but retained the ideology, main policies, and basic social structure they had inherited from Lenin and Stalin.

Domestic policies were defined mainly by the tension between Khrushchev's restless search for new ways—no matter how impractical—to solve the fundamental problems of the Soviet economy and his peers' resistance to disruptive changes that lacked clear benefits. In the early years they gambled on some Khrushchev innovations that failed. Thereafter, they greeted his proposals more skeptically.

A collage of photographs of shops, labeled from various Soviet cities (Stalingrad, Kishinev, Stalino, Moscow, Kiev, and Kazan), from 1948, intended to suggest that the Soviet Union was well supplied with food at a time when, in fact, it was suffering from near famine.
Library of Congress

Сталинград

Казань

Кишинев

Сталино

Торговля без карточек продовольственными товарами

Москва

Лист 4
Фотовыставка №10

Киев

One example is the crash development of agriculture. Some government controls were relaxed and state investment in agriculture increased greatly. Some 90 million acres of "virgin land" in Kazakhstan and Siberia were put to the plow. Much industrial production was shifted to agricultural purposes (chemical fertilizers, farm tractors, etc.). These mammoth efforts did not improve production dramatically and were largely abandoned.

Industrial policy shifted emphasis frequently between capital and consumer goods. Military, agricultural, and industrial bureaucrats insisted on continuing Stalin's forced industrialization. Others argued for improved living standards.

The police state remained. The blood purges ended and the slave-labor camps were dismantled, but the tight controls over the everyday lives of the people continued. Censorship was complete and deviation from official orthodoxy forbidden. Travel, residence, and employment were regulated and contact with foreigners was discouraged. The CPSU political monopoly survived untouched and unquestioned.

Ideology required that Khrushchev proclaim that the Soviet Union had entered another phase in history—"transition from socialism to communism." Some of its features were that "capitalist encirclement" had ended and social distinctions were disappearing between urban and rural, agricultural and industrial, intellectual and manual, men and women, personal and collective, party and state.

Life for the average Soviet citizen improved, but not dramatically. The worst terrors of Stalin's tyranny disappeared, but were not replaced by true freedom. Living standards rose somewhat, but progress was slow and uneven. Cautious hope gradually replaced desperate fear.

The Iron Curtain
Soviet foreign policy manifested the ambiguities and inconsistencies of the Khrushchev reign. Somewhat haltingly, the Soviet international position underwent major changes, both behind and across the Cold War "Iron Curtain."

"We Will Bury the Enemies of the Revolution"

Excerpts from *Khrushchev Remembers*:

Marxist-Leninists believe that progress is on our side and victory will inevitably be ours. Yet the capitalists won't give an inch and still swear to fight to the bitter end. Therefore how can we talk of peaceful coexistence with capitalist ideology? Peaceful coexistence among different systems of government is possible, but peaceful coexistence among different ideologies is not. It would be a betrayal of our Party's first principles to believe that there can be peaceful coexistence between Marxist-Leninist ideology . . . and bourgeois ideology. . . .

I always said that there can be no such thing as ideological coexistence. I always stressed that we would fight to the end, and that we were sure we would prevail.

Therefore I allowed myself at one point to use the expression, "We will bury the enemies of the Revolution." I was referring, of course, to America. Enemy propaganda picked up this slogan and blew it all out of proportion—"Khrushchev says the Soviet people want to bury the people of the United States of America!" I had said no such thing. . . . We . . . weren't going to bury anyone; the working class of the United States would bury its enemy the bourgeois class of the United States. My slogan referred to an internal question which every country will decide for itself: namely, by what course and by what methods will the working class of a given country achieve victory over the bourgeoisie? . . .

The liquidation of the capitalist system is the crucial question in the development of society. After the victory of the working class, working peasantry, and working intelligentsia, there will be neither social, national, nor any other causes for the outbreak of war in any country. But this will be only under the complete domination of the Socialist, communist system throughout the world. Mankind will then be united in a true commonwealth of equal nations. This was said long ago and scientifically proved by the founders of Marxism-Leninism. . . .

Behind that curtain, Stalin's monolithic Soviet bloc was undermined by de-Stalinization. The Chinese Communist leaders distrusted the Soviet thaw at a time when they were tightening social discipline. The tensions led, eventually, to a complete break between the two main Communist powers. Yugoslavia, which had broken with Stalin in 1948, refused to return to the fold, and other "bloc" countries cautiously asserted some independence. That led to insurrections in Czechoslovakia and East Germany (1953) and Hungary and Poland (1956), but Soviet tanks prevented overthrow of the Communist regimes. The Berlin Wall of 1961–1989 served the same purpose.

The most dramatic foreign policy change was a new attitude toward the West. Stalin's successors replaced aggressiveness by "peaceful coexistence." They argued that communism would triumph eventually through nonviolent competition. They emerged from Stalinist isolation to travel abroad and entertain Western leaders in Moscow. The most significant concrete result of this policy was the 1963 limited nuclear test ban treaty with the United States.

Stalin's heirs refrained from attempts to expand Soviet domination by force. However, they did precipitate major international crises over Berlin in 1959 and 1961 and over Cuba in 1962, and encouraged leftist "national liberation movements" in Third World countries. In part, this policy was designed to undermine Western economic and military strength. However, it also had an ideological basis, for Marxism-Leninism taught that the socialism of those movements was in step with the course of history that Marx had predicted.

Brezhnev's Stagnation

Succession to Khrushchev   Khrushchev's fall did not open a succession crisis of the post-Lenin or post-Stalin type. The oligarchs had tired of the frantic power plays of the Khrushchev period, and they lacked the personalities that had energized the previous struggles. The

result was much greater stability in the composition and politics of the leadership.

This did not mean, of course, that elite politics disappeared completely. A muted struggle was waged for the mantles of obviously ailing

Heirs Apparent

Brezhnev had been born in Dneprodzerzhinsk, Ukraine, in 1906, the son of a Russian steel worker. During Stalin's blood purges, he had become a protégé of Khrushchev. He had risen through the Ukrainian party structure to become a party secretary, had joined the party Presidium in 1952, but was dropped when Stalin died. Then he had run Khrushchev's "Virgin Lands" project in Kazakhstan. He returned to the secretariat in 1956 and the Presidium in 1957. In 1960 he was "kicked upstairs" to the largely honorary chairmanship of the Presidium of the Supreme Soviet. In June 1963 he became a party secretary again, apparently sharing with Nikolai Viktorovich Podgorny the role of heir apparent.

Kosygin had been born in St. Petersburg in 1904, the son of a lathe operator. He began as a technocratic industrial manager in Leningrad. Then he advanced through less technical governmental posts to prime minister of the Russian Republic (1943) and U.S.S.R. minister for light industry (1948). He entered the party hierarchy as candidate member (1946) and full member (1948) of the Politburo, but was demoted to candidate member in 1952. Under Khrushchev he specialized in economic planning as a moderate, junior member of the conservative faction and returned to the Presidium in 1957. Toward the end, he seemed to be a rival to Anastas Mikoyan as heir apparent to Khrushchev's prime ministership.

and aged top leaders. The immediate, principal beneficiaries of Khrushchev's demise were Leonid Ilyich Brezhnev, who succeeded to the party leadership, and Alexei Nikolayevich Kosygin, who became head of the government.

The initial succession was remarkably enduring. The only major change during Brezhnev's eighteen-year reign was Kosygin's forced retirement in October 1980 and death two months later. He was replaced as prime minister by his top-ranking deputy, Nikolai Tikhonov. Other key leaders, such as Chief Ideologue Suslov, Chief Party Functionary Kirilenko, KGB head Andropov (from 1967), and Foreign Minister Gromyko remained in place virtually throughout the Brezhnev years.

Within that stability, Brezhnev consolidated power steadily. He eliminated potential rivals carefully and increased the proportion of his supporters in the Central Committee and Presidium gradually. Unlike Khrushchev (or Stalin!), he proceeded so cautiously and with such skill that he seems never to have been challenged seriously, even when his health had deteriorated badly.

Domestic Affairs
Brezhnev's political style was evident in his domestic-affairs leadership. He abandoned Khrushchev's more radical policies and structural reforms quickly but quietly. Emphasis shifted to improving productivity through technological innovation, judicious management, increased long-term investment, strict labor discipline, avoidance of magical solutions, some decentralization of economic control, and a modest measure of "market socialism."

In Brezhnev's last years his leadership style and age benumbed the country. His care not to rock the boat may have been reassuring after the frantic Khrushchev years. However, over the long haul it fostered economic inefficiency, bureaucratic arrogance, empty rhetoric, civic indifference, corruption, and popular cynicism. Top leaders and their families—including Brezhnev's son-in-law—were implicated deeply in cases of graft and bribery that became public after Gorbachev took office. Under Brezhnev, the regime did not lurch from crisis to crisis, as under Khrushchev, but ground inexorably toward a halt, mired in muck of its own making.

Jokes about politics and society are very popular in the Soviet Union, and can help give outsiders a sense of how the Soviet people view themselves. Like all of the jokes quoted in this book, what follows is translated from Russian, and might have been overheard in Moscow or Leningrad.

In Lenin's time, it felt like being in a tunnel: dark with a light at the end.

In Stalin's time, it felt like riding on a bus: one person drives and the rest shake.

In Khrushchev's day, it felt like flying in a plane: one person pilots, everybody else is sick, and you can't leave.

In Brezhnev's era, it felt like watching a movie: Everybody is waiting for the show to end.

Like his predecessors, Brezhnev seemed bound ideologically to declare that the Soviet Union had entered yet another phase of history, "developed socialism," characterized by greater reliance on science and technology and on party leadership. That required a new constitution (1977), whose main innovation was to spell out the party's governmental authority directly and explicitly for the first time.

The Brezhnev Doctrine
Brezhnev continued Khrushchev's "peaceful coexistence" foreign policy. However, he made two important

Soviet troops moving through Salang during the war in Afghanistan.   Novosti

additions to it. First, he insisted on nuclear defense parity, or equality, with the United States. This resulted in a major covert arms buildup combined deceitfully with major arms-control negotiations. Second, he practiced the so-called "Brezhnev doctrine," intervening, with force if necessary, in the internal affairs of "fellow-socialist" countries to prevent their retreat from communism. He applied that doctrine in Czechoslovakia (1968), Afghanistan (1979), and Poland (1981). That doctrine also supported Soviet intervention in such countries as Ethiopia, Angola, and Nicaragua. As a result, Brezhnev reversed the relaxation of international tensions that had begun in 1953.

Brezhnev's Death and Succession   Although Brezhnev
was only fifty-eight years old in 1964, he was ill or infirm during much

of his term. As early as 1970, he suffered a stroke and had been clinically dead momentarily. Although he recovered, his health was never again robust and deteriorated very noticeably in the late 1970's. By the time a heart attack killed him on November 10, 1982, his aspiring successors had been jockeying for position for several years.

The Brezhnev succession was remarkable for the advanced age of the candidates. Mikhail A. Suslov had been a likely kingmaker, until he died suddenly in January 1982 at age seventy-nine. Andrei Pavlovich Kirilenko, the heir designate for several years, dropped out after a severe heart attack in May 1982 at age seventy-six. The remaining contenders were Grigory Romanov, fifty-nine, Yuri Vladimirovich Andropov, sixty-eight, and Konstantin Ustinovich Chernenko, seventy-one.

The Contenders

Andropov Andropov had been born in Stavropol province, southern Russia, in 1914, to a railway clerk. He rose through the Komsomol (young Communist) party and KGB administrations. By 1982 he had spent twenty-seven years in central administration, fifteen as KGB head. He had been a protégé of Suslov, replacing him on the Secretariat in 1982, after fifteen years on the Politburo, nine as a full member.

Chernenko Chernenko had been born in 1911 in Siberia to a Russian peasant family. He became Brezhnev's protégé in 1950 while propaganda chief in Moldava, and his entire career thereafter was service on his staff. He became a party secretary (1976) and a full member of the Politburo (1978). He had clearly been Brezhnev's preferred successor.

The rest of the oligarchy was hardly more youthful. The Politburo from late Brezhnev until early Gorbachev was one of the few genuine gerontocracies (rule by the aged) in a major modern country. The other full members of the Politburo at Brezhnev's death averaged 69.3 years of age, with only three of the twelve below the normal retirement age of sixty-five.

Several were sickly as well as aged. Andropov suffered from severe kidney disease and diabetes. Chernenko had emphysema, chronic hepatitis, and cirrhosis of the liver. Arvid Y. Pel'she died seven months after Brezhnev and Dmitri F. Ustinov in December 1984.

Perhaps the infirmities facilitated the three successions that occurred in twenty-eight months. Each new general secretary emerged within a few days. The first two chaired the Presidium of the Supreme Soviet at its next meeting, but Gorbachev deferred that honor for over three years. Andropov succeeded Brezhnev on November 12, 1982, Chernenko replaced him on February 13, 1984, and Gorbachev ended the grim sequence on March 11, 1985.

Gorbachev

Mikhail Sergeyevich Gorbachev was born in March 1931 to a Russian peasant family in Stavropol, the same province as Andropov. He had been involved in Komsomol and party administration in his home province from 1955 to 1978, until he was suddenly appointed Central Committee secretary for agriculture. With Brezhnev's obvious favor, he advanced very rapidly to Politburo candidate member (1979) and full member (1980). Andropov expanded his authority further, and under Chernenko he served as deputy party leader, acting for the general secretary during his long absences. Probably his colleagues had selected him as Chernenko's successor during the deliberations after Andropov's death and he was de facto leader already in 1984.

Gorbachev's Challenge

Gorbachev's seven-year apprenticeship in Moscow under three successive aged and decrepit chieftains prepared him well to move swiftly once he had grasped the levers of power. By late 1985 he had sacked the party bosses of Moscow, Leningrad, and twenty-three other regions: Andrei Gromyko, the perpetual foreign minister; the prime minister and fourteen other ministers; and eight departmental heads in the Central Committee. By the end of 1986 only one member of the Chernenko government remained. Gorbachev consolidated his control steadily thereafter. By early 1989, he had forced the retirement of 75 percent of the 116 republic and regional party first secretaries and of 118 of the 478 full and candidate members of the Central Committee, and had forced the Central Committee to abandon the keystone of Leninism—the political monopoly of the Communist Party. He may have lacked the iron control Stalin held in his later years, but he seemed able to secure adoption of virtually every policy he really wanted. However, his pragmatism also resulted in uncertainty, inconsistency, and sharp policy reversals.

Gorbachev is bound less slavishly to ideological formulas than his predecessors. He still pays ritualistic tribute to Lenin and speaks vaguely about a new phase in Soviet history. However, the whole thrust of his programs seems directed toward shedding the ideological straitjacket the Soviet Union has worn since 1917.

Gorbachev's dramatic impact has resulted partly from style. In sharp contrast to his predecessors, he exudes quiet self-confidence. In travels abroad he deals comfortably as a peer with the world's top leaders. At home he plunges into crowds and chats freely with ordinary people, yet he leaves no doubt among opponents and supporters alike that he is boss. He is better educated (with college degrees in law and agronomy) and probably more sophisticated intellectually than any of his predecessors, and his administrative management, public conduct, and decisions show it. However, his moderation has sometimes led to indecision.

More important than style has been the substance of his decisions. He has undertaken by far the most sweeping program of reform in the history of the Soviet Union, not only undoing six decades of Stalinism but attacking the very foundations of Leninism as well. His efforts fall generally into four categories: *perestroika*, *glasnost*, democratization, and moral renewal.

Perestroika   The cornerstone of Gorbachev's program is a drastic restructuring of the economy, called "revolutionary *perestroika*." Gorbachev had the intelligence and courage to confront squarely the harsh reality that the Soviet economic system had failed disastrously. Apparently, he concluded that past superficial remedies were insufficient and that complete collapse could be averted only by a new foundation of radically different principles.

Decentralization is a key element in *perestroika*. This means replacing Stalin's rigid centralized planning with "self-financing." Under the new system factory managers are given more authority to make decisions, and the workers receive incentives to work harder through profit sharing. Also, it means granting greater economic autonomy to the union republics.

Privatization is a second *perestroika* element. It permits individuals or families to band together to organize and operate for-profit service, small manufacturing, or farming enterprises. The details and extent of these reforms are highly controversial and may take years to work out and implement. Privatization discards implicitly two Marxist-Leninist assumptions: that profits and hired labor are incompatible with socialism and that progress from individual to collective economic endeavor is desirable and, in a "socialist" phase of history, inevitable.

Joint business ventures with foreign investors are a third major *perestroika* measure. Foreigners may now share in owning Soviet enterprises and take profits out of the country in hard currency. They may even hold controlling interest. American firms that have responded to these changes include Pepsi-Cola and McDonald's.

Glasnost

Gorbachev believed that previous economic reform efforts, especially under Khrushchev and Kosygin, had been sabotaged by the bureaucrats, who stood to lose power and wealth from decentralization. He thought that he could defeat them only if the general public—and his allies in the leadership—knew about the desperate situation and his struggle to overcome it. *Glasnost* was his means to ensure that.

Glasnost means, Gorbachev said, "that every citizen has the inalienable right to obtain exhaustive and authentic information on any question of public life that is not a state or military secret, and the right to open and free discussion of any socially significant issue." This includes the way the CPSU and the governmental organs function, socioeconomic and crime statistics, library and archival materials, and environmental situations.

However, Gorbachev limits *glasnost.* It cannot include publishing "unobjective"—even if true—information that "affects the honor and dignity of a citizen." Likewise, racism, pornography, violations of individual rights, and incitement to war and violence are not protected. Finally, "*glasnost* must not be used to the detriment of the interests of the Soviet state and society." It is not clear where these limits to free discussion will be drawn.

Democratization

The third leg of Gorbachev's program is democratization. He recognized that *glasnost* alone could not overcome his foes in the oligarchy. He had to bring the people's influence into the decision-making structures as directly and forcefully as possible. This has meant sweeping reforms of the state and party systems.

Unrest and national feeling in the republics have resulted in bloody confrontations between demonstrators and Soviet troops. But these disputes have also led to peaceful, if animated, discussions. P. Kassin/VAAP

The first big project was a new legislative structure. A Congress of People's Deputies was created, elected by two types of constituencies. Territorial districts and nationality units each elect 750 members. Gorbachev's original plan included another 750 deputies elected by official associations, but the first session of the new Supreme Soviet abolished them as "undemocratic."

The first elections, in 1989, were the freest in Soviet history, although the leadership retained significant means of manipulation. Two or more candidates contested 1,116 of the district and territorial seats, which were filled by popular vote. Campaigns were free-swinging and voter turnout high (90 percent). Many official nominees were defeated by insurgents, sometimes crushingly. Nevertheless, loyalists won 75 to 80 percent of the seats.

The Congress meets for at least one short session annually. When it first convenes, it designates 542 of its members to be the deputies who form the bicameral (two-house) legislature, called the Supreme Soviet. At each subsequent meeting it replaces, in rotation, one fourth of the deputies. It also adopts annual policy guidelines for the Supreme Soviet.

"... They Want Freedom ..."

In May 1989 the newly created Congress of People's Deputies met in Moscow in the first experiment with unfettered parliamentary debate since the Constituent Assembly of 1918. These are brief excerpts from two speeches:

Yuri N. Afanaseyev, Director of the Institute of Historical Archives:

I want to say that for a number of reasons the work of the Congress yesterday had a depressing effect on me. . . . We have cranked up the usual machinery: a few moralistic speeches . . . after which comes a stupefying vote of the majority. . . . I have scrutinized the composition of the Supreme Soviet. . . . If we . . . consider the level of professionalism required under the current conditions, we have created a Stalinist-Brezhnevite Supreme Soviet. . . . The majority that has been formed here . . . an aggressively obedient majority, which yesterday bottled up all the decisions the people expect from the Congress. . . . Yes, I am finishing, but I ask you to stop shouting and clapping, because this is what I took the podium for. So . . . we can be obedient . . . but let us not for a single moment forget those who sent us here to this Congress. They did not send us here to be graceful but to drastically change the situation in the country.

Yevgeny N. Meshalkin, Pathologist from Novosibirsk:

We Siberians . . . see Afanaseyev's and Popov's speeches as reflecting their dissatisfaction with their position at the Congress, with the fact that they are in a minority. They thought that, as at the preelection rallies outside Luzhniki Stadium, they would be able to win you over and sweep aside everything blocking their advance to the head of the Congress. . . . I am concerned as much about the situation in the country. But those who are shouting about bad work have yet to submit any constructive proposals on how it all should be except to say that they want freedom. . . . Pluralism of opinion is a must, but do you really think that pluralism of action is also a must? . . . If at the Congress there is a reasonable majority that does not allow itself to be pushed off course, this does not mean that the majority must be subordinate to the minority and refuse to state its opinion of what is going on here.

The New York Times, May 28, 1989

The Supreme Soviet meets annually for two sessions of about four months each and acts much more like a western-type parliament than the rubber stamp it had been. Both laws and decrees require its approval. Ministers are responsible to it. All this was theoretically true in the past, but nonexistent in practice.

The popularly elective president is head of state and chairs the executive bodies, including the Federation Council (composed of the union-republic presidents), Council of Ministers, and Security Council.

Other democratization measures have been put into effect or are in the works. On this long list of changes are greater internal democracy for the CPSU and an end to its constitutional "leading role," multiparty-ism, direct popular election of the president, use of genuine secret

ballots for elections, better assessment of public opinion, greater protection for freedom of worship and personal privacy, more authority for and democracy in local government councils, limits on length of tenure in public office, delegation of authority to regional and local levels of government, reduction in the size (by about 40 percent!) and authority of the bureaucracy, introduction of the legal principles of the rule of law and the presumption of innocence, reform of the judicial system and of trade unions, suspension of prosecutions for possessing anti-Soviet literature and release of many political prisoners, greater influence and autonomy for youth and women's organizations, the publication of formerly banned literary works, an end to psychiatric confinement for political dissidents, restrictions on the KGB (secret police), publication of proceedings of Central Committee meetings, liberalization of control of the press, tolerance toward orderly street demonstrations and unauthorized political organizations, a right to strike, election of factory managers by the workers, and more respect for the particular interests of the minority nationalities. If all of these changes are fully implemented, they will radically alter almost every aspect of Soviet public institutions and life as they have developed since 1917, by making the Soviet Union a pluralist, constitutional, parliamentary democracy—similar to many in the West.

Moral Renewal
Gorbachev has realized that even *glasnost* and democratization cannot ensure the success of *perestroika*. He has also identified several social evils that impair the ability of the Soviet Union to solve its economic problems. These include corruption, bureaucratic inertia, crime, and alcoholism. He has undertaken campaigns against them and related problems. His encouragement of religious revival is another part of his moral renewal effort.

The Soviet Union Joins the World
Gorbachev's foreign policies flow from his *perestroika* program. The Soviet Union cannot

deal effectively with its economic problems without reducing its military expenditures. That, in turn, requires a relaxation of international tensions.

Immediately after becoming leader, Gorbachev launched a full-scale campaign that, in effect, revolutionized Soviet foreign and defense policies. He negotiated a series of important arms-reduction measures, announced a change from an offensive to a defensive posture in strategic planning, withdrew Soviet forces from Afghanistan and Eastern Europe, undertook an exhausting round of visits to key foreign capitals, resumed cordial relations with China for the first time since Stalin, and began to cut the armed forces (by 500,000 soldiers) and the defense budget (by 33 percent). By renouncing the "Brezhnev doctrine" (see p. 138), he notified the peoples of Eastern Europe that their governments would no longer be defended by the Red Army. This led quickly to the collapse or transformation of every Communist system in the area.

In almost every way, Gorbachev seemed to be moving to reduce the distinctiveness of Soviet diplomatic and military behavior. He has said, "We should abandon everything that led to the isolation of the socialist countries from the mainstream of world civilization." This meant putting the Soviet Union on a footing similar to that of the Western countries in its relations with international organizations like GATT (General Agreement on Trade and Tariffs), the World Bank, the United Nations, the European Community, etc. He moved to normalize diplomatic relations with Israel and South Africa and aligned his country with the West on antiterrorism policy. The Soviet Union was becoming a "normal" participant in international affairs for the first time.

"Almost slaves four years ago—almost free people today." So a Soviet newspaper summed up Gorbachev's first four years. That dramatic formula probably reflected spirit more accurately than reality. Gorbachev's early years had, in fact, a very mixed record.

Failures were all too common. Some initial measures for governmental restructuring did not work and had to be rescinded. The antialcohol campaign aborted. In some respects, Gorbachev's policies backfired. For instance, *glasnost* unleashed a whirlwind of long-repressed conflict among the nationalities and serious outbreaks of labor unrest. Demands for independence by fourteen union-republics threatened to tear the Soviet Union apart. Three common evils of capitalism became significant factors in Soviet life for the first time. By 1990 inflation had reached 80 percent by unofficial estimates, unemployment 3.8 percent; and industrial strikes were idling an average of 30,000 workers each day. Other reforms were sabotaged. When planning bureaucrats were forbidden to issue production quotas, they substituted state orders.

In other ways, *perestroika* was very slow in bearing fruit. Foreign investors hesitated to form joint ventures. Many consumer goods became even scarcer. The economy came near to collapse. In 1988 agricultural production fell by 2 percent and industrial production increased by only 2 to 2.5 percent. In 1989, the latter measure fell by between 2 and 5 percent, and in 1990 the GNP fell by 7 percent.

Resistance to change was unexpectedly stiff in the leadership, the bureaucracy, the general public, and some Eastern European countries. Many Soviet citizens resented the success of neighbors who undertook cooperative ventures. Others feared the risks such endeavors seemed to entail. Similarly, as Gorbachev said, inexperience with democracy impeded its rapid, full development.

Nevertheless, a telephone survey of Muscovites in November 1989 indicated that Gorbachev is benefitting from the traditional long-suffering patience of the Russian people. Only 3.8 percent said that the Soviet economy had improved under his leadership, compared to 81.5 percent who said that it had deteriorated. Yet 57.6 percent believed that he would succeed (against 32.5 percent disbelievers) and 88.4 percent approved of his policies, while only 4.7 percent did not. This showed a trend in Gorbachev's favor, when compared to a similar survey of early 1989, but in 1990 his popularity fell and Boris Yeltsin's rose.

Even more significant was the level of participation and the voting behavior in the 1989 elections. They reflected massive dissatisfaction with the old ways that Gorbachev is trying to change. The Soviet public gave *perestroika* a whopping popular mandate.

Generations must pass before we really change. —Mikhail S. Gorbachev

In the last 20 years we have turned into something between Gogol and Orwell—an animal farm of dead souls. Now along comes a living soul [Gorbachev]. Will everyone wake up? I catch myself hoping, like an invalid who can suddenly walk 10 meters. But I just can't believe it yet.
—Soviet engineer, in Christian Schmidt-Häuer, *Gorbachev*

Perhaps for the first time in its thousand-year history, Russia has a popular, intelligent, sane, competent leader pursuing a broad, pragmatic program of modernization. Moreover, his example inspired the emergence of a similarly able leader of a legal opposition, Boris Yeltsin, president of the Russian Republic and head of a political movement even more progressive than Gorbachev. The consequences of their rivalries and collaboration for the future of the Soviet Union—and for the world where it looms so large—are incalculable, but it can well be imagined that they will have a dramatic and probably beneficial impact on both.

A Nation of Nationalities

To get a sense of the tremendous diversity of peoples and the vast extent of land in the Soviet Union, one might imagine a space satellite high above the stratosphere, focusing its lens on the Soviet Union. It floats so far distant that the entire, immense landmass is in view. The date is March 7. The camera catches the first rays of the sunrise, striking a frontier police post on the Polish border near Kaliningrad, the most westerly point in the country, at the same instant that the last glimmer of sunset is fading from the Pacific shore at Cape Dezhnev, its most easterly extremity.

These portraits are drawn from a variety of sources. Some are based on specific individuals, others on composites taken from the press and personal accounts.

7:07 A.M. Kaliningrad—Tatevik is climbing the long steel ladder of the crane she operates at a shipyard in this city of 400,000, about 30 miles (48 km.) from the border. As a young girl, she came here with her family from a small farming village in Armenia, sent by Stalin after World War II to help replace the Germans he had expelled from this former part of East Prussia. Her husband, Vladislav, came here in 1956, rather than return to his native Byelorussia, when he was released from eight years in a prison camp for having made a sarcastic remark about Stalin. From the cab of the crane, Tatevik can see the smokestack of the chemical plant where Vladislav works as a foreman. Looking out across the harbor, she catches sight of fishing boats chugging out into the Baltic Sea.

8:07 A.M. Moscow—Alicia is unbundling the last of her brood of four year olds as they arrive at the day-care center she helps to tend. She is trained as an art historian, but could not find work in that field. She will soon be forced to quit her present job. Her husband, Maxim, a physician, has left her and their small son, Sasha. When the divorce is final, they must vacate their apartment and move from Moscow. Maxim is a Muscovite, but she is Ukrainian and never obtained the necessary residence permit. She lives on the twentieth floor of a twenty-five-story building in the outskirts of the city. Only one of the hundred families who live there owns an automobile. The rest commute by bus. To travel to work she must change buses three times or walk an hour and a half through a huge, wooded park for a direct line to the center.

9:07 A.M. near Kobuleti—Shota is using a hand spade to work fertilizer into the soil around the base of a tea tree. The orchard, on a southerly slope of the Maly Hills in western Georgia, is part of the Maxim Gorki Collective Farm. Although winter still holds most of the Soviet Union in a firm grip, the tea trees are already well leafed out in this warmest corner of the country. Shota stops his spading every few minutes to pocket a few choice ripened leaves. He will pass these along to a fellow worker, who is flying to Moscow tomorrow and will sell several kilos of such pilfered leaves on the black market. Tea is the Soviet national beverage, and most of it comes from Georgia. Shota agrees with many Georgians that Gorbachev has gone too far in criticizing Stalin, another Georgian, who, he thinks, was also clever at outwitting Russians.

10:07 A.M. near Izevsk—Aïsha, a Tatar woman, is using a spade to chop up beets and potatoes as feed for the nineteen milk cows she tends on the Friedrich Engels State Farm northeast of the Caspian Sea. She has been up and about since four A.M., first cleaning the stalls and feeding the herd. The milking machines were turned on an hour later. She spent the next three hours moving the machines from cow to cow, transferring the warm liquid to the cooling vat. She likes caring for the animals, but finds the work difficult because of the shortage of equipment. Not even a cart, wagon, or wheelbarrow is available for her use. According to Soviet labor law, women cannot be required to lift more than 33 pounds (15 kg.). Yet Aïsha wastes hours each day carrying or dragging by hand much heavier loads of feed to the stanchions, manure to the pasture, milk pails to the vat, bales of hay and bags of grain to the storage bin. Her workday is broken up by rest periods of an hour or two, depending on the season, but she never finishes the evening milking before 9:00 P.M. Aïsha gets too little sleep, like 90 percent of her fellow milkmaids, who suffer from a variety of ailments as a result.

11:07 A.M. Alma-Ata Region—Zhanar has finished feeding a penful of Karakul sheep at the Novo-Shuisky Livestock Collective Farm on a high plateau in southern Kazakhstan. He is strolling toward the slaughterhouse to help butcher lambs for sale at the farm market in Alma-Ata on Saturday. The break in the weather this morning sends his thoughts six to eight weeks ahead. He looks forward to the moment when he and a dozen other shepherds will be riding horseback, driving the farm's two thousand sheep toward their summer pasture in the Zailiiski Ala Tau Mountains. Through the warm months, they will move the flock steadily higher on the slopes, searching for grassy pastures. They will sleep in crude stone huts or under the stars. Once a week, when all goes well, a motor caravan will bring them groceries, repairs for their clothing and footwear, a movie projector and film, and even baths. As summer ends, they will return slowly to Novo-Shuisky, rejoining their families and friends in late fall. Then they will resume the routine of caring for the sheep in their winter quarters.

12:07 P.M. Irkutsk—Vladimir turns off the metal-stamping machine he operates at a state automobile radiator factory in this industrial city near Lake Baikal in eastern Siberia. He has heard the grind of a worn bearing and cannot resume work until someone comes from maintenance to make the repairs. This is the third time this week that he has lost half a day's work time because of mechanical breakdowns, but he doesn't mind. He would rather spend time with some buddies in the canteen, perhaps pick up a game of chess. He worked for two months at the cooperative factory next door, but quit when he was fined 80 rubles for making a careless mistake. Vladimir was earning twice his present 200-ruble monthly pay, but he had to work "like mad." Ivan, who has a wife and two kids, stayed on at the coop. He sees the opportunity to earn "big money" as their only chance to break out of the cycle of poverty and is willing to accept the extra work and pressure. After two years, the coop has made enough profit to plan to build a housing complex for some of its workers. Ivan has a high-priority spot on the waiting list. This alone makes work at the coop well worthwhile.

1:07 P.M. in a forest in Yakutsk A.S.S.R.—Yuri is bent over, stripping the hide from an ermine he has found in one of his traps. As a full-blooded Yakut, he is pursuing a traditional occupation of his people: hunter-trapper. Yuri pauses to gaze down into the valley of the Dulgalach River. The snow is three feet deep in many places and the river is frozen solid. He sees no sign of spring. His breath hangs as ice crystals in front of him and he must swing his hands hard every few minutes to prevent frostbite. Even at midday, the temperature hovers around 0° F (–18° C). The woods are still full of fur-bearing animals, some thirty species, but Yuri's trade has become more difficult because of competition from the fur farms. Many trappers have given up their lives in the wilds to take jobs there. Yuri holds out. He likes the freedom of the forest. The government requires that he sell all his furs to its agency, but it cannot know how many pelts he collects. He can always stash away a few to peddle for premium prices to a roving black marketeer.

2:07 P.M. on the Okhotsk Sea—Oh Kon is helping his crewmates scoop a netful of Siberian and hump-backed salmon into the hold of their fishing boat. He is one of four hundred thousand Soviet Koreans, who mostly live in the Far East. The boat has nearly finished the day's run and will soon return to the huge factory ship where the catch will be loaded, processed, and canned—right there on the high seas. The fishermen will board the ship to clean up, have supper, and relax. They left Okhotsk, their home port, only last week and may not return until late summer. They will communicate with their families only by radio. In the meantime, despite the technological equipment of their fleet, they will be running many of the risks that have plagued seafarers since time immemorial: storms, fog, rough seas, ice floes, typhoons, bitter cold, and scorching sun. Their fleet belongs to the Sverdlov Collective Farm, so a good season will mean extra income for everyone. The last two years have been poor, but this one is starting out well and Oh Kon is hopeful, for he plans to get married in the fall—if the catch is good and his long-promised apartment comes through.

3:07 P.M. Karamken—Amir is putting on his blue long johns, heavy cotton work clothes, parka, and hard hat, preparing to go to work in one of the large, deep-lode gold mines in the Kolyma River valley of Magadan Province in the northeastern corner of Siberia. He will work with the blasting crew. A clearing crew and two shifts of digging crews will follow, each laboring for six hours. He has come 3,500 miles from his native Uzbekistan, because jobs are plentiful here and pay well. He earns 700 rubles a month, about four times as much as on the cotton farm back home. The premium pay reflects the harsh climate, primitive living conditions, and economic importance of the mines. Gold from

Magadan mines accounts for two thirds of the province's industrial production and has helped make the Soviet Union the world's second-largest gold producer. Recently, Amir's mine went to the "self-financing" plan. It can use any profits to build new housing to replace the crude wooden barracks in which most miners now live. Amir must decide whether to transfer to construction work. The Karamken complex is only nine years old and, therefore, was not one of the slave labor camps that made Kolyma so notorious during the Stalinist period. In fact, Karamken is so far from being a prison that the workers actually elect their supervisors—another of Gorbachev's reforms.

4:07 P.M. Petropavlovsk—Stepan is working at his desk in the Kamchatka District office of the Communist Party, preparing for an evening meeting of the Petropavlovsk city soviet. As the local party secretary, he must ensure that the municipal budget on the agenda conforms to party policy. His mother is Koryak (Koryaks are a native Kamchatka people), and his father Russian. He is proud to be the only member of the local political elite to have Koryak ancestry, but his job is less fun than before Gorbachev. Because of the new austerity program, he must tell the city soviet to cut the subsidies to the local timber-processing plant and ship-repair shop. He resents the implication of Gorbachev's *perestroika* campaign that the Party has not been doing a good job. He has lost two staff members to cutbacks and has virtually given up hope for transfer to the Timber Industry Ministry in Moscow. Stepan had secured an unopposed nomination to the Congress of People's Deputies to enhance his prospects for that assignment, but more than half of the voters struck his name from the ballot. Now he will be lucky to keep the job he has. From his office window he can see two of the active volcanoes that loom over the city, lighting it with an eerie glow at night, and he thinks of the beauty and many natural wonders of this Far Eastern peninsula—the geysers, hot springs, and soaring mountains—"After all, I would be homesick in that cold, unfriendly city."

5:07 P.M. near Ugolny, Chukchi National Area—Chula is running across the frozen tundra, a stick in hand. Since she returned from school at 3:00 P.M., she has been helping her father search for three stray reindeer from the family herd. She is a twelve-year-old Chukchi; like the Inuit, the Chukchi are one of the "peoples of the North." Oil has been discovered in their homeland in northeast Siberia and their way of life is changing fast. The tundra is being destroyed, the number of reindeer has fallen by three fourths, and fish no longer swim in the district's rivers. Even the Chukchi are being swamped by new residents, mainly Russians. Only fourteen thousand Chukchi remain in a total population of three fourths of a million in their homeland. To buy even a loaf of bread, Chula must go on foot or dogsled to a neighboring village and wait in line for hours, for her own settlement has no shops, radios, or telephones, and most of its inhabitants still live in skin tents.

The great size and diversity of the Soviet land combined with the peculiarities of historical development to produce a large and greatly varied population. More than one hundred distinct nationalities occupy Soviet territory. That human kaleidoscope confronts the Soviet Union with still another paradox. The wealth of that diversity provides the country with its most valuable resource. Yet it also has great potential to divide, maybe even to tear the Soviet Union apart.

Population and Demographics

The population of the Soviet Union was 286.7 million in 1989. That made it the third most populous country in the world, far behind China (1 billion) and India (750 million). (The U.S. population is 250 million.) United Nations projections indicate that it will retain that ranking for the foreseeable future.

The population of the Russian empire grew rapidly in the decades before the Bolshevik Revolution, increasing by 37.3 percent from 1890 to 1913. Because of civil war, famine, and terrorism, it rose only 0.7

percent from 1917 to 1939. After World War II the growth resumed, expanding by 44.5 percent between 1950 and 1977. From 1979 to 1989 it grew by 9.3 percent. That figure conceals wide variations, ranging from 4 percent in Ukraine to 34 percent in Tadzhikistan.

The population density of the Soviet Union is 31 persons per square mile (12 per sq. km.). (The population density in the United States is 65.3 persons per square mile, 25.2 per sq. km.). However, enormous disparities exist among regions. Immense areas of Soviet Asia are almost uninhabited, while Soviet Europe is much more densely populated than the United States, ranging as high as 321.9 per square mile (124.3 per sq. km.) in Moldava.

Much migration has occurred since 1917, some of it involuntary. During and after World War II, Stalin forcibly relocated from Soviet Europe to Asia nearly 3 million people, including eight entire nationality groups (Crimean Tatars, Volga Germans, Kalmyks, Karachais, Chechens, Ingushi, Balkars, Meskhs) as well as some Poles, Greeks, and Kurds. At least 1 million died as a result. Later Khrushchev conscripted millions of European workers for his Virgin Lands program in Siberia and Kazakhstan. Voluntary migrations have drawn other millions from economically backward areas of Asia to more advanced European regions and from Europe and rural Asia to new industrial centers in the Urals and Asia.

Another form of migration has been from country to city. Forced industrialization moved millions of peasants to cities. Other millions followed, looking for jobs, as the industrialization process continued. The proportion of urban dwellers in the total population increased from 32.5 percent in 1940 to 66 percent in 1989 (in the United States it is 80 percent).

Those population trends have largely offset one another to maintain the diversity the Bolsheviks inherited. The Central Asians' higher birthrates and the net migration to Soviet Asia have increased, while urbanization has reduced, the extreme diversity. This is especially evident when viewed through the kaleidoscope of Soviet nationality groups.

The Peoples of the Soviet Union

Marxism-Leninism holds that all human conflicts result from differences in the ownership of the means of production. Once capitalism is eliminated, those conflicts should disappear. In fact, ethnic tensions have been repressed during the seven decades of Soviet communism, but have diminished little and remain one of its most perplexing problems.

Most Soviet nationalities have quite distinctive cultures, though some are closely related. They differ in language, religion, family practices, life-styles, art, dress, food, folkways, etc. Many Balts seem as Scandinavian as Swedes, while some Soviet Far Easterners are indistinguishable from Chinese.

Soviet nationalities differ markedly from ethnic groups in the United States. Except for American Indians, all American groups are relatively recent immigrants. As we have seen, some Soviet nationalities have lived in their present homelands for over a thousand years. Compounding the problem, most of the minority nationalities inhabit the Soviet borderlands, with many of their ethnic fellows residing in neighboring countries.

The Russian empire became multinational largely through colonialism, similar to the imperialism of western Europe after 1492 and during much the same time period. Unlike those in the West, however, Russian conquests were overland. This made it easier to resist the anticolonial movements of the twentieth century. Thus, while the European colonies in Africa and Asia have all achieved independence, only Finland has left the Russian empire. The Soviets could justify their control by

Principal Nationalities in the Soviet Union

NATIONALITY FAMILY	NATIONALITY	HOMELAND	POPULATION (IN THOUSANDS)[1]	PERCENT IN HOMELAND[2]	PERCENT OF HOMELAND[3]	PERCENT OF U.S.S.R. TOTAL[1]
	All citizens of the Soviet Union	U.S.S.R.	286,700			100
Eastern Slavic	Great Russian	R.S.F.S.R.[4,5]	137,397	82.7	82.6	51.5
	Ukrainian	Ukrainia[5]	42,347	86.5	73.6	16.2
	Byelorussian	Byelorussia[5]	9,463	80.0	79.4	3.6
Baltic	Lithuanian	Lithuania[5]	2,851	95.5	80.1	1.1
	Latvian	Latvia[5]	1,439	94.1	53.7	0.6
	Estonian	Estonia[5]	1,020	93.7	64.7	0.4
	Karelian	Karelia[6]	138	54.5	10.0	0.1
	Finn	none	77	[7]	[7]	[8]
Other European*	Moldavan	Moldava[5]	2,968	90.2	63.9	1.1
	Romanian	Moldava[5]	129	[9]	[9]	[8]
	Polish	none	1,151	[7]	[7]	0.4
	Bulgarian	none	361	[7]	[7]	0.1
	German	none	1,936	[7]	[7]	0.7
	Greek	none	344	[7]	[7]	0.1
	Hungarian	none	171	[7]	[7]	0.1
Caucasian	Georgian	Georgia[5]	3,571	96.6	68.8	1.4
	Armenian	Armenia[5]	4,151	65.5	89.7	1.6
	Azerbaijani	Azerbaijan[5]	5,477	86.0	78.1	2.1
	Balkars	Kabardino-Balkar[6]	66	[9]	[9]	[8]
	Karachayev	Karachayevo-Cherkess[10]	131	[9]	[9]	[8]
	Kumyk	Dagestan[6]	110	[9]	[9]	[8]
	Nogai	Dagestan[6]	36	[9]	[9]	[8]
	Dagestan	Dagestan[6]	1,657	81.6	80.2	0.6
	Chechen	Checheno-Ingush[6]	756	[9]	[9]	0.3
	Ingushi	Checheno-Ingush[6]	186	[9]	[9]	0.1
	Kabardin	Kabardino-Balkar[6]	322	[9]	[9]	0.1
	Adygien	Adygei[10]	109	[9]	[9]	[8]
	Cherkess	Karachayevo-Cherkess[10]	46	[9]	[9]	[8]
	Abazian	Karachayevo-Cherkess[10]	29	[9]	[9]	[8]
	Abkhazin	Abkhazia[6]	91	[9]	[9]	[8]
Central Asian	Uzbek	Uzbekistan[5]	12,456	84.9	68.7	4.8
	Kazakh	Kazakhstan[5]	6,556	81.0	36.0	2.5
	Turkmen	Turkmenistan[5]	2,028	93.1	68.4	0.7
	Kirghiz	Kirghizia[5]	1,906	81.1	43.8	0.7
	Karakalpak	Karakalpak[6]	303	99.7	33.5	0.1
	Uigur	Alma Ata[10]	211	[9]	[9]	0.1
	Tatar	Tatar[6]	6,317	23.7	44.0	2.4
	Bashkir	Bashkiria[6]	1,371	70.0	25.0	0.5
	Chuvash	Chuvashia[6]	1,751	52.0	70.0	0.7

NATIONALITY FAMILY	NATIONALITY	HOMELAND	POPULA-TION (IN THOUSANDS)[1]	PERCENT IN HOMELAND[2]	PERCENT OF HOMELAND[3]	PERCENT OF U.S.S.R. TOTAL[1]
	Tuvinian	Tuva[6]	166	90.0	60.0	0.1
	Gagauzi	Moldava[5]	173	83.8	3.5	0.1
Iranic	Tadzhik	Tadzhikistan[5]	2,898	77.0	59.0	1.1
	Ossetian	[11]	542	[9]	[9]	0.2
	Kurd	none	116	[9]	[9]	[8]
	Tat	Azerbaijan[5]	22	[9]	[9]	[8]
	Talyshi	Azerbaijan[5]	100	[9]	[9]	[8]
Mongol	Buryat	Buryat[6]	353	[9]	[9]	0.1
	Kalmyk	Kalmykia[6]	147	[9]	[9]	0.1
Uralian	Mordovinian	Mordovia[6]	1,192	[9]	[9]	0.5
	Umdurts	Umdurt[6]	714	[9]	[9]	0.3
	Mari	Mari[6]	622	[9]	[9]	0.2
	Komi-Zyrian	Komi[6]	327	[9]	[9]	0.1
	Komi-Permiak	Komi-Permiak[12]	151	[7]	[7]	0.1
	Khanty	Khanty-Mansi[12]	21	[9]	[9]	[8]
	Mansi	Khanty-Mansi[12]	8	[9]	[9]	[8]
	Saami	Kola Peninsula	2	[9]	[9]	[8]
	Samoyed	Siberia	34	[9]	[9]	[8]
Altaic	Yakut	Yakutia[6]	328	87.0	43.0	0.1
	Dolgany	Siberia	5	[9]	[9]	[8]
	Tofa	Siberia	1	[9]	[9]	[8]
	Tungus-Manchurian	Siberia/Far East	56	[9]	[9]	[8]
No Family	Paleo-Asiatic	Siberia/Kamchatka/Sakhalin	32	[9]	[9]	[8]
	Jewish	Jewish[10]	1,811	[8]	15.0	0.7
	Gypsy	none	209	[9]	[9]	0.1
Foreign	Turkish	none	93	[9]	[9]	[8]
	Korean	none	389	[9]	[9]	0.1
	Persian	none	31	[9]	[9]	[8]
	Assyrian	none	25	[9]	[9]	[8]

1. Population figures, along with their percentages of the total population of the Soviet Union, are based on 1979 census figures.

2. Percent in homeland refers to the percentage of the members of a nationality who reside in its designated homeland.

3. Percent of homeland refers to the percentage of the population of a homeland that is constituted by members of the designated nationality.

4. Russian Soviet Federated Socialist Republic. This is used rather than "Russia" because the R.S.F.S.R. includes several times as much territory as Russia itself: Siberia, the Far East, Karelia, Sakhalin, Kamchatka, etc. In all other cases, the political unit and the historical homeland coincide closely.

5. Union Republic (S.S.R.)

6. Autonomous Republic (A.S.S.R. or A.R.)

7. Not applicable

8. Less than .05%

9. Figures are unavailable

10. Autonomous Oblast (A.O.)

11. The homeland of the people of the Ossetian nationality is in the Caucasus, especially in the North Ossetian A.S.S.R. and the South Ossetian A.O. of the Georgian S.S.R.

12. National Region (N.R.)

*Moldavia changed its name to Moldava in 1990.

claiming that they were bringing the benefits of Marxism-Leninism to more and more peoples.

Stalin implemented his nationalities policy by providing separate territorial units in the state structure for the fifty-three principal national groups. For instance, Ukraine is organized as the Ukrainian Soviet Socialist Republic.

The Russian Soviet Federated Socialist Republic, which covers more than three quarters of the territory of the Soviet Union, is a major exception to this rule—and a tacit admission of Russian imperialism. It includes the historic Russian homeland plus seventeen other nationality-based territorial units in Europe, as well as an Asian area (Siberia and the Far East) that is triple the size of the European portion and consists entirely of tsarist colonial conquests.

In the 1970 census, Soviet residents identified themselves with more than 800 ethnic and linguistic denominations. The government grouped them into 104 nationalities (down from about 200 in the 1926 census), many more than in any other country, and reported over 150,000 persons with "other nationalities." The official categories ranged in size from the 143.6 million Russians to Siberian tribes with a few hundred members. The state identifies each citizen with an official nationality and stamps all internal passports accordingly. The determination of nationality is often based on culture more than ancestry.

In reality, the categories are less neat. One seventh of all marriages are mixed in nationality and 7 percent of the people have mother tongues different from their official nationalities. Furthermore, much migration by the Slavic groups occurs among the homelands.

Russians are especially mobile. They have moved massively into the Asian parts of the R.S.F.S.R. and form 19 percent of the population of the other union republics. For instance, Kazakhstan's 1970 population was 40.8 percent Russian, 6.1 percent Ukrainian, and only 36 percent Kazakh. Other union republics with large Russian populations were

Latvia (32.87 percent), Kirgizia (29.2 percent), Estonia (27.9 percent), and Ukraine (21 percent).

Ethnic conflicts—called "bourgeois nationalism" in Marxist-Leninist ideology—take many forms. They include boundary disputes, of which some thirty-five are current. Others have been declarations of independence or autonomy or manifestations of religious militancy. Under *glasnost,* demonstrations, riots, and ethnic assaults have occurred in at least ten of the fourteen non-Russian union republics. In just one recent year such violence cost 304 lives and 6,100 injuries and produced 360,000 refugees. The most serious conflict in the 1980s was the virtual civil war between Armenians and Azerbaijanis.

The variety of Soviet peoples may be indicated by surveying the largest ones. Space limitations prevent adequate description of their enormous diversity. However, even the highlights suggest the richness and tenacity of their traditions.

Eastern Slavs

By far the largest group of nationalities is the Eastern Slavs. It includes three of the four most numerous nationalities (Russians, Ukrainians, Byelorussians). They are among the Slavonic peoples, Indo-Europeans (a language family) who dominate Eastern Europe.

Slavs inhabited the region between the Carpathian Mountains and the Dnieper River by the sixth century A.D. and may have been the original settlers. By the ninth century they had divided permanently and settled in nearly the same areas they occupy now, except that the Russians have become very widely dispersed eastward from their historic homelands.

Russians or *Great Russians* are much the most numerous nationality, with 51.5 percent of the population. If they formed a separate country, its population would rank fifth in the world—behind China, India, the United States, and Indonesia. However, their share of the Soviet population is declining, because their birthrate is only about 60 percent of the national average.

Russians have disproportionate political and economic importance. All top Soviet leaders from Lenin through Gorbachev, except Stalin, have been Russian. In 1988 nineteen of the twenty-three Politburo and Secretariat members and two thirds of the Central Committee were Russian. Sixty-four percent of the Soviet population declared Russian as their native tongue in 1979, and another 18 percent claimed fluency in it.

Russians tend to dominate Soviet cities, the political and economic centers. In 1970 they numbered 65.6 percent of the urban dwellers. On the other hand, Russians trail Jews, Georgians, and Armenians in percentage pursuing higher education.

Ukrainians or *Little Russians* form the second largest Soviet nationality, yet they are less than one third as numerous as the Russians. Less widely dispersed then the Russians, they constitute only 2.7 percent of the population outside the Ukrainian S.S.R.

The Ukrainians are Slavs who were ruled and influenced by Lithuanians and Poles for centuries. They have had an active, organized nationalism since the mid-nineteenth century, but formed an independent political entity only briefly during the Civil War. Yet they are more numerous than all but four of the nationalities (English, German, French, Italian) that form European nation-states. Between the world wars 7.5 million Ukrainians lived in pieces of their homeland held by Poland, Czechoslovakia, and Rumania.

Initial Ukrainian reaction to the nationalist opportunities of *glasnost* was relatively moderate, but later, under pressure from western Ukrainians, they were demanding independence. As much the largest national minority, they pose potentially the greatest danger to Soviet unity.

Byelorussians or *White Russians* have had even more difficulty than Ukrainians in securing a separate state, being wedged among Ukraini-

"Good-bye to Winter"

The annual "Good-bye to Winter" festival is traditionally organized throughout Ukraine on one of the Sundays in March. It symbolizes the meeting of winter with spring, during which winter gives over its powers to spring and informs the latter on how people have prepared for it.

In many administrative districts and regions of Ukraine, farm equipment is inspected and fairs are held for spring and summer consumer goods.

Squares, stadiums, public gardens, and parks serve as locations for the festivities. Preparations begin well in advance. Father Frost (Santa Claus), Snow Maiden, and their assistants ride along the streets in open cars or sleighs inviting people to participate and announcing the time and place.

In Kiev, Ukraine's capital, the festival is held on the grounds of the Exhibition of Economic Achievement of the Ukrainian S.S.R. and in the city's parks. Various concerts and shows are staged on temporary platforms. Amateur performing collectives and professional actors participate in them. Improvised cafés and shops are set up on the sidewalks to serve tea and pancakes with different stuffings and toppings. Visitors are offered rides in *troikas* (sleighs). Spring, played by a festively dressed girl, greets the crowds.

Each town and village organizes the festival in its own way, but its songs, dances, games, shows, and competitions take place throughout Ukraine.

Adapted from *Ukraine*, No. 3, 1988

ans, Russians, Poles, and Lithuanians. Their glimpse at national independence during the Civil War was even briefer. Furthermore, their homeland is less clearly delineated by natural boundaries and is not entirely included in the Byelorussian S.S.R. This may explain why Byelorussia has been relatively untouched by nationalist agitation under *glasnost.*

Balts   The northwestern rim of the Soviet Union is formed largely of land occupied by four Baltic nationalities. All have small populations and areas. Yet each is distinctive in culture, language, and national character.

Lithuanians are the most southerly and much the most numerous of the Balts. However, their low population growth rate (6.6 percent) and Russian immigration threatens their hold on their homeland.

Lithuanians have a long, distinctive national tradition. They settled in their present homeland as early as 1500 B.C. and began to organize a state in the ninth century A.D. At times during the thirteenth to eighteenth centuries they ruled vast areas of Poland, Byelorussia, Ukraine, and Russia, as far as the Black Sea. From the seventeenth century on, Russia eroded Lithuanian control until in 1795 it absorbed Lithuania itself.

Lithuanian nationalists remained active. They led a cultural rebirth and regained independence during World War I. After twenty years of turbulent separate existence, Lithuania was annexed by Stalin in 1940. Under Gorbachev, Lithuanians have formed a large nationalist political organization (Sajudis), and in 1989 the Lithuanian branch of the Communist Party and the official State organs—with the apparent support of an overwhelming majority of the people—began with determination to try to regain the country's independence, the first open secessionist effort since the earliest years of the Soviet Union.

Antis, a leading Lithuanian rock band noted for its strongly visual style. Gintaras Babravicius

The *Latvians* or *Letts*, whose homeland borders Lithuania on the north, are endangered even more than their neighbors. Though Latvia is only half as populous as Lithuania, Russian immigration is as great, and its natural growth rate is much lower (4 percent). An example of Russian domination is the kindergarten system in the capital city, Riga. Russian is the sole language in 71.2 percent of the schools, Latvian in 19.5 percent; 9.3 percent are bilingual.

Latvia lacks Lithuania's long tradition of national independence. Its location on a natural trading route made it the frequent prey of more powerful neighbors. German Teutonic knights, Poles, Swedes, and Rus-

Scene from the patriotic Latvian opera Black Power, *featuring the heavy-rock band* Jumprava.   Juris Berzins

sians succeeded one another as conquerors. Nevertheless, nationalist sentiment developed during the nineteenth century, stimulating cultural development and a successful independence movement during World War I.

In 1940 Latvia was annexed like Lithuania. Under Gorbachev, the Latvians joined Lithuanians in demanding their independence. Popular demonstrations have commemorated Stalin's annexation and the deportation of 200,000–300,000 Latvians. In 1989 the nationalist Popular Front won twenty-six of Latvia's thirty-four seats in the Congress of People's Deputies.

Estonians—between Latvia and the Gulf of Finland—have the highest per-capita income in the Soviet Union. Estonians are related to the Finns, the Hungarians, and some "peoples of the North." Their ancestors immigrated from the Ural region in prehistoric times. Between 1219 and 1721, Estonia was ruled, in turn, by Danes, Teutonic knights, and Swedes, and since then by Russians, except for its 1918 to 1940 interlude of independence.

"Eestlane Olen"
["Born Estonian"]

A nationalist rock song by Estonians Alo Mattiisen and J. Leesment.

No less than a thousand beginnings.
Not brief shining moments [1]*, but a thousand years rising.*
To deny your own nation
Is worse than selling yourself into slavery.

Refrain
I was born Estonian, I am now Estonian,
And it is Estonian I shall remain.
Being Estonian, proud and good
Free as my grandfather was [2]
Yes, truly free, as my grandfather was.

The voice of a thousand thunderclaps queries.
The open sea. Ancestral homesteads.
Sacred Soil.
A thousand times, and a thousand have remained—
Despite all troubles, they keep the
holy fire alive.

Repeat Refrain

Translated by Peter Riggs

1. Literally, "Not a swan's first flight"—signifying that Estonians have faced such tribulations before and are well used to the struggle.
2. The reference to "grandfather" is quite deliberate—referring to the generation of the 1920's that fought successfully against Russian occupying forces to establish an independent Estonian state.

Under *glasnost* Estonian nationalists have the support of the local CPSU and government in calling for independence. They have formed the largest legal non-Communist political organization in the Soviet Union since the Revolution and held massive popular demonstrations. Even the Estonian parliament has defied Moscow by adopting nationalist laws.

Karelians are the least numerous and distinctive Baltic nationality. Their homeland lies north of Leningrad, between Finland and the White Sea. It is the largest, most northerly, and least densely populated Baltic land. Karelia is not entirely within any territorial unit, and much of it lies across the Finnish border. The Karelians are thoroughly submerged by Russians, who form 70 percent of the Karelian A.S.S.R. population.

Karelians differ from Finns mainly in having been ruled by Russia since 1485, while the Finns were under the Swedes (1249–1809). Karelians have shared in the nationalist excitement of *glasnost* by demanding that the adjacent Kola Peninsula be attached to their republic. (See *The Land and People of Finland.*)

Other Europeans

Several significant European Soviet nationalities are parts of groups that reside mainly in neighboring countries. This results largely from the impossibility of fitting international boundaries to the complex ethnic patterns of Eastern Europe. It also results from Soviet repossession of all pieces of the Russian empire, except parts of Finland.

The *Moldavan* nationality is a Soviet designation for Romanians residing in the Moldavan region (called Bessarabia by Romania) of their homeland, the most southwesterly corner of the Soviet Union. A similar number inhabit Romanian Bessarabia. Soviet citizens assigned Romanian nationality originated in other regions of that country.

Romanians are descended from Dacians, who settled that area in prehistoric times. A long succession of invaders conquered their strategic location on the Asian face of southern Europe. Moldava was independent only briefly in the late Middle Ages, after which the Turks ruled it from 1415 until it became a Russian protectorate in 1812. Between the world wars, Moldava rejoined Romania. That the Moldavans continue to consider themselves Romanian is indicated by their recent successful demand to have their language officially redesignated Romanian, by their name change from Moldavia to its Romanian form, and by their organizations and demonstrations for independence.

Poles. Émigré groups say that Soviet Poles may be double the number reported in the official census. They live mainly in the three union republics bordering Poland: Byelorussia, Lithuania, and Ukraine.

The Soviet Poles are the legacy of a thousand years of conflict and boundary changes between western and eastern Slavs. Poland was a powerful nation at times, such as in the sixteenth century, but Prussia, Russia, and Austria split it up in the late eighteenth century. It reappeared from 1918 until 1939, when Hitler and Stalin partitioned it again. The World War II settlement re-created it on the most westerly land it had ever occupied, with the Soviets recovering all the territory that Russia had held from 1795 to 1918. Despite massive transfers of population, many Poles remained in the Soviet acquisition. Under *glasnost* some of them have called for creation of a Polish autonomous republic in southern Lithuania and northwestern Byelorussia.

The Soviet *Bulgarians* live mainly in the Moldavan S.S.R., along the Azov Sea coast, and in southwestern Ukraine. The Bulgars were a Turkic people who migrated from the Volga-Ural area to the lower Balkan peninsula in the sixth century, conquering indigenous southern Slavs. Gradually, the Slavs assimilated the Bulgars and adopted their name. These peoples formed the Bulgarian state and nation that have existed intermittently since 679.

Soviet *Germans* are mainly descended from settlers recruited by their compatriot Catherine the Great, to develop agriculture in the lower Volga basin and along the Black Sea. The promise of certain privileges, such as exemption from military service, that led them to immigrate were not kept or were withdrawn later, and many left for America. Some fifty thousand were exiled to Siberia in 1915, most of them dying en route.

In the mid-1920's the Bolsheviks created an autonomous German republic in the Volga basin. During World War II Stalin, suspecting disloyalty, abolished the republic and deported the Germans to Siberia and Central Asia. They were rehabilitated in 1964, but were not allowed to return to their homeland. In 1989 steps were taken to reestablish their autonomous republic. They reside mainly in the Urals, Central Asia, and southwestern Siberia, but are very widely dispersed. Recently, well over two hundred thousand Soviet Germans have emigrated, mainly to West Germany.

Caucasians   The peoples of the Transcaucasian region form an incredible mosaic. Six major groups of nationalities and many lesser ones divide, subdivide, and intermingle in a pattern too complex for easy categorization. The groups and subgroups range in size from a few hundred families to several million persons. They derive from many origins and have dwelled together in a relatively small area since prehistoric times without losing their distinctiveness. Almost necessarily, such complexity produced deep-seated ethnic tension. Despite long Soviet repression, it has reappeared under *glasnost.*

Kartvelian peoples include Georgians, Mingrelians, Meskhs, and Svans. These nationalities formed gradually in the Caucasus mountains by the fourth century B.C., but usually have been ruled by more powerful neighbors (Romans, Byzantines, Persians, Arabs, Turks, Mongols). They became Christian in the third century. Several Georgian principalities maintained a shaky independence in the fifteenth to eighteenth centuries, but fell under Russian control after 1783. The Meskhs converted to Islam in the seventeenth century. Early in the Civil War, Georgia formed an independent Transcaucasian Federation with Armenia and Azerbaijan. That soon broke down, and Georgia came under

Dancers at the annual Tbilisoba folk festival in Tbilisi, Georgia. Novosti

firm Bolshevik rule by 1924. In 1944 Stalin deported all 110,000 Meskhs to Central Asia, perhaps because he doubted their loyalty at a time when he was considering the possibility of invading Turkey. In 1968 they were released from exile, but are forbidden to return to their homeland in southwest Georgia. Many Georgians are intensely proud of Joseph Stalin, a native son, but this has not prevented recent outbreaks of nationalist violence, including demands for independence, even by the republic's Supreme Soviet (parliament).

Armenians are the most southwesterly Caucasian peoples. Outside their own republic they form sizable minorities in the Azerbaijan, Georgian, and Russian republics. About two million of them formerly lived in northeastern Turkey, an area that covers about five sixths of historic

Armenia. After massacres by Turks between 1895 and 1916, only about thirty-five thousand remained. The other survivors dispersed into the Soviet Union, the Middle East, and overseas. About five hundred thousand settled in the United States. (See *The Land and People of Turkey.*)

Armenians are descended from peoples who fused under the leadership of the Armens and who invaded from the east in the sixth century B.C., toppling a two-hundred-year-old kingdom. In 70 B.C. an Armenian empire extended from the Mediterranean to the Caspian Sea. Since then, Armenians have maintained a distinct national identity and culture, based mainly around a form of Christianity that they have practiced since approximately A.D. 300, though others (Persians, Greeks, Romans, Byzantines, Arabs, Tatars, Mongols, Iranians, Turks, Russians) often ruled them.

An Armenian mourning the loss of his entire family in the ethnic riots in Sumgait, Azerbaijan, in 1988.   P. Kassin/VAAP

In 1828 Russia took most of eastern Armenia from the Turks. During the Civil War, Armenia was a battleground between Bolsheviks, Armenian nationalists, and Turks. By 1921 the Bolsheviks had won control definitively. Armenian nationalism has found renewed expression under Gorbachev, particularly in massive popular agitation to transfer the Armenian-populated Nagorno-Karabakh Autonomous Oblast from the Azerbaijan to the Armenian S.S.R., in violent clashes with the neighboring Abkhazians and Azerbaijanis, and in secessionist demands.

The Soviet Azerbaijanis (or Azeris) constitute about two thirds of the total Azerbaijani population. Most of the rest reside in northern Iran. The *Balkars, Karachayevs, Kumyks,* and *Nogai* are close relatives.

The earliest known inhabitants of Azerbaijan were Kurds, at least five thousand years ago. Later, Persians, Arabs, Turks, Mongols, and Iranians invaded and controlled the country. Local chieftains usually avoided complete foreign rule, and the original population gradually assimilated the invaders. In the eighteenth century Russian power expanded into the area and by 1828 absorbed the northern half. During the Civil War Russian Azerbaijan was controlled successively by Bolsheviks, Azerbaijani separatists, and British troops, and it joined the Transcaucasian Federation. In 1922 the Red Army attached it definitively to the Soviet Union. After World War II Stalin attempted to annex southern Azerbaijan from Iran through a short-lived puppet regime. The main reaction of Azerbaijani nationalists to *glasnost* has been increasingly violent hostility to Armenian demands for Nagorno-Karabakh.

Dagestan lies immediately north of Azerbaijan. Dagestanis have inhabited the eastern Caucasus Mountains since time immemorial, almost always ruled by others but never fully subjugated. The numerous mountain valleys and the Dagestanis' resistance to or acceptance of invaders has fragmented them enormously. They include more than forty distinct groups, some of which include only one hundred to two hundred persons. Their complex linguistic and cultural affinities and differences

Now that people in the Soviet Union have greater freedom to express themselves, political arguments are often public and heated. E. Savelyev/VAAP

have confounded ethnologists, who cannot agree on their origins or relationships.

Central Asians *or* Turkestanis

The Turkestani homeland is a vast Central Asian region, two thirds as large as the United States and divided among China (29 percent), Afghanistan (4 percent), and the Kazakh (48 percent), Turkmen (9 percent), Kirghiz (3 percent) and Uzbek (7 percent) republics of the Soviet Union. The Turkestanis number about 52.5 million, of whom about 8.25 million inhabit China, 1.2 million Afghanistan, and the remainder (82 percent) the Soviet Union.

As a family of Soviet nationalities, the Turkestanis are exceeded in number only by the Slavs. Moreover, their population is growing faster than any other major group.

The earliest known Turkestanis were Aryan tribes in the seventh century B.C. At that time, Iranic peoples infiltrated and became dominant. Later conquerors included Greeks and Chinese. By the thirteenth century the Turkestani civilization had formed, largely by successive invasions of Persians who supplied the culture, Arabs the Islamic religion, and Turkmen the language. The Russians conquered them between 1717 and 1885, but native revolts continued until about 1930.

Two gentlemen take a tea break in Bukhara.   Jan Knipper Black

Turkestani "bourgeois-nationalist" tendencies have plagued all Soviet leaders. Nearly all Turkestanis retain their Moslem faith and practices, despite the militant atheism of Marxism-Leninism. Under
Brezhnev, Turkestani nationalism often took the form of rampant corruption by local politicians. Gorbachev has cracked down on the crimi-
nals, but has hardly subdued the underlying Turkestani nationalism,
which has erupted in sporadic demonstrations and rioting.

The main Turkestani nationalities are:

Uzbeks, the most numerous Turkestanis and the third largest Soviet
nationality. They and the Tadzhiks have the highest birthrate (3.4 per
100 population). About 1 million Uzbeks live in Afghanistan.

Kazakhs are the second largest Turkestani nationality. They separated from the Uzbeks in the fifteenth century and settled in northern
Turkestan. Because of the great influx of outsiders seeking to develop
their country economically, Russians outnumber Kazakhs in their own
homeland. About five hundred thousand Kazakhs live in China and
Mongolia.

Turkmen or *Turkmenians* live in the most southerly and most desert
union republic. It straddles the medieval Great Silk Route between
China and Europe, which may account for the oriental appearance of
its people.

The *Kirghiz* are descended from nomads who were driven out of the
Yenisei River basin by the Mongols and intermarried with earlier inhabitants of their present mountainous homeland.

Karakalpaks are related closely to the Kazakhs.

The *Uigur* nationality originated in the Chinese branch of the Turkestani. They reside mainly in the Alma-Ata region of the Kazakh S.S.R.
and the Fergana Valley of the Uzbek S.S.R.

Other Turkic peoples have homelands outside Turkestan. They include the following:

Tatars poured out of Central Asia in the later Middle Ages and ruled
Russia for more than two hundred years. After their power was broken,

they settled in the middle Volga-Ural region and the Crimea. The Crimean Tatars were not finally conquered until the late eighteenth century. Early in World War II, when they numbered about 250,000, Stalin suspected them of disloyalty, merged their Crimean Tatar A.S.S.R. into the Ukrainian S.S.R., and moved them forcibly beyond the Urals. Nearly half of them died. The survivors were rehabilitated in 1967, but have not been allowed to return to their homelands yet despite continuing agitation.

The Tatars are scattered more widely than any nationality except the Russians. After World War II, many Volga Tatars migrated eastward. Over 4 million live in a broad swath along the Urals, including the Tatar A.S.S.R. of the R.S.F.S.R. and the adjacent Bashkir A.S.S.R. Nearly 2 million live in the Turkmen S.S.R. and about 100,000 in the Tadzhik S.S.R. A few thousand live in the Soviet Far East.

The *Bashkirs* live mainly in the Bashkir A.S.S.R. in the middle Volga region of the R.S.F.S.R.

The *Chuvash* are Bulgars who remained in the central Volga basin. They formed a state from the seventh to the thirteenth centuries.

The *Tuvinians* are Buddhists whose homeland borders China in eastern Siberia.

The *Gagauzi* live mainly in the Moldavan S.S.R. but also in Ukraine, the northern Caucasus, and the Kazakh S.S.R. They settled in the Balkans in the ninth through the fourteenth centuries. Recently, they have called for an autonomous Gagauzi republic in Moldava.

Iranic Peoples
The nearness of Iran to the Caucasus and Soviet Central Asia, and the wash back and forth of peoples over the ages, has inevitably left a deposit of Iranic peoples in that area.

The largest Iranic nationality are the *Tadzhiks,* whose homeland borders Afghanistan and China in the most southeasterly corner of Central Asia. More than 2 million live in northern Afghanistan and several thousand in western China. The Tadzhiks are descended from

Cotton harvester operator Mukhiddin Momenkulov sharing a meal with his family in Tashkent District, Uzbekistan. Novosti

the ancient Soghdian and Bactrian peoples of that area, with a heavy overlay of Iranian culture and ethnic stock.

Iranic peoples in the Caucasus include the *Ossetians, Kurds, Tats,* and *Talyshi.* Their homelands are scattered widely through the region. The Ossetians are descended from the medieval Alan peoples. The Kurds are a branch of a people who number about 5 million persons, mainly in Iran, Iraq, and Turkey.

Mongols
Two Soviet nationalities are descendants of the Mongols, who ruled the largest land empire in the history of the world in the thirteenth and fourteenth centuries. Three million Mongols survive, about one third of them in the Mongolian People's Republic, which lies between Siberia and China. (See *The Land and People of Mongolia.*)

The larger Soviet Mongol nationality is the *Buryats,* most of whom live in the ancient Mongol homeland south and east of Lake Baikal in eastern Siberia. Others live in two other nearby enclaves, and tens of thousands inhabit Mongolia and northwest China.

The other Soviet Mongol nationality is the *Kalmyks,* who fled Mongolia in the seventeenth century and settled in the Volga region. They live mainly near the mouth of the Volga River. During World War II Stalin suspected them of disloyalty, exiled them to Siberia, and abolished their republic. They were rehabilitated in 1957, their republic was reestablished, and most of them returned to their homes.

Peoples of the North

Some twenty-nine nationalities, totaling 3,492,400 persons in 1979, have homelands in the arctic and subarctic regions. They include groups that belong to the Uralian, Altaic, and Paleo-Asiatic linguistic-ethnic families. That means their languages and cultures are thought to fall into these three groups. About a third of their homelands form distinct administrative territorial units. However, Russian immigration has been so great that very few retain a native majority.

The largest (86.9 percent) category is the Finno-Ugrian branch of the Uralian language family, related to the Estonians, Karelians, and Finns. They include the *Mordovinians, Udmurts, Mari, Komi-Zyrianes, Komi-Permiaks, Khanty, Mansi,* and *Saamis.* Their homelands are mainly in the European north from the Kola Peninsula to the northern Urals.

The Samoyedic branch of the Uralian family is found mainly east of the Uralians. The three nationalities in this branch total only 34,400 persons.

The Turkic branch of the northern Altaic language family consists mainly of *Yakuts,* who have dwelt in eastern Siberia at least since the seventh century. The other northern Turkics are the *Dolgany* and *Tofa.*

The *Tungus-Manchurian* branch of northern Altaics form seven nationalities totaling only 56,100 persons. They are scattered over an

The Tamigin brothers, hunters from Til-Tim village in Khanty-Manski Autonomous District. Novosti

immense area of eastern Siberia and the Far East, including Sakhalin Island.

The so-called Paleo-Asiatic peoples are not a linguistic-ethnic family, but a miscellaneous group of eight nationalities unrelated to other northern families. They total only 31,600 people and live in the extreme northeastern corner of Siberia and on the Kamchatka Peninsula and Sakhalin Island. They are descended from the earliest inhabitants of northern Asia and include 1,500 to 1,900 *Eskimoes* or *Inuits*—who are found in larger numbers in Alaska (30,000), Greenland (42,000), and Canada (30,000)—and about 500 *Aleuts*.

Other Nationalities   Several official nationalities do not have
territorially defined homelands.

Jews are the largest and most important of these nationalities. They
are treated as a nationality regardless of religious practice or affiliation.
According to some historians, many of them are descended from Khazars, a people who ruled much of the Volga-Dnieper basin in the seventh
to ninth centuries and converted to Judaism en masse in the eighth
century. Others are descended from a large colony of Jews who settled
in Ukraine when it was ruled by a religiously tolerant Poland.

Russia and the Soviet Union have a long history of anti-Semitic
sentiment. For instance, after 1791 Jews were confined to an area in
southwestern Russia, called the Pale of Settlement, where they were
subject to periodic attacks called "pogroms". Most of them remained
there after the Bolsheviks abolished that restriction. Stalin created a
Jewish Autonomous Oblast in the Far East in 1934, but only 0.7 percent
of Soviet Jews live there and only 6 percent of its population is Jewish.
When the German armies occupied the former Pale during World War
II, most of its Jews fled or were annihilated.

Since then, Soviet Jews have been very widely dispersed. About 88
percent live in Ukraine, Byelorussia, western Russia, Moldava, and the
Baltic republics. Jews are mainly urban, except for a group in the
Caucasus called the "mountain Jews." The 1970 census showed that
Jews numbered more than 1 percent of the population in five union
republics: Moldava, 2.7 percent; Ukraine, Byelorussia, and Latvia,
1.6 percent each; and Georgia, 1.2 percent. In recent decades about
500,000 Jews have emigrated to the United States, Israel, and elsewhere in the West.

Gypsies numbered 209,000 in the 1979 census, but unofficial estimates place them nearer 500,000. Soviet Gypsies are part of a world-
wide nationality of 1.5 to 2 million persons. As nomads, they have no
specific Soviet homeland. Originally from northwest India, they mi-

grated to Persia in the ninth century A.D. and to southern Greece in the late eleventh century. The main groups of Soviet Gypsies entered Russia from the Balkans in the fifteenth and sixteenth centuries and from Germany and Poland in the sixteenth and seventeenth centuries. A separate group of about eight thousand Gypsies lives in Central Asia. Gypsies have resisted quite successfully persistent governmental efforts to persuade or force them to abandon their nomadic ways.

The many Soviet peoples described in this chapter are greatly diverse. They live differently, look different, and speak many languages. Their foods are distinct. So are their clothing and homes. Some are nomads. Others dwell mainly in cities or on farms. Their homelands include mountain slopes, arid deserts, lush subtropical forests, arctic tundra, and treeless steppes. Each group has its own customs, sports, and leisure activities.

The difficulties of ruling such a variegated population have plagued all governments since tsarist times. The tsars subjugated the non-Russian peoples by open force. Lenin concealed the dictatorial, centralized control of the CPSU, backed by the Red Army and the police, behind the fiction of "national in form, socialist in content." That system collapsed with Gorbachev's liberalization program. He proposed to substitute a new voluntary "treaty of union" establishing a confederation of autonomous states with central government authority limited to a few areas like foreign relations, defense, and monetary policy.

Few traditions of the Soviet nationalities are so deeply implanted as their various forms of religious belief and practice. Despite centuries of tsarist effort to impose a common religion and seven decades of rule by militantly atheist communism, religion in many forms remains an important part of the lives of the Soviet peoples. The next chapter examines that aspect of Soviet life.

Religion

Religion in the Soviet Union is another paradox. Marxism-Leninism calls religion "the opium of the people" (Marx) and "every religious idea . . . unutterable vileness" (Lenin). The ruling Communist Party is committed to active repression of religion, and its members must be avowed atheists. Yet until 1990 the government recognized and regulated religion and was allied with the largest denominations. Despite two generations of systematic, sustained hostility until the late 1980's, the traditional spiritual religions remain powerful forces in the lives of the Soviet people.

The Russian Orthodox Church was the dominant religious organization in the Russian empire. As an official religion, it was supported by the tsars and served them loyally. It tapped a deep mystical and messianic strain in the Russian soul and held the devotion of an overwhelming majority of the Russian people. In 1914 its members worshipped in 54,000 churches and 25,000 chapels. Other religions were tolerated or persecuted.

Lenin launched a harsh campaign against churches and believers from the moment he took power. His government separated church and state, confiscated all church property, denied civil rights to the clergy, and restricted religious activities severely. Opponents of those policies were treated as counterrevolutionaries.

Stalin continued Lenin's policies, with characteristic viciousness. He enacted the repressive 1929 Law on Religious Associations, closed scores of thousands of churches and mosques, and imprisoned tens of thousands of clergy and millions of believers. In 1932 he adopted a five-year plan to eradicate religion, declaring that "not a single house of prayer will be needed any longer in any territory of the Soviet Union, and the very notion of God will be expunged."

His reversal during World War II permitted the number of Orthodox churches to increase from 4,255 to 22,000 and the number of priests from 5,665 to 33,000. He reopened some monasteries and seminaries and eased the repression of some minority religions.

Khrushchev began by urging greater religious toleration, but after 1959 waged a virulent campaign that reduced the number of Russian Orthodox churches from 25,000 to 8,000 and restricted church activities even more narrowly than had Stalin. Typically, things changed little under Brezhnev. He continued the repression but with less zeal and made a few modest concessions, especially in his last years. In 1975 he liberalized the 1929 law somewhat. Nevertheless, by 1986 the number of Orthodox churches had fallen further, to 6,794.

Toleration   Gorbachev seems ambivalent toward religion. He was reared in a religious home. His mother is a believer and continues to worship regularly. However, he is an atheist and occasionally lectured Communists on the importance of combatting religion. Early in his tenure he called for an "uncompromising struggle against religious manifestations and strengthening of . . . atheistic propaganda."

He seems to see religion as a means of moral renewal and doubts that communism is an adequate alternative. In the words of one of his aides on religion, he wants a change in "the moral climate in the country by emphasizing the moral aspect of religious belief."

Greater religious toleration is an aspect of *glasnost,* and includes a policy of allowing the church to "carry out its activity without any outside interference." Gorbachev has denounced past repression, ordered the 1929 law liberalized, and interpreted its provisions less strictly. In 1989 the Council on Religious Affairs rescinded its 1961–83 antireligious decrees and in 1990 the Supreme Soviet voted, 341–1, to end official atheism and state control of religion.

This has meant allowing baptisms without interference, relaxing restraints on parish priests, permitting churches to engage in charitable and religious educational activities, authorizing the printing or importation of large numbers of Bibles and prayer books, and joining in an elaborate celebration of the one-thousandth anniversary of Russian and Ukrainian Christianity. Jews have been allowed to open a Jewish cultural center and a Judaic studies center and to teach Hebrew, and mosques may now teach Arabic.

One of Gorbachev's most important policies toward religion has been increased tolerance for religious congregations. From 1977 to 1988, 650 churches, mosques, and meeting houses were reopened, and for the first time in Soviet history a few new churches were built. Then, in the next fifteen months, state authorities returned 1,377 churches and mosques and four monasteries to worshippers and, in the first six months of 1990, gave permission for the construction of 424 new places of worship and registered 1,241 new religious congregations.

Legal Status   Nevertheless, until the new law on the freedom of conscience was enacted in 1990 and while the CPSU retained its antireligious commitment and political dominance, repression of religion

The Peal of Bells

Christian traditions are being restored to our villages. The bright
sun is now shining over the gloomy heritage of the stagnation
period, and the peal of bells can be heard from all over. After being
silent for fifty years, the Moldavan bells have come back to life. It
is hard to convey the great happiness of seeing a church restored,
the joy of hearing the *tip-tap* of a tinsmith covering its dome.

Under this roof the people have for many centuries been
preserving their original ethnic culture, their language, history and
faith in better times. Small wonder that in these fifty years, when
the locked-up churches rotted before our very eyes, the language,
the people's specific features and moral principles were destroyed,
too. Excommunicated from his church, man turned into a lonely
blade of grass in a bare field, and the cherished dream of the
stagnation adherents—total estrangement and indifference to other
people—in Moldava became almost a reality. Almost, but not quite.

Spring in Moldava this year is truly unique.

Adapted from Ion Drutse, People's Deputy of the U.S.S.R., in *Moscow News*, No.
16, 1989

---

continued. Official texts reflect the paradoxical character of the church-
state relationship. The 1977 constitution guarantees "freedom of conscience . . . and . . . worship." However, it protects "atheistic [but not
religious] propaganda" and prohibits "incitement of hostility or hatred
on religious [but not atheistic] grounds."

Furthermore, until its 1989 revision the constitution proclaimed the
CPSU to be "the leading and guiding force of Soviet society," and the
party statutes require all members to "combat resolutely all manifesta-

tions of . . . religious prejudices." Those provisions clearly empowered the state and public organizations to repress religion.

The Council of Religious Affairs   The professed separation of church and state is not practiced. The Council for Religious Affairs, headed by a CPSU militant, is an agency of the U.S.S.R. Council of Ministers to police religious practice. It licenses congregations in twenty-three recognized denominations; controls the use of church buildings; approves admissions to seminaries, ordinations, and parish assignments of clergy, and the composition of congregational councils; and authorizes the publication and importation of all religious materials. All religious activity not sanctioned by it is illegal. For instance, for many years it has banned the Ukrainian Catholic Church, Hare Krishna, and some fundamentalist Protestant denominations.*

The state has used its authority aggressively against religion. It permits far fewer congregations than the number of believers requires. Before 1988 official estimates placed the religious population at 28 to 56 million and the number of congregations at 15,000 (50,000 in 1917). This meant 1,867 to 3,734 worshippers per parish. Western estimates put the figure closer to 7,000. Moscow, with 8.7 million people, was allowed only 47 churches (560 in 1917). Similarly, Dagestan, with 1,360,000 Moslems, has only 27 mosques (1,500 in 1914). Nor is the approval of clergy appointments a mere formality, because, officially, "the choice and the designation of priests is the business of the Party."

The Soviet state represses religion in other, more subtle ways as well. By reserving the leading positions in society to CPSU members and limiting CPSU membership to atheists, it thwarts the ambitions of believers. It harasses churchgoers and clergy by fabricating charges of

---

*This section describes the situation before the religious freedom law was passed in 1990.

An Easter procession at a Russian Orthodox church in Estonia.   Novosti

tax evasion or embezzlement, denying job security or eligibility for better housing, and punishing absences from school or work for religious observance. It permits and even encourages militant atheists to disrupt worship services.

Despite that hostility, Stalin's reconciliation with the Russian Orthodox Church in World War II restored, in effect, the church-state alliance of tsarist times. Since then the church has supported the domestic and foreign policies of the government, refused to intervene on behalf of victims of religious persecution, and endorsed official claims of religious freedom.

Recently the state has had problems imposing its will on other official denominations. Devout Moslems in Central Asia and Kazakhstan forced the resignation of the chief religious leaders for being too political, while many Moslems worship with unauthorized clergy. In Dagestan, for instance, only 84 of the 384 mullahs, or active religious teachers, are licensed. In another recent act of defiance, Protestant dissidents persuaded religious leaders to take back their concessions to the state on a religious matter.

Religious Revival   Despite the repression, subversion, and
state hostility, religion survives. Indeed, it may be growing in strength. The official Communist youth newspaper complained recently that "religious tendencies have become more noticeable," especially among young people. The religion commissar has admitted that religious worship is "tending to increase" in some regions. Christenings of children quadrupled and religious funerals increased by one third between 1963 and 1988. As early as 1966 an official survey showed that 47 percent of collective farm households had religious icons. A 1990 survey of Muscovites showed the Russian Orthodox Church to be the institution in which they had the greatest confidence, with 64 percent expressing support, compared to 38 percent for the CPSU and 28 percent for the government. Also, after seven decades of antireligious campaigning by

Moslem worshippers in a mosque in Central Asia. Novosti

the state, only 12 percent of Soviet citizens declare themselves to be confirmed atheists.

Estimates of the number of baptized members of the Russian Orthodox Church range as high as 90 million, about the same as in 1917. (However, since the total population has grown, the percentage of the population that is baptized has fallen by half.) About 50 million are active participants. In addition, there are 30 to 35 million Moslems, and 10 to 12 million members of other religions. Officials are especially concerned over the "strengthening" of denominations other than Russian Orthodox. Gorbachev himself has worried publicly that too many local party officials in Uzbekistan attend mosques. Throughout the Moslem areas, traditional religious ceremonies are practiced by nearly everyone for marriages and funerals.

Easter

Hedrick Smith describes an Orthodox Easter:

Russians celebrate Easter with a Saturday midnight mass that lasts for several hours. . . . In Vladimir . . . the ceremony of Christ's Resurrection had transformed the cathedral into a place of mystical enchantment. It was ablaze with forests of candles that illuminated ikons, encased in gold or silver and lavished with the kisses of the faithful. Bearded priests in gilded robes were swinging censers or passing an ornamented Bible studded with pearls and precious stones. The repetitive litany and the melancholy chants of the choir, somewhere up in the lofts, had a hypnotic effect. . . .

It was a terribly Russian scene with its Eastern, Byzantine emphasis on the beauty and power of the ritual creating a pious state of mind rather than Western Protestant sermonizing to appeal to the individual conscience. There were no pews. The worshippers, hundreds strong, filled the cathedral, watching, waiting, listening patiently for two or three hours. As the climactic moment approached, the church was so jammed I found it impossible to move, even a few inches. Yet there was something soothing in the communal presence, in the mesmerizing hum of the priests' chants and the quiet crackling of waxed candles. . . . People bought them at the rear of the church and then passed them forward . . . and instructions were whispered, stranger to stranger, so that each new candle would be lit before the chosen ikon of its distant, invisible owner.

[The service ended with the priests leading] the faithful in a candlelight procession to pass three times around the church, symbolizing the search for Christ's body in the sepulchre. . . .

Hedrick Smith, *The Russians*, 1976

Communism as a Religion   Despite the atheism of Marx and Lenin, they founded what is, in effect, a secular religion. It has all the usual attributes of a religion. Its God is materialism; its saints are Marx, Engels, and Lenin; its Old Testament is the writings of Marx and its New Testament those of Lenin; and its church is the CPSU. It has hymns, ceremonies, sermons, and rites of passage. Communism attempts to perform all the services and fill all the human needs that are met by spiritual religions elsewhere.

The main religious denominations in the Soviet Union tend to be based largely on the various nationalities that were described in the preceding chapter. Indeed, one of the great dangers to Soviet unity, during this period of *glasnost,* is the extent to which religious and ethnic ties coincide. Domination of minority nationalities by ethnic Russians and suppression of minority religions by militant Marxist-Leninist atheists have given rise to a double grievance for many Soviet citizens. The main religions are:

Russian Orthodox. In addition to the official church described above, the fundamentalist Old Believer sect is a major dissident denomination that dates to the seventeenth century.

Evangelical Lutherans, who number about 510,000, mainly among Latvians, Estonians, and Germans.

Other Protestants, including about 3 million Baptists, Pentecostals, Mennonites, Seventh-Day Adventists, and other evangelical Christians, who are found mainly among descendants of Slavs who were converted by missionaries in the nineteenth century. About 500,000 baptized adults belong to congregations affiliated with the officially recognized All-Union Council of Evangelical Christians and Baptists. They are one of the most dynamic and rapidly growing religious groups.

Roman Catholics, who number 4.5 to 5 million. Catholicism is a matter of national pride among Lithuanians and Poles, about three quarters of whom remain faithful to that church. The Ukrainian Uniate Church was Roman Catholic until Stalin forcibly merged it with the

Russian Orthodox Church. Until Stalin the Ukrainians maintained a separate Orthodox Church as well. Most Ukrainians identify their branches of both Catholic and Orthodox denominations with Ukrainian national identity and resent the Stalinist unification. Dissidents maintained separate churches, illegally until 1990.

Georgian Orthodox. Christianity came to this region in the fourth century, before the Russians or the Ukrainians were converted. As a result Georgian Orthodoxy differs from other Orthodox churches and remains very strong today.

The *Armenian Apostolic* church dates to the third century and shows great continued vitality. It retains the loyalty of 60 to 75 percent of Armenians and baptizes virtually all Armenian babies. Religious motivations partly explain the high emotions in the Armenian conflict with Moslem Azerbaijan.

Most peoples of Central Asia are *Moslem.* About 80 percent—some 30 to 35 million—remain faithful to Islam, although they were allowed only about 1,500 legal mosques and only 25 to 30 pilgrims to Mecca per year. Because of their high birthrate, Islam is probably growing in strength. Many practicing Moslems and clerics evaded the organization imposed on their religion by the Council of Religious Affairs and worshiped in 1,800 unregistered mosques. Most Soviet Moslems are Sunnis, but Shi'ites are found in the Caucasus and Ismailians in the Pamir Mountains.

Jews. Judaism has suffered perhaps the greatest inroads among Soviet religious denominations. Due, largely, to governmental persecution only about 60,000 to 100,000 of the 1.8 million Jews are active in their faith. Only 1 to 3 percent of European Jews are practicing, compared to about 20 percent in the Caucasus and Central Asia.

Buddhism is the predominant religion among the Buryat, Kalmyk, Korean, and Tuvi peoples, who total about 1 million persons.

Occupations and Education

Work

The way people work, the kinds of jobs they hold, and how much they earn in the Soviet Union reveal another paradox. Despite an intense seventy-year period of forced modernization and the reputation of being a major world economy, the Soviet labor force remains at a rather primitive level of development. It falls far short of the advanced industrial character required by Marxism-Leninism as the substructure for communism.

Command Planning   Centralized command planning was the basis of the Soviet economy until Gorbachev. Under that system, a government agency in Moscow works out a plan that tells every farm, factory, and office what and how much it must produce and then tries to ensure that the necessary resources are distributed among them to enable them to reach those goals. The enterprises, in turn, set similar production quotas for their workers. Thus, their job efforts are directed entirely toward producing the greatest amount of product, with no incentive for quality or creativity. Most Soviet leaders now agree that command planning has failed and should be replaced by a western-style free-market economy, but the conversion is far from complete.

Farming remains far more prominent in the Soviet Union than in most western countries. In 1985, 25.4 percent of the economically active population was employed in agriculture (four fifths as farm workers) (the comparable figure for the United States is 2.7 percent).

The value of the Soviet ruble in comparison to the U.S. dollar is very difficult to express. For decades, the official exchange rate hovered around $1.60, which is the figure used for conversions in this book. However, that calculation grossly exaggerated its true worth. The black-market price ranges widely, but probably averages between 10 and 20 U.S. cents. Even those figures are misleading when applied to purchasing value, because most prices in the Soviet Union are artificially set by the government and have no necessary relation to market value. One ruble equals 100 kopecks. In 1989 the Soviet government began a laborious process of devaluing the ruble that is intended to give it a realistic exchange value and free convertibility on the international market eventually. It established a "tourist ruble" worth only $0.16.

Such a large army of farmers should be a great economic asset. Yet it has very low productivity. One American farm worker produces as much as ten Soviets. This is because of adverse soil and climate conditions and because the Communist system imposes an inefficient bureaucracy and withholds incentives.

Soviet farm work may be identified with five occupational categories: full-time state farm workers, full-time collective farmers, household-plot farmers, private leaseholders, and part-time farm workers. Besides farm workers, agricultural occupations include auxiliary agricultural activities, such as farm-equipment maintenance. About 70 percent of farm workers are manual laborers.

State farm workers are government employees paid salaries or wages

To Market

Tonya Chernyayeva has gone to the Butyrsky Market in Moscow every Saturday for thirty years to sell her home-produced cheese, cream, and milk. She is a retired veterinary assistant and her husband, Nikolai, is a forest ranger.

The couple had a hard start in life. They built their own house because their wages were so low, and relied mainly on homegrown vegetables and fruits and on their cow while raising two sons. Then came the 1961 anticow campaign.

The bureaucrats reasoned that if villagers gave up their privately owned livestock, they could work more efficiently on the collective farms. Owners of cows were harassed. The number of farm animals in personal possession plummeted, as did private production of meat and dairy products.

However, the collective farms did not start flowing rivers of milk. Instead, villagers joined the lines outside food shops in towns, and prices at the markets skyrocketed.

Strictly speaking, there was no law against keeping livestock or selling their products at market. However, mowing hay was forbidden on public land—even on wasteland, in ravines, or along

to work on the state farms (*sovkhoz*). They number about 11.1 million, an average of 483 per farm. The *sovkhoz* average about 43,000 acres (17,400 hectares) each. Their managers are appointed by the state, and whatever they produce is state property.

State farms being the most "socialist" type of agricultural enterprise, Soviet leaders have felt bound ideologically to promote them. Consequently, between 1950 and 1985 the percentage of state farm workers

roadsides. The militia seized illegally mown hay.

The Chernyayevs kept their cow anyway. They cultivated every square meter (yard) of their plot and fed their cow food scraps. At night they quietly mowed grass on the bog and along the village canal. They often went without themselves to keep their cow alive.

In the 1970's, haying on wasteland was permitted again and Nikolai was allowed to cut hay in the woods. So they bought a second cow. Each cow produces twice as much milk as the national average. As overhead, the Chernyayevs pay nearly 500 rubles ($800) per cow for insurance, artificial insemination, a cow herder, mixed feed, etc.

Even if prices at the market are three times as high as the 28 kopeks ($.45) per liter at the state shops, the Chernyayevs sell their supply of milk quickly, because it is fresher and better. Their sales for a Saturday might be 150 to 160 rubles ($240 to $256), while Nikolai's pay as a forester is 85 rubles ($136) and Tonya's pension is 62 rubles ($99) a month. That extra income has enabled them to buy a car for themselves and one for their son and to enlarge their house, luxuries that few ordinary Russians can afford.

Adapted from *Moscow News*, July 1988

A poultry farm in Azerbaijan. Novosti

increased from 8 to 34.6 of agricultural employees and the number of *sovkhoz* rose from 4,900 to 23,000. Gorbachev is attempting to reverse this trend, despite the ideology.

Collective farmers are members of cooperative organizations (*kolkhoz*) that work government-owned land. They contract to deliver to the government a specified amount of produce at a set price as rent. They earn income from any amount of food that they grow or raise above that quota, which they sell to the government, through consumers' cooperatives, or at public markets. In theory, the farm is run by a manager and board elected by a general meeting of all members. In practice, all important decisions are imposed by local representatives of the Ministry of Agriculture and the CPSU. The 26,000 *kolkhoz* (1985) average about 16,000 acres (6,500 hectares) each. About 10.5 million persons work them (1989), averaging 403 per farm. The overwhelming majority are manual laborers, and 20 percent operate tractors and other machinery. Collective farm employment declined from 64.1 percent of agricultural workers in 1950 to 36.2 percent in 1985. Moreover, besides converting many *kolkhoz* to *sovkhoz*, the state has merged many of them into larger units, dropping their number from 93,000 in 1953.

Private household plots are worked by state farm workers, collective farmers, members of their households, and rural and semirural residents. They provide the equivalent of full-time employment for about 10.4 million persons. Each rural family may use a piece of land no greater than 1.24 acres (.5 ha.) for gardens, orchards, pastures, vineyards, etc. However, in 1985 only 10.6 million acres (4.3 million ha.) were available for that purpose for 25 million farm workers and 9 million other rural workers, an average of only .31 acre (.13 ha.) per worker. Ninety-nine percent of all collective farmers and 80 percent of other rural workers have such plots.

Ideologically, household plots are less desirable than *sovkhoz* or *kolkhoz*, because they resemble capitalist private enterprise. Yet they are also more successful, producing 30 percent of the milk, meat, eggs, and vegetables; 60 percent of the honey, potatoes, fruit, and berries; and nearly 25 percent of the total agricultural production, while occupying only 0.7 percent of the agricultural land. Only about 12 percent of the produce reaches the market; most is consumed by the growers.

Private-leasehold farming is a recent experiment that builds on the success of household plots. It permits families or groups of farmers to lease land from state or collective farms for fifty-year terms and work them as private enterprises. Gorbachev has proposed "that all agriculture . . . should follow this path." The *sovkhoz* and *kolkhoz* would cease farming and become service centers for the leaseholders.

Fresh fruits and vegetables are available at private markets like these, but cost much more than at the poorly stocked government stores.   N. Stepanenkov/VAAP

Part-time workers are a crucial supplement to the agricultural labor force. Nonagricultural enterprises assign about 10 percent of their work forces to help with the harvest, and many schools close to let their pupils do the same. In 1984, for instance, about 18 million persons put in an average of one month each as part-time farm workers.

Industrial Occupations

Marx viewed factory workers as the "proletarian" social class that would overthrow capitalism and lead the way to communism. Lenin added landless peasants to the proletariat and claimed to be acting on its behalf. His successors have continued to regard industrial workers as the "most advanced" social class. Furthermore, Marxism-Leninism teaches that industrialization is an essential phase in the evolution toward communism.

Despite that ideology, the typical Soviet citizen ranks industrial workers at the bottom of the scale of occupational preferences. Yet industrial workers earn about 110 percent of the average income, compared to 89 percent for *sovkhoz* and white-collar and 68 percent for *kolkhoz* workers.

In 1985, 27 percent of the Soviet labor force was employed in industry, mainly manufacturing (compared to 20.4 percent in the United States). In keeping with the industrialization obsession, manufacturing workers are concentrated heavily in those industries needed to expand the industrial base. Metallurgy, machine building, and metalworking account for about 60 percent of manufacturing employment (the U.S. equivalent is 40 percent). The overwhelming majority (84

We need growth in the high-tech sectors of our economy, like computers. But in the rest of the economy we produce a real surplus of trash. We produce more steel than we need, more tractors of bad quality and make more shoes of poor quality than anyone else. We have huge stockpiles and inventories of these goods. For five years or so we need zero rates of growth for most of the economy because of these stockpiles. We may need minus growth in these areas.

Nikolai P. Shmelyov, Head, Economics Department, Institute for the U.S.A. and Canada, Moscow, in *The New York Times*, April 30, 1989

A broom maker peddling his products.   N. Stepanenkov/VAAP

percent) of industrial workers hold blue-collar jobs. Two thirds are skilled and semiskilled workers, and the remainder are unskilled.

Service Occupations

The Marxist-Leninist ideological obsession with production neglects as "nonproductive" occupations that provide services, such as banking, education, the retail trade, etc. Gorbachev's *perestroika* reverses this attitude. He denies that "the service sector is somehow secondary or supplementary." Nevertheless, service occupations remain relatively inferior with 29.3 percent of the labor force (as compared to 58.4 percent in the United States). The share of Soviet employment in the services is rising by only about 3 percent annually.

The largest service occupation is the rough equivalent of commerce or trade in the West. It employs 24.3 percent of service workers. This includes the sales clerks in the giant GUM department store on Red Square, where 1 million Muscovites and another million visitors shop every day. More typical are the workers in tens of thousands of shabby, poorly stocked shops, where sullen clerks dole out scarce, shoddy goods to interminable lines of grumbling customers. Other significant service occupations are education, health and social services, housing and communal services, and science and scientific services.

The Soviet ideological commitment to create a socialist society reduced employment in private service occupations from 4.8 percent of service-sector workers in 1950 to .01 percent (6,000 workers) in 1985. Then, *perestroika* legislation permitted the creation of private "cooperatives" in twenty-nine types of businesses. By 1990, 193,000 cooperatives were employing 4.9 million workers, selling goods at a rate of more than 40 billion rubles annually, and providing services at a 31.9-billion-ruble yearly pace, about 5 to 6 percent of the total gross national product. Some of the larger coops conduct over 100 million rubles in business per year. In addition, illegal private enterprises employ 17 to

Peddlers selling handmade wooden "nesting" dolls and other toys typical of Russian folk crafts. Igor Gayday/VAAP

20 million workers and generate 14 to 16 billion rubles ($22.4 to $25.6 billion) worth of trade in the services annually. An economist at the State Planning Commission estimated the total annual business of the black market at $145 billion.

Although occupations in the legal private sector remain few and limited, Gorbachev has implied clearly that the state should own only the "commanding heights" of the economy, while all but the largest industrial and service enterprises should be private. Other predictions on the future size of the private sector have ranged from 14 to 40 percent of the goods and services.

The T-Shirt Cooperative

The cooperative named Symbol has started baking *perestroika* in an ordinary electric oven. At a temperature of 518.9°F (270.5°C) the colorful silhouette of the U.S.S.R. map sticks fast to the front of a T-shirt. The word *perestroika* running across the map, with the hammer and sickle replacing the Russian letters "C" and "T," also gets firmly imprinted on the fabric. Valery Drannikov, chairman of the cooperative, maintains that these symbols cannot be removed from the garment.

He bought the secret of this permanent paint from a talented chemist for 500 rubles. The cooperative has been keeping the formula secret for a year now. In their opinion, this is the guarantee of success.

"Our cooperative turns out T-shirts with 'Spartak,' 'Dynamo,' '*perestroika*,' '*glasnost*,' and 'democracy' written on them," says Dannilov. "We also have drawings of Leopold the cat, the main character from a popular cartoon, and his words: 'Kids, let's be friends!' "

Items made by the Symbol cooperative are sold at the state-owned Moskovsky department store and Spartak shop. Irina Goncharova, head of the knitwear section at Spartak, said that her staff had no idea the T-shirts would be so popular. "They are selling like hotcakes, especially to foreign tourists. But it is strange that the state-run light industry does not produce anything like this. It had better get around to it because the prices fixed by cooperatives are rather high—knitted tops may cost 35 to 40 rubles."

"Of course, this price makes it profitable for us," says Drannikov. "We produce a maximum of two thousand T-shirts a month. We employ women who work at home, sewing on old machines. In short, our production is a bit Stone Age. However, the state sector ties our hands with its monopoly and planned economy.

We can't buy equipment or materials and so think of something original to reduce prices. Nevertheless, I hope that with our enterprising approach we shall give a boost to the economy. We are soon going to lease a textile mill. I have a dream: I want the heads of industry to buy our T-shirts, so that they will look more often at the word *perestroika*.' "

Adapted from *Moscow News*, No. 16, April 17–24, 1988

Other Occupations

A final segment of the Soviet economy includes miscellaneous occupations which employ about 22.2 percent of the labor force (in the United States they employ 18.2 percent). Much the largest industries in that sector are construction (43.9 percent) and transportation (41.8 percent).

A unique, unofficial Soviet occupational category is BICH, an acronym for "formerly cultured person." "Biches" are people who were established in solid careers, often professional, and were expelled from their normal social relations as a result of family or professional failure. They tend to become homeless, seasonally employed drifters who migrate to the Far East, often engaging in antisocial activities. Their number is unknown, but probably reaches hundreds of thousands.

Another result of the Marxist-Leninist preoccupation with industrialization has been the official elimination of unemployment. The state endeavors to mobilize all human resources for the overriding task of building socialism. No workers can be spared from that effort. Indeed, able-bodied persons without gainful employment may be guilty of "parasitism" and punished accordingly. Yet an estimated 1 percent of the labor force are "parasites" and another 2 percent at any time are unemployed temporarily while changing jobs. The official estimate of the total number of unemployed puts the figure at 3.8 percent for 1989,

Pepsi is sold from kiosks like this.
David Brown.

*McDonald's in Moscow, with a typical line
waiting to be served.*

including by unofficial sources, 20 to 30 percent of the labor force in Central Asia and the Caucasus.

In addition, Gorbachev has disclosed widespread underemployment. Official figures place the number at "nearly 6 million," but some economists put 25 percent of the work force in that category. *Perestroika* measures to correct that are producing official unemployment for the first time since at least the early days of Stalinism. So far, the number of unemployed workers is modest and the government provides retraining programs to keep them occupied until they find new jobs.

Education

Job training is one of the three main purposes of Soviet education, the others being ideological indoctrination and social discipline. That is, schooling is designed to train people to perform the tasks of industrialization, to understand and accept Marxism-Leninism, and to submit to the controls of an authoritarian system.

The 1977 constitution guarantees "citizens of the U.S.S.R. . . . the right to . . . free education of all types," promises "state stipends and other benefits" and free textbooks, and establishes compulsory education, now for ten years. It enshrines the occupational objective by emphasizing the importance "of linking study with . . . production."

Quantity over Quality   Substantial public expenditure gives effect to the constitutional commitment. The state bears about 95 percent of direct education costs. The Soviets spend more on education per person than any Western country except the United States. The result is a very large number of students. Nearly 40 percent of the population (109.7 million) is enrolled in educational or training programs, 52.4 million in grades one through eleven (1989).

On the other hand, many educational facilities are poor in quality. Half the schools lack central heating, running water, and sewers. A

A scene at an agricultural school.   Novosti

typical classroom is very old-fashioned by American standards. Even in the lower grades, the children spend most of the day working quietly at their desks or reciting lessons on command from the teachers.

Teachers are underpaid and overworked. They earn about 70 percent as much as industrial workers. Yet in rural areas they spend 32 to 39 hours per week in class, plus time for preparation, grading, etc.

Marxism-Leninism inflicts on Soviet education another mindless application of the principle that quantity is more important than quality. The state plans that 98 to 99 percent of the students pass their courses. Teachers whose classes fail to meet the plan are punished accordingly. So they promote substandard students, adversely affecting the classes above.

The productivity principle applies even to preschool. To free parents

Schoolwork

An excerpt from Cathy Young's very readable account *Growing Up in Moscow*

Schoolwork is governed by strict requirements: one has to use standard-ruled, twelve-sheet notebooks (quad-ruled for math).

In the second half of the first year, each pupil was issued a journal, which signified that we were now serious students. The journal, an innocuous-looking thick notebook with a blue cover, was the principal stick. Each two-page spread was allotted to the records of one week, divided horizontally into six sections (Saturday was a schoolday, too) and vertically into three columns, the one on the left for the class schedules, the one in the middle for the homework assignments, and the one on the right for the teacher to put grades in. The bottom of the page was reserved for such uncomplimentary remarks as "fidgeted in class," "talked in class," "misbehaved during the break," or even stronger criticisms. The journal had to be kept in perfect order. If you wrote down a homework assignment in your notebook but not in the journal, you had to copy it into the journal by the time of the next

for economically productive work during the school day, the state provides nurseries and kindergartens and covers 80 percent of their cost. The overwhelming majority of children under the normal school-entering age of six attend them. For the same reason, schools offer day care after class hours.

From the age of six, children with special talents are transferred to specialized schools designed to develop that talent. These include schools for art, music, ballet, military training, sports, circus performers, science, mathematics, and languages.

inspection by the teacher; doing the homework wouldn't get you off the hook for not writing it down in the right place. We were also graded on "keeping the journal."

At the end of each week, the journal had to be signed by the teacher and by the child's mother or father, and many children submitted theirs to their parents with fear and trembling. ("Please don't write in my journal that I behaved badly in class!" one of my mother's piano students—a very high-strung one, it's true—would plead tearfully. "You cannot imagine what my daddy is going to do to me!" This was quite an exaggeration, as far as Mamma knew.)

A journal was more than a daily report card; it was a record of all your school activities, as well as an ID of sorts, which you had to be able to present whenever you were in school—a sort of schoolchildren's equivalent of the Soviet passport. I remember how my heart would sink when I plopped down at my desk in the first class period of the day, opened my schoolbag, and found that the journal was not in it—I had left it on the table where I'd been doing my homework. Losing a journal was even worse, and for a teacher to take away a student's journal temporarily was a very serious and unpleasant punishment.

On the positive side, the journal did develop our organizational skills.

In academic high school all students must take courses related directly to production and all schools are attached to industrial enterprises for work orientation and training. Every student must learn a trade. For part of each summer they work on farms or in factories or service industries. In addition, about 4.1 million students are enrolled in vocational secondary schools and 4.5 million in specialized secondary schools where they receive both secondary education and vocational training.

Full-time workers are encouraged to continue their education, especially through job-related courses. About 50 million persons at a time are enrolled in training courses. Another one million students annually receive secondary-school certificates from other adult education programs.

By law, schools must indoctrinate the students with Marxism-Leninism and Soviet patriotism. Children learn official doctrine from the first grade on. About 10 percent of class time in the upper grades is devoted to the virtues of communism, collectivism, and the Soviet Union and its leadership, and to the vices of capitalism, individualism, and religion. University students take five full courses in "political education." This slavish reliance on an official line received a rude shock in 1988, when Gorbachev abandoned the old orthodoxy abruptly and canceled history exams until new textbooks could be written to fit his interpretation.

The constitution guarantees "school instruction in the native language." Minority nationalities allege that this works only one way. Russian students attend Russian-language schools outside Russia, but schools in other languages are available only in their homelands. All minority-nationality students must learn Russian, but Russians are not obliged to study other Soviet languages even if they live in a minority homeland.

Secondary-school students may take in-depth higher education preparatory courses during their senior year. About 20 percent do so and pass highly competitive examinations to enter one of the 896 universities or institutes that train students for some 430 professions. This is about half the proportion of the United States.

Higher education has the same production orientation. Its main goal is to develop the students' skill at applying scientific knowledge. The state encourages this by offering free tuition to all students and financial aid to part-timers who must take time from their jobs to take exams or write papers.

There are two types of institutions of higher education. Technical institutes train about three fourths of the 5 million full-time students for specific professions. Universities provide the remainder with a more general education. Another 15 million part-time students at a time pursue some 50,000 training programs, called "people's universities," that are related directly to their jobs.

The official emphasis on education has produced a tremendous increase in the educational achievements of the Soviet population. In 1914 only 28 percent of the population of the Russian empire was literate. Today illiteracy has been virtually eliminated.

Soviet education still lags well behind the United States. Students number 185 per 10,000 population (as compared to 264 per 10,000 in the United States), and much more Soviet than American higher education is in vocational training, rather than general education. Quite apart from its stress on production, Soviet education emphasizes rote learning and intellectual and social discipline, in contrast to the American stress on individuality, spontaneity, and creativity. This may be changing under Gorbachev, for a major point in his *perestroika* program is radical reform of the educational system to introduce many practices that are routine in the United States.

Daily Life

Paradoxes

The paradoxes of Marxism-Leninism are most evident and poignant in the daily lives of Soviet citizens. Perhaps no social and political system has such a clear commitment to enhancing the living conditions of its citizens or draws on such rich physical resources. Yet more than seven decades after the Bolshevik Revolution, most Soviets still live in grinding poverty. Soviet living standards—that is, how well people live, what they can buy, how well they are cared for—average about one third those of the United States.

The Marxist-Leninist obsession with quantity production permits only very limited varieties of even life's necessities. Thus, Soviet citizens can rarely express their individuality through possessions or lifestyle. They go through life buying and doing only what the government prefers, rather than what they might choose themselves. For instance, the average rural woman must always wear the same type of flower-print cotton dress, because no other style is available, though the privileged can obtain Western fashions at high cost. Some émigrés who have settled in the United States refuse to wear floral dresses because they remind them of the "uniforms" they left behind. The parent who shops for a toy car for a child's birthday present can buy only the one or two models available in even the largest toy stores. The couple wanting an apartment takes the one offered when its turn comes on the list or goes back to the bottom, perhaps to wait another fifteen or twenty years.

For decades, the lack of significant improvement in living standards was blamed on the Civil War, World War II, and the Stalinist tyranny. After 1945 progress was made. However, recently, the economy has stagnated and daily life has become bleaker and more difficult again. By one Soviet calculation, Russia ranked seventh in the world in per person consumption in 1917, but had fallen to seventy-seventh by 1990. Even *glasnost* and *perestroika* have brought little, if any, relief.

Personal and Family Life

Sex, Love, and Courtship

Marxism-Leninism treats the family as part of society's superstructure. Family life is thought to reflect and be determined by the character of the economic relations. The abolition of private productive property should eliminate the tensions and problems of family life under capitalism.

In practice, the Soviet leadership has reversed that relationship. It treats personal and family life as a means to increase the rate of progress toward communism. The government justifies intervention in private life that would be unacceptable in western countries.

Tractor Love. One object of such official attention is romantic love. For instance, Marxist-Leninist films and novels provide an approved version of the eternal triangle: A state farm worker's passion is torn between a girlfriend and a tractor. The tractor wins, but then the girlfriend joins the same work brigade and the three of them live happily ever after—building socialism together.

The State

This song by Mikhail Barazikhin shows how some young Soviets react to being under the constant control of the state.

> *They monitor us from birth,*
> *Our kind uncles and aunts,*
> *We grow up an obedient breed,*
> *We sing what they want,*
> *We live how they want.*
> *Looking out at the terrorists above,*
> *I say to you: Get out of control,*
> *Tear down these walls,*
> *Sing what you want, not what you're told*
> *Get out of control, we can be free.*

Translated by Paul Easton

In reality, Soviet love life falls far short of that ideal. Soviet men, women, and tractors fall in and out of love much as they do elsewhere. Immediately after the Bolshevik Revolution, some zealots preached free love, arguing that monogamy, marriage, and the family were bourgeois institutions, incompatible with Marxism.

Though that view faded fast, the Soviets remain quite permissive in sexual mores. For instance, 50 percent of happily married Soviet women approve of extramarital sex. Only 7 percent of young people who engage in sex intend to marry their partners. The rate of out-of-wedlock births is 9.5 percent of all births in the Soviet Union (U.S. 8.1 percent). In one study of 1,000 first pregnancies, 616 of the women were single.

Soviet love and courtship practices vary immensely. This results mainly from national and religious diversity. Central Asians follow Moslem traditions. Soviet Inuits behave like their cousins in Alaska and Canada. Moldavan romances resemble Romanian ones, and so on.

Public policy does affect courtship in some ways. Planned economic development transfers large numbers of workers, predominantly men in heavy industry and women in light industry. This causes surpluses of men in some areas and of women elsewhere; it also separates courting couples, straining their relationships. The CPSU sometimes interferes in the love lives of its members more directly. For instance, it may punish a member for dating a devoutly religious person.

Marriage and Divorce

Marriage regulations are very simple. The spouses must be eighteen years of age, give their consent, file thirty days' notice with the marriage registration bureau, and appear for a civil ceremony.

The overwhelming majority of Soviet citizens marry, and 83 percent live in families (U.S. 92 percent). Over 79 percent of women (U.S. 66 percent) and over 78 percent of men (U.S. 57 percent) age 25 to 29 are married. However, only about 40 percent of Soviet women over 54 (U.S. 52.5 percent) are married.

Marriages for convenience are fairly common. Muscovites are especially desirable, because their spouses can secure permission to reside in the capital. These fictitious unions inflate the marriage and divorce rates.

Despite official efforts to promote the mixing of social groups, most

Wedding Palace

For a Soviet marriage to be legal, the couple must appear for a civil ceremony, usually at a municipal "wedding palace." The bride wears white and carries a bouquet, the groom dresses formally, and family and friends attend. The party gathers in a waiting room at the palace. At the appointed time, the couple leads the procession into the ceremonial hall to the strains of a march. A member of the local council performs the rite and pronounces them husband and wife. They exchange rings, and they and their witnesses sign the marriage register. The ceremony is very brief, as dozens may be scheduled there each day. The wedding party may then visit the local war memorial or statue of Lenin (where the bride leaves her bouquet) en route to a reception and dance. In Moscow, newlyweds have priority in the line at the Lenin mausoleum and brides toss their flowers on his casket. A religious couple will hold a church service after the civil ceremony.

Bride and groom during a marriage ceremony in the wedding palace in Alma Ata, Kazakhstan. Novosti

marriage partners have similar backgrounds. About 70 percent of spouses have similar occupations, 85 percent the same nationality, 90 percent comparable education.

Spouses have been legally equal since the Revolution. However, much practical inequality remains. Wives continue to do most household chores, even when employed full-time.

Childless couples can obtain uncontested divorces easily. They simply file forms at a municipal office and pay 100 rubles ($160). Contested divorces and those involving dependent children are taken to court after a mandatory three-month delay, which the court may extend to six months. Divorces are common, numbering 3.3 per 1,000 inhabitants (U.S. 5 per 1,000).

Marriage and divorce practices vary considerably among the nationalities and between urban and rural areas. Central Asian men marry later and women earlier than do Europeans. Divorce rates are much higher in cities than in the country and in the Slavic and Baltic nationalities than among the Caucasians and Central Asians.

Children

The Soviets are said to dote on children. An official publication calls them "the only 'privileged' class in the Soviet Union." Westerners say they are "pampered, spoiled, and protected." Strangers offer children flowers and other gifts at farm markets and in shops. They sometimes get priority attention in restaurants and hotels, and special treats in their shortage-plagued land. Some parents work extra jobs in order to buy nice clothes for their children, often going without themselves. Few children under age ten are allowed to be alone in public, even walking to school.

But, quite naturally, the treatment of children varies enormously by the nature of the family. Overtired, alcoholic, or unhappy parents have little time for their children. Teachers in Moscow report the same types of problems in dealing with neglected and abused children as are encountered by some American teachers in troubled neighborhoods.

The Second Sex

Hedrick Smith on women in the Soviet Union:

On paper, Soviet women already have it made. They are officially liberated. Abortions are legal. Four-month paid maternity leaves are written into law, and jobs must be kept for new mothers for a year. A network of state-subsidized day-care centers has been set up nationwide and cares for ten million preschoolers. Equal pay for equal work is established as a principle. A higher proportion of Soviet women work than in any other industrialized country and a modest number have achieved career successes. Vast numbers have completed higher education and work beside men in science, industry, and government.

Yet despite these achievements and the enormous propaganda hoopla about women in the Soviet media, Soviet women remain a distinctly second sex. If any large segment of the population has been exploited by the system, it is women. Even three decades after World War II . . . women still do the bulk of the low-paying, backbreaking, dirty manual labor. They shoulder a wearisome double burden of work plus what Lenin termed "domestic slavery." Justifiably, they complain of inadequate relief from the competing tensions of career and family.

Female workers on their lunch break.   Igor Gayday/VAAP

Comparative Birth and Family Rates

U.S.S.R.	*U.S.A.*
Average Number of Births:	
19.6 per 1,000 population	15.8 per 1,000 population
1.7 per family	1.24 per family
Infant Mortality:	
38–41 per 1,000 live births*	Under 10 per 1,000 live births
Abortions:	
2.08 per 1,000 live births	.4 per 1,000 live births

*Western estimates

Official policy encourages parents to have many children, with propaganda, awards, subsidies, extended maternity leaves, tax breaks, early retirement benefits, etc. The results are quite uneven.

Family size varies enormously by republic and between urban and rural areas. Central Asian birthrates are as much as six times as high as Russian and Baltic. Only 1 percent of families in urban Russia have four or more children, compared to 25 percent in urban Turkmenistan.

The common presence of grandparents adds to the size of the family. The percentage of three-generation households (grandparent, parent, and child) varies from 15 in Moscow to 48 among Bulgars. However, half of all elderly pensioners do not want to live with their offspring, an attitude matched by 88 percent of those children. The smaller family is becoming increasingly predominant.

Income

Marxism-Leninism holds that capitalists exploit workers by paying minimal wages and selling their products for handsome profits. It teaches that socialism abolishes profits and therefore pays workers full value. Until well into the Gorbachev era, the constitution and legal system applied that principle by forbidding the hiring of labor for private gain.

In fact, Soviet socialism exploits workers more than contemporary capitalism. Soviet workers receive only 36.6 percent of the value of their product (U.S. 64 percent). As a result, Soviet incomes are low.

Many citizens receive "social consumption funds." These are state grants and subsidies for education, housing, pensions, maternity leaves and child allowances, health care, vacations, child care, etc. They average 46 rubles ($73) monthly per person. A fair approximation of the U.S. counterpart to Soviet "social consumption funds" is $300.

Men may receive retirement pensions at age sixty if they have worked

Earnings and Income

Average monthly earnings (per person): 195 rubles ($312) (U.S.: $1,531)

Collective farm profits: 159 rubles ($255)

Garden profits: 50–60 rubles ($80–$95) in rural areas
5 rubles ($8) in urban areas

A suburban family needs 2,000–2,500 rubles per month ($3,200–$4,000) to live comfortably. Suburban incomes are generally higher than the national average, black-market earnings common.

Only 31 percent of individuals earn more than 150 rubles per month. Average national family income per month: less than 500 rubles ($800) and 20 to 28 percent live below the official poverty line (officially, 205.6 rubles—$329 per month—for an urban family of four). In the United States 14 percent live below the poverty line.

for twenty-five years and women at fifty-five after twenty years. Workers in some difficult or dangerous occupations may retire earlier. About 57 million people—20 percent of the population—receive some kind of pension (U.S. 20 percent). Most pensions are meager, averaging 87 rubles ($139) monthly, 12 rubles above the government standard for "minimum material security." The value of those pensions is being eroded by an inflation rate estimated at 11 percent annually.

Elderly musicians at the Alaverdoba harvest festival in Telavi, Georgia.   Novosti

Housing

Engels called "the state of the workers' houses" a measure of their "general standard of living." This makes the lot of Soviet citizens doubly paradoxical. Their system is based on the Marxist commitment to material comfort, and their country is the world's most spacious. Yet they have grossly inadequate housing.

Two types of housing exist. About 40 percent is owned by the residents privately or in cooperatives. The state owns the rest and rents it for a nominal amount, less than one fourth of the meager cost of its upkeep. In 1989 for the first time the government began to sell public housing to tenants, but it had very few takers, 36,000 the first year.

Apartments are notoriously cramped. The typical family of four has about 110 square feet (40.8 sq. meters) of floor space (U.S. 520 sq. ft.), and about 20 percent of households share living quarters with others. Another 5 percent live in factory dormitories. Nevertheless, this is much better than the early 1950's, when only half as much space was available and 75 percent of apartments were communal.

Housing is especially short in major cities, because their greater convenience and job opportunities draw people from throughout the country. To ease the pressure, the authorities pursue a Catch-22 policy. To obtain a residence permit, a person must have housing; but housing cannot be acquired without a residence permit. As a result, housing is obtained largely illegally through personal connections, influence, and bribery. Ordinary people wait nearly twenty years for larger apartments. In 1987, 22.3 percent of the urban population was on waiting lists. In 1990, 1.5 to 3 million people were homeless.

The general dissatisfaction with housing produces intense pressure to build huge volumes of additional units without regard to quality. Consequently, housing deteriorates quickly, requiring extraordinary maintenance efforts that are not provided. Even minor repairs take eight to ten years, and preventive maintenance is nonexistent. Thus,

Family Finance: The Bayevs

The Bayevs are an average Soviet family, living in Skhodnya, 19 miles (30 km.) from Moscow. Sergei, thirty-four, is an adjuster of weaving looms and a CPSU member. Tatyana, thirty-five, is a medical laboratory assistant. Their children are Misha, ten, and Seryozha, eight.

Tatyana makes 140 rubles a month and Sergei makes 300, but for the last three years their total monthly income was only 305 rubles. While Sergei attended a technical school, he earned 165 rubles as a senior foreman. During that time, says Tatyana, there was never enough money. They didn't make a single major purchase.

The Bayevs have a 2,000-ruble nest egg. They saved half of that before Sergei went to technical school. The rest is Sergei's insurance. They plan to use this money to buy furniture when they receive their new three-room apartment.

Tatyana is already making about as much as she ever will. However, Sergei could earn another 200 to 300 rubles a month by working overtime. Sergei thinks that he should earn 2,000 to 2,500 rubles a month to take proper care of his family. Then they could vacation every year at a southern resort (at least 1,500 rubles for four). They could buy everything they need and Tatyana could stop working.

This is unrealistic, Sergei knows. Says Tatyana, "This will never happen."

The Bayevs try not to economize on food. Still, they avoid buying costly delicatessen items and sausage sold at cooperatives. They buy most of their food in Moscow. Tatyana usually comes home lugging bags. The essentials are available in Skhodnya—milk, sugar, butter, and bread (much worse than in Moscow)—but usually only in the morning. Meat, fish, vegetables, and fruit are generally available only in Moscow.

Everything the Bayevs have is old. They have a small black-and-white TV; a small twenty-five-year-old refrigerator that came from Tatyana's parents; a washing machine; the necessary furniture; one pair of boots apiece; and a tape recorder bought with money they got from selling Tatyana's winter coat, another present from her parents.

When the boys were infants, they fell ill with a mild but unpleasant skin disease. The doctors' only advice was to take them south, which the Bayevs could not afford.

The four Bayevs are registered as living in a two-room, 335-square-foot (31-sq.-m.) apartment where Tatyana's grandmother, eighty-five, her sister, and her sister's daughter are also listed. Seven people couldn't live in an apartment that size. So they rented another one-room apartment for 50 rubles a month. Then Tatyana's parents got a 195-square-foot (18-sq.-m.) apartment and traded places with the Bayevs. It was still crowded, but at least there were just the four of them.

Having less than 54 square feet (5 sq. m.) per person, the Bayevs are on priority waiting lists for rehousing at the local Executive Committee and at Sergei's work. They have been promised a three-room apartment, but if Tatyana's grandmother dies, they will lose their priority. In that case, they would not get better housing for years.

Since Sergei has no residence permit for Moscow, when the new apartment becomes available, he must find a family in the Moscow region that has such a permit and exchange housing with them within a month.

"We can't buy a cooperative apartment," says Sergei, "because we don't have rich parents to pay the first installment. Also, in the

Moscow region it's probably harder to join a housing cooperative than to get a state apartment."

Sergei commutes seventy minutes and Tatyana forty minutes to work each way. The boys can walk easily to school. When they return home, their grandmother feeds them dinner. Then they play outdoors. They do their homework when Tatyana gets home.

On weekends the family often goes skiing or bicycle riding. They vacation separately (Tatyana has twenty-four days, Sergei has eighteen days), each taking the boys to visit nearby relatives. They never go to the theater and rarely visit friends.

"So here we are thirty-five years old," says Tatyana. "We've both worked most of our lives. But we haven't earned anything yet—neither an apartment nor furniture, nor any good things."

"It's all right. We'll get everything," replies Sergei.

---

even recently built housing is shabby. Typically, a family moving into an apartment spends $1,500 repairing and completing it, in addition to some $800 of postconstruction work by the state.

The poor housing construction was tragically evident in the 1988 Armenian earthquake. Official reports blamed the 25,000 deaths and 500,000 homeless largely on the "shoddy construction" of high-rise apartment buildings "that fell apart like matchboxes" in the tremor. Many other structures deteriorate well before their time, at enormous cost in labor, materials, and the comfort of their occupants. While 54 million apartments were built between 1961 and 1986, 24 million were demolished. Replacements for demolished structures account for 12 to 14 percent of new construction.

Housing is poorly equipped, especially in rural areas. About 60 percent of rural and 8 to 10 percent of city residences lack running water, sewers, or central heating. About 16 percent of urban homes lack baths or showers. Only 28.5 percent of households have telephones (U.S. 92.5 percent).

Household supplies, furniture, and appliances are scarce, expensive, and poor in quality. Severe shortages of such basic goods as soap, detergent, towels, toothpaste, toilet paper, razor blades, lotion, and light bulbs require widespread rationing. The average person must work seventeen minutes to earn the price of a bar of soap and twenty-two days for a washing machine (U.S. 3 mins./35 hrs.) Television sets are unreliable and dangerous. Sixty percent of Moscow apartment fires result from faulty TV's.

Rents are stable and low. Most rents have not risen in sixty years, and the average citizen spends far less on housing than does an American, requiring only 3 to 4 percent of family income. A 538-square-foot (50-sq.-m.) apartment averages $16.83 per month (U.S. $370). Rents are low because the state subsidizes about two thirds of housing costs. However, if wage levels and amount of space are considered, the Soviet advantage disappears. The average Soviet worker spends 50 percent more time earning rent than does an American for the same amount of space.

The housing shortage has harmful side effects. Cramped quarters generate family tensions and impair hygiene and health. Much time is spent unproductively searching for better housing. All that leads to lowered morals, morale, and job performance.

Food and Diet

Soviet meals vary enormously by region and income level. Typically, Slavs eat hearty breakfasts of meat, potatoes, and tea—but never coffee. Lunch is similarly ample, often taken at a workplace cafeteria. The most common dish is borsht, a meat-and-vegetable stew, colored in Ukraine with red beet juice. Sausage, fish soup, mashed or fried potatoes, tomatoes, pickled mushrooms or cucumbers, and cabbage are other typical foods. Sour cream is often used as a dressing or thickener. Fruit may be included, stewed or jellied with potato flour. Supper, at about 6 P.M., is the lightest meal. Bread is eaten at nearly every meal, as are various sorts of pancakes.

Though regional variations are great, the average citizen eats more poorly than in 1913. The bare necessities are inexpensive, but supplies are seriously deficient in quality, quantity, and variety. Much time, effort, and money are required to obtain fruit, good cuts of meat, and vegetables other than cabbage and potatoes. Even bread and potatoes are scarce sometimes.

Prices for standard fare (bread, beer, cabbage, meat, and potatoes) are very low and have not changed in state shops since 1955, due to strict price controls and large governmental subsidies. In 1988 these amounted to over 50 billion rubles ($80 billion) [U.S. $16.5 billion]. Bread is so cheap that it is sometimes used as animal fodder. Many other foods, however, are expensive. A key element in Gorbachev's *perestroika* program is reduction and eventual elimination of price controls and subsidies. In that event, food costs will certainly soar. Even without those drastic measures, the prices of such staples as bread, potatoes, and vegetables rose 18 percent in 1986 to 1988.

If labor time expended to earn the money to purchase food is considered the comparison becomes much less favorable to the Soviet Union. The average Soviet family works more than three times as long to pay for food as does its American counterpart.

Another indicator is family budget share spent on food: U.S.S.R. 59 percent, U.S. 15 percent. Moreover, the typical family eats only 58 percent as much as its American counterpart and about 75 percent as much as its government recommends for good nutrition. To attain that standard would require 71 percent of the family budget.

Price is a less serious food problem than supply. The Soviet Union cannot feed itself. Every year, good harvest or bad, it buys tens of billions of dollars' worth of foodstuffs from the West ($26 billion in 1989). One survey found only four of one thousand types of goods to

Comparative Food Prices
Some representative food prices in dollars are:

	Washington	Moscow		Washington	Moscow
Bread*	$ 0.30	$ 0.14	Tea, 3.5 oz.	$ 1.37	$ 1.12
Beef*	2.38	1.35	Coffee beans*	3.41	13.43
Chicken*	0.92	2.28	Beer, qt.	1.38	0.36
Sugar*	0.33	0.63	Vodka, qt.	16.68	28.43
Butter*	2.04	2.35	Milk, qt.	0.46	0.50
Tomatoes*	1.14	0.34			
Eggs, doz.	0.89	2.50			

*per pound
Adapted from *Moscow News*, No. 20, 1988

be readily available. During a recent holiday season shops lacked chocolate, chicken, coffee, tea, sugar, yeast, salami, cheese, cake, candy, meat, butter, and even that staple of Russian diets, cabbage.

The problem begins with insufficient production. For instance, supplies of fruit are perennially short, yet the size of orchards fell by 30 percent from 1974 to 1989. Careless handling and storage on the farms makes this worse. During harvesting the grain crop shrinks by 8 to 10 percent, and 80 percent of the potatoes are damaged. Another 30 to 40 percent of each crop spoils or is stolen in storage. Processing plants are primitive and packaging shoddy.

Even more galling for the consumer is the poor distribution system. Marxism-Leninism treats distribution as unproductive and gives it very low priority for resources. Transportation is neglected and expensive. Forty percent of the cost of bread, meat, and milk is for transporting it, and 20 to 40 percent of agricultural products rot en route to market.

Warehouses are inadequate and poorly tended. Food is distributed with little regard for potential demand. For instance, one municipality one hundred miles from Moscow ships sixteen thousand tons of meat to the capital each year and its residents bring seven thousand tons back on shopping trips.

The most obvious distribution weakness is retail food stores. They are grossly insufficient in number, poorly equipped, and badly understaffed. For instance, the giant GUM store in Moscow has sales of 700 million rubles annually with only five thousand clerks. Shops are redecorated every twenty-five years (U.S. five). Long lines form at any store with food in stock, regardless of type, amount, or quality. An estimated 65 billion hours a year are spent in shopping lines, more than on farming, construction, and science and technology combined. The average housewife spends the equivalent of one workday a week waiting in line.

Every housewife carries a string bag everywhere and joins any shopping line she sees. With luck, the supply lasts until she reaches the sales counter. She selects an item and enters a second line to pay. Then,

Glimpses of Soviet Life in Crisis, 1990

No eggs, meat, milk, fruit, vegetables, salt, matches, or bread in government shops. Only 30 percent of needed medicines. Little gasoline. Monstrous queues. Panic buying and hoarding. A flourishing black market for basic goods at very high prices (milk at $12 a quart) or by barter. Rats and, in Aralsk, bubonic plague. Fifty million people in ecological disaster zones. Soaring crime rate. Roving armed bands. The army authorized to shoot civilians. The central government defied or ignored. Fourteen of the fifteen union-republics claiming autonomy or independence. Gorbachev unable to leave to claim his Nobel Peace Prize.

armed with a receipt, she stands in a third line to receive her purchase. She may buy more than she needs of available items to hoard or to share with neighbors. They will reciprocate another time.

Because each shop sells only one type of product, the shopper must repeat this process several times. Nor are there many choices. If the meat shop has sausage, she buys sausage or goes without. Frequently, she spends two or three hours a day shopping merely to feed her family. She must be eternally vigilant to avoid being cheated by clerks. One official investigation discovered that fifty-seven of fifty-eight fruit and vegetable retail workers in Moscow cheated.

More food is available in large cities than in smaller communities. Therefore, shoppers flock to the cities, especially Moscow. Six million people visit Moscow every day and buy 40 percent of its food and 57 percent of its consumer goods.

QUESTION IN KIROV REGION: *How do you plan to solve the food problem?*
ANSWER: *By asking for another shuttle train to Moscow.*

The Soviet elite and foreigners have access to special shops with much larger and better quality supplies, including imported goods not available otherwise. These are uncrowded and provide home delivery.

The food situation is eased somewhat by the private gardens. Collective and garden farmers sell fresh and appealing produce at farm markets at substantially higher prices than the state stores. For instance, one journalist reports seeing a bunch of carrots for 16.5 cents at an official market and a similar one for $4.62 from a private gardener.

Almost every minority nationality has typical foods. Lamb or mutton, often roasted on a spit (shish kebab), is popular in the Moslem cultures.

So is pilaf, a rice dish with various other foods (raisins, nuts, bits of meat, vegetables) added. Fish soup is popular with Siberians, as is a meat dumpling that they prepare in fall and store in the snow. The peoples of the north eat the meat of reindeer, wild horses, and fish, especially salmon.

Comparative Annual Consumption of Food Items (In Kilograms Per Person, 1986)

	U.S.S.R. Gov't. Recommends	Actual U.S.S.R.	U.S.		U.S.S.R. Gov't. Recommends	Actual U.S.S.R.	U.S.
Meat	82	62.5[2]	101.3	Vegetables	130	103	116.3
Dairy	405	332	270.4	Fruits, juice	91	52	67.7
Eggs[1]	292	266	255	Bread	115	130	97
Fish	18.2	18.4	23.5	Potatoes	110	104	57
Sugar	40	41.5	28.8				

1. Number of eggs.
2. Includes lard and "meat products"; by 1989 this figure had fallen to 45–50 kilograms per person.

Restaurants are few, expensive, unreliable, overcrowded, and poor in quality. Moscow has 122 restaurants for 8.7 million people, one fourth as many as in 1900 and catering to a much larger population. (Monroe County, NY, with one tenth the population, has over six times as many.) Ordinary people dine out only on special occasions. The average family spends only 8 percent of its meal money in restaurants (U.S. 33 percent). Good restaurants are reserved for foreigners and the elite. This situation may be changing. Restaurants are a favorite business for cooperatives, and twenty McDonald's are opening in Moscow.

· 235 ·

Though access to western clothes is limited, many Soviet women do their best to dress fashionably. N. Stepanenkov/VAAP

Clothing

Given the Soviet Union's northerly climate, good clothing seems essential. However, in style, variety, and quality, attire is poor. Moreover, all but the shabbiest clothes are expensive.

Typical Soviet citizens buy less than half as many clothes and shoes as Americans, yet they spend 17 percent of their income on them (U.S. 6 percent). A pair of jeans costs nearly $100, and a light Dacron man's suit twice that much. It takes a worker 37 hours to earn the price of a pair of shoes (U.S. 6 hours). Moreover, because ready-made clothing is poor in quality many clothes are handmade.

Poor quality is especially galling and uneconomical in clothing and shoes. Shoddy products wear out quickly. Clothing is not very fashionable. Only 10 percent of young people can afford stylish clothes. Most Russian women wear brightly colored floral-print cotton dresses. Standard wear for male office workers is gray gabardine sports jackets and trousers of another shade of gray.

Shopping for decent-quality clothing is as great an ordeal as for food. Because good clothing is less perishable, the frustrating, demoralizing, and uneconomical favoritism, bribery, black marketeering, price scalping, hoarding, and under-the-counter sales are even more common.

Transportation

The Soviet obsession with production combined with the government's policy to restrict personal liberty to limit the availability of private transportation. Automobile production is low and prices high. Most buyers must wait years for delivery. Used cars cost more than new ones.

The life of the private motorist is difficult. Gasoline costs more than

---

Comparative Transportation

	U.S.S.R.	U.S.
Automobiles	10.5 million (1:26 inhabitants)	135 million (1:1.8 inhabitants)
Cost of average new car	$12,559	$6,000
Fatalities in traffic accidents	58,000 (1989)	45,000 per year
Railroads	92,000 miles (148,000 kilometers)	140,000 miles (225,000 kilometers)
Railroad travel per person	857 miles (1,380 kilometers) per year	49 miles (79 kilometers) per year
Air travel per person	420 miles (675 kilometers) per year	1,342 miles (2,159 kilometers) per year
Subway	7 to 8 million passengers per day (Moscow)	3.7 million passengers per day (New York)
Bus	15 million passengers per day (Moscow)	1.4 million passengers per day (New York)

twice as much as in the United States. Parts and repairs are virtually unobtainable. Roads are relatively few, poor, and unsafe. The Soviet accident rate is 165 times as high as the United States. The Soviets have one traffic fatality per year for every 181 passenger vehicles (U.S. 1:3,000). As a result, most Soviet transportation is public. The average Soviet person travels much more by rail, bus, and subway than the United States counterpart. Also, passenger travel on rivers and canals is much heavier.

Health

Some Soviets call their medical and hospital services the best in the world. By several statistical indicators they compare very favorably with other countries. However, the ideological emphasis on quantity has sacrificed quality.

The main basis of pride in their health-care system is the constitutionally guaranteed availability of free medical care to all citizens without charge. To meet that commitment, an elaborate network of facilities has been developed. It provides more hospital beds (1 per 80 inhabitants) and physicians and dentists (1 per 267 inhabitants) than any other country. (U.S. 1 per 171 inhabitants and 1 per 418 inhabitants).

However, Soviet medical care is notoriously low in quality. Medical personnel are poorly trained. Forty percent of medical school graduates cannot read X rays or cardiograms. They are paid less than the average industrial worker ($200 to $250 monthly for general practitioners) and treat patients rudely and impersonally, using hasty consultations and inflating performance reports to meet work norms.

Moreover, many supposed merits of the system are illusory. The overall picture conceals great variations by social hierarchy and region. Government big shots receive much better care than ordinary workers. The special medical service for about 69,000 top leaders had a 1989 budget of 1,884 rubles ($3,014) per person, compared to 73 rubles

($117) per person for the administrations that served the rest of the population. Latvia spends 70 rubles ($112) per person annually on health care compared to 42 rubles ($67) in Tadzhikistan (U.S. $2,000). The absence of fees is meaningless, because of indirect charges and widespread bribery that amounts to 8 billion rubles annually.

Facilities and medical equipment are grossly inadequate. Of 4,000 district hospitals, 1,000 lack sewers, 2,500 hot running water, and 700 any plumbing.

Supplies, including pharmaceuticals, are often unavailable. Thirty percent of required medicines and bandages are lacking. So consumption of medicines is a third to a half of Western norms. In recent years, only 5–10 percent of the single-use syringes needed have been available, leading to dozens of accidental AIDS infections in babies and diphtheria outbreaks.

The results of the poor system are evident in the state of health. All major forms of illness are more prevalent than in Western countries. Chronic diseases afflict 50 percent of men and 60 percent of women, including about 5 percent who suffer from clinical forms of mental illness.

Some diseases—such as tuberculosis and cholera, which have virtually disappeared in the West—are serious problems in the Soviet Union. Four million workers miss work every day because of illness. The Ministry of Health says that 53 percent of schoolchildren lack good health. One teenager in four needs psychiatric treatment. So far, however, Soviet citizens have contracted very few cases of AIDS, with only 150 reported by early 1989.

The health situation has worsened in recent years. For instance, the death rate per 100,000 population from cardiovascular disease increased from 247 in 1960 to 535 in 1983 (U.S. 408) and for lung cancer from 26 per 100,000 population in 1961 to 74 in 1982 (U.S. 56). The overall death rate among young men rose 11.1 percent from 1979 to 1988.

Dr. Edward Koronevsky, a hypnotist, treating alcoholics.   Novosti

Alcoholism   The gravest Soviet health problem is alcoholism.
Annual consumption has increased alarmingly, from 1.62 quarts (1.85
liters) of pure alcohol per adult in 1950 to 14 quarts (16 liters) by the
early 1980's. Official studies estimate that 40 million persons are
medically certified alcoholics. Only 0.6 percent of men and 2.4 percent
of women abstain (U.S. 30 percent). In 1988 6.5 million persons were
arrested for public drunkenness. Moreover, the number of alcoholics
had been increasing before 1985 (while U.S. alcohol consumption de-
creased by 17 percent from 1980 to 1987).

Such drinking is devastating. Alcoholism is the third leading cause
of death, accounting for one fifth of all deaths. The rate of deaths from
acute alcohol poisoning is 65 times(!) higher than the world average.
Drinking accounts for 17,400 (1989) vehicular deaths annually (U.S.

A song about drinking by the rock group Kino:

I came home,
As usual alone again,
My house is empty.
The telephone suddenly rings,
They will knock on the door
And shout from the street
That I've slept enough,
And a drunken voice will say:
"Give us some food."
My friends always go through life
At a march,
Waiting only at
Beer kiosks.
My house is empty;
Now it's full of people
For the thousandth time,
My friends are drinking wine there.
Someone's been in the toilet a long time
And broken the window.
To tell the truth, I couldn't give a damn,
I laugh,
Though it's not always funny.
I get very angry
When they say to live
Like I do now is impossible.
After all, I live,
And no one can deny that.

Translated by Paul Easton

25,000 for more than ten times as many cars). It contributes significantly to the spread of venereal disease and mental illness and to the high (6 to 7) percentage of children born physically or mentally handicapped. Alcohol is a significant factor in 63 percent of drownings, one third of ambulance calls in Moscow, and nearly half of all suicides or suicide attempts.

Alcoholism has many other side effects. It adds to the problems of poverty and crime. The average household spends 15 percent of its income on alcohol (U.S. 1.8 percent). About half of all crime—including 90 percent of murders, 76 percent of rapes, 80 percent of robberies, and 90 percent of vandalism—are committed under intoxication. Alcoholism contributes to 40 percent of divorces and to job absenteeism that results in a loss of 15 to 17 percent of industrial productivity.

Alcohol abuse reaches the highest levels of the leadership. Khrushchev told of Politburo meetings when Stalin and the entire leadership became roaring drunk.

In April 1985 Gorbachev launched an antialcohol campaign. He cut alcohol production, closed some liquor stores and restricted the hours of sale at others, dismantled breweries and distilleries, destroyed vineyards, banned alcohol at public events, raised liquor prices, stiffened penalties for public and workplace intoxication, hiked the legal drinking age, etc. To provide alternatives, he boosted fruit juice production, expanded recreational opportunities, and authorized the first Soviet Alcoholics Anonymous chapters.

The effects were immediate and dramatic. Consumption of state alcohol fell by 56.5 percent and alcoholism by 29 percent. Crimes and auto accidents caused by intoxication dropped 37 percent, industrial absenteeism dwindled by 33 percent, workplace accidents caused by drinking dropped 20 percent. The death rate slipped from 10.6 per 100,000 in 1985 to 9.7 in 1986.

However, the campaign had unanticipated side effects. Some alcoholics turned to drugs. Production of moonshine vodka rose enormously, depleting retail sugar supplies. Lines at the remaining liquor stores became intolerably long, requiring police to maintain order. Thefts and black-market sales from state stocks increased. Perhaps most seriously, the loss of revenue from alcohol sales (about 37 billion rubles, or $59.2 billion, 1985 to 1987) worsened an already catastrophic state budget deficit.

In 1988 the campaign was cut back, though not abandoned. Consumption rose again, by 10 percent. So did alcohol-related crime, by 19.6 percent. Obviously, this disastrous problem has no easy solution.

The result of those various health problems is a short lifespan. Life expectancy at birth is an average of 69 years, 64 for males and 74 for females (U.S. 75, 72, and 80 respectively). More seriously, the situation has worsened in recent years. Between 1972 and 1984 Soviet life expectancy fell by two years for men and one year for women. In Moscow it declined by two years from 1983 to 1985.

The medical industry does not bear full blame for the catastrophic state of Soviet health. Other major causes are the harsh climate, poor living and working conditions, and the drab social environment.

Crime

Marxism-Leninism holds that all criminal behavior results from capitalist competition for profits. Crime should disappear quickly under communism. Despite that, the Soviet Union is far from abolishing crime. Under Gorbachev the reported crime rate has been rising dramatically. In 1988 the number of reported crimes was 657 per 100,000 population (U.S. in 1987, 5,662), an increase of 17.8 percent over the previous year (U.S. +2.2 percent), including a rise in murders by 14.1 percent— to 5.9 per 100,000 population (U.S. in 1987, 8.4). In 1989 crime jumped another 32 percent. About 15 percent of crime is "grave."

Offenses that resemble Western crime—violence against property or persons, theft, harassment, traffic violations, breaches of public order, etc.—constitute about 80 percent of the 750,000 criminal cases that Soviet courts try annually, with a 99.7 percent conviction rate and 32 percent receiving jail sentences. Drunkenness, vandalism, and street crime are common, especially in areas of large job turnover, such as industrial development and construction sites far from traditional extended families and cohesive neighborhoods.

Until recently, Soviet authorities denied the existence of such Western criminal problems as organized gangs, prostitution, drug traffic, etc. Gorbachev has dropped this pretense. One hotel admitted banning 332 prostitutes and 406 black marketeers from its premises. Soviet police estimate that the country now has 3,500 organized criminal gangs. A recent Uzbek criminal conspiracy involved "killings of rivals, street skirmishes, racketeering, sumptuous funerals for victims." Official statistics reported 10,000 drug-related offenses in one recent six-month period and the total number of drug addicts is estimated unofficially at 1.2 to 1.4 million.

Juvenile delinquency has become serious. One medium-sized city was wracked by youth warfare involving 150 gangs. In 1988 Moscow militia arrested 35,000 teenagers and stopped forty gang fights, including one with nearly one thousand participants.

Although official statistics show higher crime rates in American cities, this is not reflected in popular attitudes. A poll of residents of Moscow, New York City, Detroit, Boston, and San Francisco indicated that only New Yorkers were more afraid than Muscovites "to go out alone at night in the street where you live."

Marxist-Leninist doctrine has created two new crime categories. One is economic. It covers economic acts that conflict with the task of "building socialism." The ideology holds that society evolves toward communism through successive stages. Any private ownership incompatible with the current stage is illegal. In the present phase, individuals and families may not own more than one principal residence. Therefore, ownership of a second home is an economic crime.

Crime

One consequence of *glasnost* has been much more open reporting of crime. The following paragraphs summarize a discussion of crime problems held by the U.S.S.R. State Bank and Ministry of Internal Affairs:

The illegal "shadow," or black market, economy is huge, but not even an approximate estimate of its size can be made. Figures of 5, 40, and 150 billion rubles have been suggested. The criminal world accounts for not more than 5 percent of the total, but assessments are difficult because economic crimes and criminal offenses are interwoven.

Organized crime seems to be increasing. Criminal groups are growing in number and developing Mafia-like structures with internal discipline and strict distribution of roles. Ten years ago, these gangs averaged ten members. In every recent case they have numbered at least fifty.

Increasingly, crime involves the entire controlling structure of an enterprise, from bookkeepers and auditors up to directors and heads of public organizations. Each group seeks personal bodyguards and high-level protectors. Not infrequently, they recruit leaders at the regional or national level.

The new system of cooperatives cannot be expected to drive out the shadow economy. In fact, because they have such difficulty obtaining the raw materials they need on the legal market, half of them resort to the shadow economy themselves. State enterprises must do the same to such an extent that two thirds of the raw materials necessary for Moscow's everyday services can be obtained only through bribery.

One economist has gone further, identifying a "fictitious" economy composed of false production reports. She alleges that forty percent of the gross national product has not been produced, but is duplicate reporting.

Adapted from *Moscow News*, No. 15, 1988

Another economic crime is "speculation." In this historical stage, purchase and resale of goods for private profit is deemed illegal. Similarly, the store clerk who sells scarce items at a premium price and skims off the profit subverts the pricing and distribution systems that the state has established to advance socialism and commits an economic crime. So do the fifteen thousand shopkeepers a year who are convicted of hoarding goods and those who steal 19 million rubles a year, just from Moscow shops. A newly created economic crime is extortion from cooperatives. About 10 percent of all crime is economic.

Courtroom scene during the trial by the Military Collegium of the U.S.S.R. Supreme Soviet of high-ranking Ministry of Internal Affairs officials charged with receiving bribes and other crimes. P. Begelman and K. Yakhyaev, former Deputy Minister and Minister of Internal Affairs of Uzbekistan, are shown in the defendants' dock. Novosti

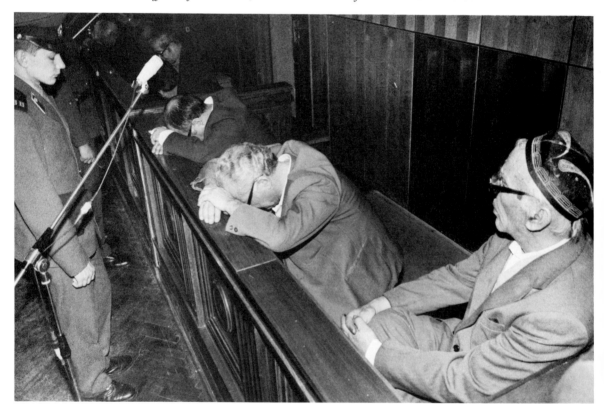

A monumental economic crime under Brezhnev was an Uzbek conspiracy that fleeced the state of some 4 billion rubles ($6.4 billion). It overreported cotton production to earn investment funds, some of which the Uzbeks stole. Less spectacular overreporting of production is done to claim undeserved bonuses. Many, perhaps most, industrial enterprises engage in that practice.

Other economic crimes are part of daily life for the average citizen. Bootlegging liquor, buying a place in a line, exercising a trade reserved to the state, hiring human labor privately, exchanging favors involving state services or goods, misrepresenting production capacity, and refusing to take gainful employment ("parasitism") are among the hundreds of economic crimes affecting scores of millions of ordinary citizens every day. They are so pervasive that in a desperate effort to stamp them out, the state established the death penalty for the most serious economic offenses, only to rescind it in 1989 because it had failed to deter crime.

The other new category of crime is political, noneconomic acts that slow the drive toward communism. Anything defined as undermining the unity or morale of the Soviet people or their confidence in the leadership is "anti-Soviet propaganda or agitation" under the Criminal Code. This includes saying or writing anything reflecting ill on the state or its leaders, forming unauthorized organizations, attempting or applying to emigrate, publicly disapproving of official action, refusing to obey an official, and the like.

A very prominent political crime under Gorbachev is agitation to incite hatred among ethnic nationalities. The Armenian-Azerbaijani conflicts have been the most conspicuous, but the American C.I.A. counted some three hundred public disturbances over ethnic issues in 1987 and 1988.

Ironically, much political and, especially, economic crime has great social value. It provides a secondary production, distribution, and management system that usually works more rationally and efficiently than the official one. Factory managers meet production goals only because they obtain black market supplies and equipment that are unavailable legally. Ordinary citizens evade bureaucratic roadblocks, find decent food, ease the tensions of living, and gain otherwise forbidden pleasures and satisfactions, by engaging in such petty criminal activity.

The Ultimate Paradox   Indeed, the Soviet Union may be the only political and social system in history whose success and even survival depend on the willingness of its citizens to disobey its laws, especially those that are its peculiar contribution to legal theory and that could not exist elsewhere. Perhaps that is the ultimate paradox of daily life in the Soviet Union.

Leisure

Given the grim daily life, a discussion of leisure activities in the Soviet Union might seem irrelevant. After spending an average of forty-one hours a week on a regular job, several hours meeting "socialist obligations," ten to twelve hours shopping, several hours in civic "volunteer" activities, and the normal fifty-six hours sleeping, typical Soviet citizens would seem to have little free time.

Nevertheless, substantial leisure time is available. Urban men average thirty-four to thirty-five hours per week in such activities, urban women average twenty-four to twenty-five, and rural women average about twenty (U.S. men average 40, women 39).

Consistent with Marxism-Leninism, state agencies, such as trade unions and economic enterprises, organize most leisure activities. Soviet leisure is mainly on weekends, eight legal holidays, and annual vacations. Forms of recreation vary considerably by region and age. Part-time instruction for occupational improvement was the most common leisure endeavor, but television replaced it recently. Workers age sixteen to twenty-nine spend one third of their free time viewing TV, 11.5 to 12 hours per week on the average. Television is even more popular in the countryside, occupying about half the leisure time.

Other leading leisure activities are amateur art and other social activities; walks and sports; reading; and theater, movies, and concerts. A typical peasant sees fifteen movies annually, many more than in any other country, at a cost of only 30 to 70 kopecks each.

Travel is another important recreation. About 70 percent of the people take at least one trip each year, although not necessarily for tourism. About 60 percent vacation an average of twenty-one working days, spending 8 percent of the family budget. Some 63 million people each year visit sixteen thousand "health-building resorts," including 10 million at trade union resorts. The state pays expenses fully for 2 percent of vacationers and partly for 18 percent.

Going ice fishing is one way to enjoy the long winter. A. Bochinin/VAAP

Use of Time: Pskov, R.S.F.S.R. and Jackson, Mich.

This chart is based on a joint 1986 survey study by Soviet and American sociologists, comparing the use of time by residents of "representative" cities in the two countries: Pskov, a Russian city of 200,000, and Jackson, Michigan, with 80,000.

	Pskov	Jackson
Working time, men[1]	49	41
women[1]	39	24
Leisure time, men[1]	37	41
women[1]	31	42
TV viewing[2]	109	149
Reading[2]	42	27
Movies, etc.[2]	25	18
Food preparation[2]	50	34
Housecleaning[2]	27	43
Laundry[2]	20	11
Other housekeeping[2]	17	24
Housekeeping, women[2]	140	95
Socializing[2]	22	65
Child care[2]	27	17
Shopping[2]	21	29
Sleeping/resting[2]	497	474
Eating[2]	48	61
Grooming[2]	55	71
Conversation, women[2]	13	25
Have enough leisure	40%	50%
Own microwaves	—	32%
Own dishwasher	6%	39%
Live in apartments	83%	33%
Hold jobs, women	78%	55%

[1]Hours per week
[2]Minutes per day

Reported in *Washington Post Weekly*

Most vacations are in the summer. The Black Sea, Baltic, and Baikal shores, the Caucasus Mountains, and the vast forests and innumerable smaller lakes are popular destinations. So are river and canal cruises and visits to historic sites.

Two massive CPSU youth affiliates organize many leisure activities for children. The Young Pioneers (ages 9 to 14) and Komsomol (ages 15 to 27) enrolled virtually all children at one time, though membership has fallen by one quarter in recent years. They offer pastimes from neighborhood games to summer vacation camps. Several hundred thousand youth have traveled in groups to foreign countries, mainly other Communist states, but also Western Europe.

Hobbies similar to those in the West are widespread. The All-Union Society of Stamp Collectors has about 4 million members in five thousand clubs. Other hobbies are more distinctively Soviet. Chess is the national game and is far more widely played than anywhere else. Other Soviet club activities are winter outdoor swimming, song writing, and poetry reading.

Chess is popular at all ages.   Novosti

Sports and physical fitness are major recreations. Some 270,000 clubs, factories, farms, trade unions, and schools and universities run an elaborate system of facilities and organizations. Some 35 million citizens participate in sports, and 62 million take part in organized or individual physical training programs. Physical training is compulsory, and sports optional, for students from grade one through the second year of college. Some 4 million children with exceptional athletic talent receive daily training for sports careers in eight thousand special schools.

Boxing is one of many sports in which teenagers compete.   A. Bochinin/VAAP

Seventy different sports are recognized officially for group activity. The most popular is track and field, with 7 million registered participants. Volleyball (6 million) and skiing and soccer (5 million each) are next. Thirty million athletes hold ratings in a national system of performance standards set for fifty-six sports. For instance, to qualify as International Master of Sport in the 100-meter dash, a man must cover the distance in 10.3 seconds. Many minority nationalities have sports peculiar to their traditions.

The tremendous Soviet effort in competitive sports has paid handsome dividends in international prestige. Since 1956 they have won six of the eight summer Olympics in which they participated (they boycotted the 1980 games) and seven of nine winter Olympics. However, they have been criticized for providing state support for their Olympic contenders in ways that violate the amateur status they claim. The most important such state aid is a system of forty "sports schools" that some 23,000 potential star athletes attend and fifty "sports colleges" that train their coaches.

Culture and Science

The World's Richest Cultural Legacy

The Soviet Union inherited the world's richest cultural legacy. During its last century the Russian empire outshone all other countries with its array of talent. Tolstoy, Dostoyevski, Pushkin, Gogol, Turgenev, and Chekhov were required reading for the well educated everywhere. Glinka, Mussorgsky, Rimsky-Korsakov, Glazunov, Borodin, Scriabin, Rachmaninoff, and Tchaikovsky were mainstays of the international symphonic and operatic repertories. Anton Rubinstein was among the most celebrated pianists. Russian ballet dominated the dance world. Diaghilev's Ballets Russes, Anna Pavlova, and Vaclav Nijinsky were the greatest dancers. Stanislavsky's "method acting" revolutionized dramatic performance, and Stravinsky invented modern symphonic music. Such avant-garde painters as Kazimir Malevich changed the art world by creating wholly abstract art.

Moreover, turn-of-the-century Russia was absorbing the immensely varied cultures of the minority nationalities it ruled. From Moldava and the Baltic to the Pacific coast, a great kaleidoscope of cultural traditions was enriching the Slavic core.

Less than a generation later, Soviet culture stagnated at home and lacked serious influence abroad. Its international audience had evaporated because its creative juices had dried up or drained away. Its greatest artists, performers, and writers lived and worked in exile. They enriched the world, but not their homeland. The Soviet dictatorship had driven them out and isolated the country from the main currents of world culture by rigorous censorship and border controls.

Marxist-Leninist ideology had suffocated Russian culture with its promise of liberation. Marx had taught that the arts, culture, and science are parts of the "superstructure" of society. Capitalism enslaved them in the interests of a small ruling class, but socialism would unleash their creativity.

However, Marxism-Leninism required that art inspire, culture nurture, and science inform the Soviet people in their efforts to build socialism. In Lenin's words, culture became "party work," subject to party control, or as Stalin said, cultural workers must be "engineers of the human soul." The doctrinal framework they built on that ideological foundation remains intact, though *glasnost* is undermining it.

Its main principles are:

1. "Popularization of art, culture, and science." The Bolsheviks alleged that before the Revolution only the bourgeoisie benefitted from those works. Lenin said, "Art belongs to the people. It must be understood and liked by them."

2. "National in form; socialist in content." Arts and culture should use the languages and styles of the minority nationalities, but only for the purpose of "building socialism."

3. "Socialist Realism," that is, "socialist in content, realist in form." Art and culture must present socialism as the leaders want the people to think it is—glorifying the heroes and great events of Soviet socialism,

ignoring their defeats and defects, and villifying their adversaries—in clear, simple, direct, traditional forms that all can understand.

4. "Democratic centralism." Official "unions" monopolize all artistic, cultural, and scientific endeavors. Theoretically, their leaders are responsible democratically to the members. In fact, they are lackeys of the CPSU. Each union makes the rules and admits the members to practice its art or science. The CPSU "agitation and propaganda" directorate supervises that system. Lately, its control has relaxed greatly.

Socialist Realism: Arts and Culture

Those principles led to domination of artistic and cultural life by the CPSU. The various artistic "unions" are overseen by a seventy-seven-member Academy of Arts. Writers, painters, dancers, musicians, etc., can work publicly in their fields only if the CPSU permits. All must express in various forms and forums only orthodox ideological views. They must subordinate their individuality to the collective consciousness of Soviet society as interpreted by the party and address the widest

---

This is an example of the application of Socialist Realism principles: Ignati Dvoretsky's The Man from Outside *has been produced in many theaters in the Soviet Union. Its protagonist is the young engineer Alexei Cheshkov, invited from the outside to help organize the work of an enormous modernized foundry in a machine-building factory. It would seem a dull theme, but the play arouses the audience, not only because production here appears as a symbol for the ethical and humane in people. The playwright exposes a very important social conflict: society's ripening demand for a new style of work and new work relationships.*

From *Soviet Life*, August 1974

possible "proletarian" audience. Deviations from those norms have been punished by banning offending works, expelling perpetrators from the union, imprisonment, exile, or death.

Engineers of the Human Soul

With few exceptions, truly gifted persons have been unable to flourish or even survive productively under that regimen. Most of them have rebelled and been punished, fled abroad, or fallen silent. Those who have accepted the yoke of the dictatorship have been mainly mediocrities whose potboilers are scorned by their counterparts abroad. Indeed, mediocrity is an explicit goal of Soviet cultural policy. "Good writers" are "incomprehensible to the masses; their style is too complicated."

Control has varied somewhat in harshness over time. In the chaos of War Communism (1918–1921), the state gave little attention to cultural activities. During NEP (1921–1928) sincere supporters of Bolshevism enjoyed considerable freedom, but others were persecuted. Under Stalin (1929–1953) repression increased greatly and orthodoxy narrowed. Under Khrushchev repression waxed and waned. Brief, partial thaws occurred in 1953, 1956, and 1961. Each time jittery leaders soon lost their nerve and cracked down again. Brezhnev imposed firm control consistently, though not with Stalinist brutality.

Gorbachev's *glasnost* seems an obvious invitation for writers and artists to express their creativity freely. To a great extent that has happened. Criticism of Gorbachev's predecessors has been free and open, and he has largely replaced Socialist Realism by what some observers call "critical realism." This requires that the shortcomings that Gorbachev wants to reform be discussed with unprecedented candor. However, that license does not include views he considers obnoxious. Moreover, the state control apparatus remains intact and functioning, and its previous rigor can be restored at any time. In a sense its work has increased, for Gorbachev ordered it to review all suppressed works and release those no longer considered unacceptable. Of the first eight thousand titles examined, 95 percent were cleared.

In one respect the situation has changed greatly since Stalin. Unorthodox work is produced outside officially sanctioned channels much more freely. Throughout the long period of repression some talented artists and writers created privately—even secretly—works that could not be published or shown publicly because of official disapproval. Under Stalin such activity was suppressed brutally. Khrushchev and Brezhnev were ambivalent and inconsistent.

Gorbachev has been consistently tolerant. By encouraging individual enterprise, he sanctions unofficial, commercial culture. That unofficial-but-tolerated or gray market in culture seems much livelier and healthier than its official counterpart. The *samizdat* (underground press) that began under Khrushchev flourishes, and some legal private art galleries have appeared. This competition may be encouraging state cultural organizations to relax their interpretation of acceptability.

From Revolutionary Art to Village Prose

The most evident and sustained example of broadened acceptability is "village prose," by such novelists as Valentin Rasputin and Feodor Abramov. This school of writing began appearing in official media in the early 1960's and has never been suppressed systematically, even though it deviates from Socialist Realism. It focuses on questions of universal importance to the human condition, especially spiritual, moral, and emotional matters of inner being. These ideals often conflict squarely with current public policy. The heroes of these novels do not build socialism, nor do their plots glorify Soviet triumphs. They portray grim realities of Soviet knavery and failure. Yet the rulers from Khrushchev to Gorbachev have tolerated them, perhaps because they are not directly political nor explicitly critical—or maybe because they express better than anything cultural since 1917 the age-old Russian spirit that still abides in the Soviets—even in dictators.

The Best of Soviet Literature

Despite the general mediocrity of Soviet literature, some outstanding works have been written. Tragic events have provided the main themes of its greatest fiction. Mikhail Sholokhov's *And Quiet Flows the Don* (1928) portrayed the sufferings of the Don Cossacks at the hands of the Bolsheviks during the Civil War, hardly a Socialist Realism theme. Its sequel, *The Don Flows Home to the Sea* (1940), and his later works were much more orthodox ideologically. So were his 1953 and 1957 revisions of his masterpiece, lending credence to allegations of plagiarism.

Boris Pasternak's complex and beautiful novel *Doctor Zhivago* (1957) depicts the life of a physician in the turbulent years from 1905 until the early 1920's. Pasternak's earlier creative writing had been mainly poetry, and he had limited himself to translations as he became increasingly unwilling to fit the official literary mold. When *Doctor Zhivago* was published in Italy—against his wishes—after being banned in the Soviet Union, officialdom hounded him to his 1960 death.

Another writer who has mined the rich vein of World War I and the Civil War is Alexander Solzhenitsyn, easily the leading Russian author of the twentieth century. His unfinished epic series of historical novels, *The Red Wheel*—beginning with *August 1914* (1972–1983) and *October 1916* (1984)—may be his masterpiece. It may even overshadow his monumental three-volume indictment of Stalinist terror, *The Gulag Archipelago* (1973–1975), perhaps the greatest single work of contemporary world literature. Through massively compacted detail and a relentlessly oppressive style, Solzhenitsyn conveys the atmosphere and character of Soviet tyranny with inescapable force and vividness. The tone of the third volume lightens dramatically, reflecting the exhilaration of the post-Stalin thaw.

Those works and such lesser books as *First Circle* and *The Cancer Ward* (1968) are staggering feats of organization, imagination, recall, and evocation. They are overpowering expressions of a Christian, Russian-nationalist conscience in the slavophile tradition. Indeed, Solzhe-

Excerpt from *One Day in the Life of Ivan Denisovich*

Aleksander I. Solzhenitsyn spent eight years in one of Stalin's prison camps. After his release he wrote *One Day In the Life of Ivan Denisovich,* a novel centering on life in one of those camps. It appeared under Khrushchev's patronage in 1962 as the first account of Stalinist tyranny published legally in the Soviet Union.

Shukhov took off his cap and put it on his knee. He dipped his spoon in both his bowls to see what they were like. It wasn't bad. He found a bit of fish even. The gruel was always thinner than in the morning—they had to feed you in the morning so you'd work, but in the evening they knew you just flopped down and went to sleep.

He began to eat. He started with the watery stuff on the top and drank it right down. The warmth went through his body and his insides were sort of quivering waiting for that gruel to come down. It was great! This was what a prisoner lived for, this one moment.

Shukhov didn't have a grudge in the world now—about how long his sentence was, about how long their day was, about that Sunday

nitsyn seems to have absorbed those characteristics so fully that he has the gaunt, intent, otherworldly appearance of an ancient Orthodox icon.

Publication of Solzhenitsyn's *One Day in the Life of Ivan Denisovich* (1962), based on his prison-camp experiences, was a key event in the post-Stalin literary thaw. However, his fierce independence soon aroused official enmity, and his later books were suppressed until well into the Gorbachev era. He stolidly resisted a campaign to force him to emigrate, but by 1974 had exhausted Brezhnev's patience and was deported.

they wouldn't get. All he thought now was: "We'll get through! We'll get through it all! And God grant it'll all come to an end."

He drank the watery stuff on the top of the other bowl, poured what was left into the first bowl and scraped it clean with his spoon. It made things easier. He didn't have to worry about the second bowl or keep an eye on it and guard it with his hands.

So he could let his eyes wander a little and look at other bowls around him. The fellow on the left had nothing but water. The way these bastards in the kitchen treated a man! You'd never think they were just prisoners too!

Shukhov started to pick out the cabbage in his bowl. There was only one piece of potato and that turned up in the bowl he got from Caesar. It wasn't much of a potato. It was frostbitten of course, a little hard and on the sweet side. And there was hardly any fish, just a piece of bone here and there without any flesh on it. But every little fishbone and every piece of fin had to be sucked to get all the juice out of it—it was good for you. All this took time but Shukhov was in no hurry now. He'd had a real good day—he'd managed to get an extra helping at noon and for supper too. So he could skip everything else he wanted to do that evening. Nothing else mattered now.

Two other leading Russian novelists emigrated after the Revolution and never returned. Ivan Bunin, the first Russian Nobel laureate, was a gloomy pessimist who dwelled on the contrast between the grim frustrations of transitory human life and the eternal beauty of nature. Vladimir Nabokov, who was also a collector of butterflies, was a highly imaginative stylist who engaged in complex, subtle, and highly sophisticated literary exercises.

Probably the most important novel of the Gorbachev period is Anatoly Rybakov's *Children of the Arbat* (1987), the first major literary effort to depict Stalin and everyday life in his Moscow honestly and fully. Within two years of its publication, 7 million copies were in print. In 1989 he published a sequel, *1935 and Other Years.*

Poetry occupies a special place in Soviet culture. Poets command the popular adulation that is reserved to sports heroes and movie stars elsewhere. They fill soccer stadiums for public readings. This was true in the days of Pushkin and has withstood even Socialist Realism. Two young poets, Yevgeny Yevtushenko and Andrei Voznesensky, generated much of the excitement of the Khrushchev thaws. Their faintly veiled eloquence expressed the frustrations and hostilities that usually were ferociously suppressed in the official media. They remain popular, though slightly faded. Other leading poets, like Nobel Prize winner Joseph Brodsky, have emigrated, and no young poets of their caliber have emerged.

Ironically, the quality of Soviet literature has declined as literacy has risen. That literacy has created the world's largest reading audience. The Soviet Union publishes more books and booklets annually (85,000 titles), including more translations of foreign authors, in more copies (2.5 billion) than any other country, 25 percent of the world output. American favorites include Jack London and Mark Twain. Some printings run more than 10 million copies. The Soviet Union holds the world's record for number of libraries (326,000), aggregate holdings (5.6 billion volumes), and number of members (234 million).

Theater The artistic effervescence of the Russian theater in 1917—perhaps the most vigorous and innovative in the world—did not end with the Bolshevik Revolution. Many of its leaders supported the new regime and served it eagerly. They experimented enthusiastically with radically new dramatic forms and ways to transform theater into a mass medium, heeding Lenin's command to "bring the theater nearer to the masses and their socialist ideals." In return, the Bolsheviks nationalized all theaters and turned them over to left-wing producers and directors.

From 1923 the Bolsheviks required theaters to present "primarily the heroic episodes in the struggle of the working class." After 1928 theater was ground systematically under the Socialist Realism heel. Experimentation, imagination, and aesthetics became taboo. "Industrial drama," patriotic and historical docudramas, and ideological melodramas became the required repertory.

The giants of the first decades passed from the scene, and their successors were skillful technically but uninspired artistically. Producers, directors, managers, playwrights, and performers were purged ruthlessly, and theaters closed at the least sign of unorthodoxy. Some theaters evaded the rules through satire, puppetry, children's plays, or classical works whose heretical messages were heavily disguised.

Since the late 1960's, Yuri Lyubimov has been the brightest star in the Soviet theatrical firmament, with his unconventional productions at Taganka Theater. He emigrated in 1984, but returned in 1989 and resumed his leadership.

The theater's importance as a mass medium made it a special target of Gorbachev's *perestroika*. He urged it to draw "the public's attention to the many alarming developments of the seventies and early eighties" and to "focus on the burning issues of today." When the theater establishment resisted that appeal, he launched an experimental program, giving a group of seventy companies unprecedented financial, managerial, and artistic autonomy. The new freedom has generated some two hundred experimental studio theaters in Moscow alone, but no great artistic creativity so far.

Soviet theater is dominated by Russians. Minority nationality companies, playwrights, and performers are encouraged officially and play important roles in their cultures. However, productions rarely cross ethnic lines or influence the Russians significantly.

Despite its monotony in theme and subject matter, Soviet theater is the most popular in the world. About three hundred professional residential companies and countless amateur and touring troupes perform in forty-five different languages in the 630 public legitimate-theater houses. Performances are nearly always sold out, with the total number of tickets sold reaching some 120 million annually.

Theatergoers are undoubtedly attracted by the ingenious stagecraft and performance skill and by the fleeting opportunities to see censorship foiled by innuendo, veiled analogy, and the like.

Cinema   The first Russian motion picture was made in 1908, and by 1917 twenty-four Russian production companies were making more than one hundred films a year for 1,045 cinemas with an aggregate seating capacity of over 350,000. Cinema attracted a larger audience than all other entertainment media combined.

Lenin regarded cinema as "the most important of all the arts" as a tool in marshaling support. The Bolsheviks nationalized the industry in 1919 and used it to produce and disseminate propaganda. Roving "agit-trains" with portable cinema theaters were an important Bolshevik device for gaining popular support during the Civil War and early Soviet years.

During the 1920's Soviet cinema was a great caldron of technical and artistic activity, development, and change. The innovative dramatic techniques of Sergei Eisenstein and others influenced moviemaking throughout the world. In ten years the number of moviegoers grew to over 300 million annually. As its audience and propaganda value grew, political control tightened.

Increasingly harsh imposition of Socialist Realism stifled imagination and output. Fewer and fewer, worse and worse, films were produced and shown to more and more people. For five years during World War II, only thirty-four feature films were produced and only five were completed in 1952.

Stalin's death reversed that trend. Ideological control was relaxed somewhat, and the number of feature films returned to the 1917 level by the late 1950's. However, no truly outstanding cinematic artists emerged and the productions were generally mediocre.

Until Gorbachev the cinema industry was heavily subsidized by the state to ensure inexpensive access (50 cents per ticket) to its Socialist Realism message. However, in May 1986 younger members of the Filmmakers' Union rebelled against its leadership, elected renegade filmmaker Elem Klimov their president, and demanded successfully that the government ease its control over the release of films. The industry was restructured on a "self-financing" basis.

Glasnost requires that films portray the shortcomings of society more candidly. As a result, some previously banned films have been released and some new productions reflect greater "critical realism." The most notable new film has been *Repentance* by Georgian director Tengis Abuladze. It depicts the tragic effects of Stalinist tyranny and, universalizing from that, all evil on the lives of ordinary people.

Dance
Ballet, the dominant Soviet dance form, rivals poetry as the artistic passion of the country. Some Bolsheviks demanded its suppression after the Revolution, because it had been distinctively identified with the tsarist nobility and upper class. It was saved from oblivion by the timely discovery that its dominant naturalistic style of dance-drama was ideologically sound.

Nevertheless, artistic creativity in ballet suffered the same ideological straitjacketing as in the other arts. The Bolsheviks required that it develop a mass audience, a "heroic" style of performance to portray Soviet achievements, and full-evening scenarios featuring emotional human dramas in revolutionary settings, with much propaganda and pantomime but little dancing. Leading choreographers (Mikhail Fokine, Sergei Lifar) and dancers (Vaclav Nijinsky, Anna Pavlova, future choreographer George Balanchine) emigrated after 1917 and became mainstays of the most distinguished ballet companies in the West. Others (such as choreographer Leonid Jakobson) remained in the Soviet Union, but their works were suppressed. A second wave of émigrés (Mikhail Baryshnikov, Rudolf Nureyev, Natalya Makarova, Valery and Galina Panov) followed during the Brezhnev period. They became leaders of Western ballet, but have had little influence in their homeland.

Soviet ballet has emphasized highly disciplined training, virtuoso individual performances, and skillful use of music and decor. Spectacular leaps and sweeping, graceful movements provide its most cherished moments. Some full-length productions, such as *Romeo and Juliet* (with music by Prokofiev), achieved wide popularity around the world.

Ballet was the slowest of the arts to respond to the opportunities of *glasnost.* Yet by 1989 works by Balanchine were being performed in the Soviet Union for the first time and émigré dancers were being invited to return.

Despite the lack of innovation, ballet's popularity has grown enormously. Before 1917 two theaters presented forty to fifty performances a year to audiences totaling some 33,000. Now thirty-four professional companies, ranging in size from 40 to 225 dancers, and hundreds of amateur ones give thousands of performances to millions of viewers. The greatest of them are the world-famous Kirov and Bolshoi companies of Leningrad and Moscow. Some twenty professional ballet schools train the dancers.

Music

Music survived Socialist Realism better than some other arts, despite the relatively late arrival of modern concert, chamber, and operatic music in Russian culture. The Bolsheviks recognized the propaganda value of music at once and set about to control it. They nationalized musical education and publication in 1918 and invented "agitational music" to provide "new music capable of reflecting the heroism and pathos of the revolutionary struggle and the labor exploits of the Soviet people, and of expressing their thoughts and feelings."

Moreover, they decreed that "music in the Soviet Union, in fact, is not for entertainment."

Those ideological requirements alienated many composers and performers. Stravinsky remained in Paris, where he had lived since 1911. Rachmaninov (in 1917), Prokofiev (in 1918), Alexander Grechaninov (in 1922), and Alexander Glazunov (in 1928) emigrated. Prokofiev returned in 1933 and remained in the Soviet Union until his death in 1953, although he was reprimanded repeatedly and forced to revise some works, while others were suppressed.

Despite that loss of talent and the stultifying effect of Socialist Realism, several Soviet composers produced work of international renown. In general the works that earned those reputations were denounced officially for "formalism" and "bourgeois decadence."

Dmitri Shostakovich (1906–1975), the leading Soviet composer and one of the greatest in the world, was prodigiously productive. His music was admired internationally for its originality, imaginative power, and humor. He was alternately praised and lambasted officially and did penance by revising disapproved works and writing new pieces to fit the Socialist Realism mold. Shostakovich had the last word, however. In his posthumously published memoirs and a satirical cantata, he denounced the Stalinist tyranny over the arts.

Two other world-class composers, Aram Khachaturian (1903–1978), an Armenian, and Dmitri Kabalevsky (1904–   ), are especially noted for their skillful use of folk melodies, a quality that endears them to the government because of its "popular" character. Nevertheless, even they have suffered for occasional lapses from orthodoxy.

Few present-day Soviet symphonic composers have significant international reputations. One is the Volga German Alfred Schnittke (1934–   ), whose avant-garde music is expressionistic and surrealistic. Another is the more conventional former head of the Russian Composers' Union Rodion Shchedrin, who, nevertheless, has availed himself of *glasnost* to compose a Slavonic Mass. The leading popular composer is the Latvian Raimonds Pauls, who writes jazz and rock. Recently, annual modern-music festivals in Moscow and Leningrad have showcased composers outside the Socialist Realism mold.

As in the other arts, performers have suffered less from Socialist Realism than creators. The Russian tradition of emotional, highly talented, tightly disciplined, and enormously energetic virtuoso musicians has survived. The pianist Leonid Kogan and violinist David Oistrakh (died 1974) are notable examples. Yet many great instrumentalists and conductors emigrated, including cellist-conductor Mstislav Rostropovich and his wife, the soprano Galina Vishnevskaya; conductor Serge Koussevitsky; violinists Jascha Heifetz, Isaac Stern, Mischa Elman, and Nathan Milstein; cellist Grigory Piatigorsky; and pianist Vladimir Horowitz.

The fount of talent is kept flowing by the "tracking" system of specialized schools and dozens of annual musical competitions throughout the country. At the apex of the training structure are the Moscow and Leningrad Music Conservatories. Apart from the stars, professional musicians earn less than the typical factory worker and complain about the poor quality of the concert halls and their lack of artistic freedom.

A Soviet rock singer at a concert in Moscow honoring the 30th anniversary of the Beatles. N. Sinitsyna/VAAP.

Jazz and rock were long suppressed in the Soviet Union as bourgeois corruptions. Since the late 1970's they have gained a certain grudging official acceptance and great popularity, especially among young people. A few western groups such as Abba and a selection of heavy-metal bands performed in the Soviet Union, even before Gorbachev, inspiring hundreds of homegrown emulators, some quite good. A number of them, including the Ganelin Trio and Viktor Tsör's Kino group, have performed with success in Western Europe and America.

"Rock 'n' Roll's Dead"

What weird faces,
Beware of trouble.
I know there used to be sky
But I forgot where it was.
We'll meet again and say "hello"
But something's gone wrong in all that
For–rock 'n' roll's dead and I'm not yet
Those who love us
Stare at our back
Elbow to elbow, a brick makes a wall
We stood up too proud
So we pay a double price
For those who were with us
For those who wait now
For those who'll never forgive us for the fact that
Rock 'n' roll's dead
And I'm still alive

A song by Boris Grebenschikov, whose former group Aquarium is popular in the Soviet Union and has toured the United States.

Another form of popular musical culture in the Soviet Union with a very long tradition and wide following is the solo or choir song, sung formally or informally. Usually the words and music have folk origins but have been rendered more "revolutionary." Sometimes they are performed by mass choirs of thousands of amateurs.

Still another type is the "author's song." A balladeer, usually amateur, sings or chants verse informally, while strumming a guitar. The best-known of these performers was Vladimir Vysotsky, an actor at the Taganka Theater, who died of alcohol-related illness at age forty-two and has become a cult figure.

Folk music is exceptionally well developed. Its rich and greatly varied traditions among the Soviet peoples before 1917 met a double need for Socialist Realism. They are readily accessible to the common people and they express the minority-nationality cultures.

Graphic Arts
In 1917 the Russian graphic artists were perhaps the world's most daring and imaginative innovators. Protagonists of four principal abstractionist approaches vied for acceptance: imaginists, rayonists, suprematists, and constructivists.

Many leading artists were revolutionary politically and allied themselves with the Bolsheviks enthusiastically. They claimed to have been a "prelude" to the political revolution. Ironically, some of that artistic effervescence paved the way for the monotonous tyranny of Socialist Realism. In particular, constructivists like Vladimir Tatlin proclaimed themselves "artist-engineers" or even "productivists" and strove to erase the line between aesthetics and industrialization.

From 1926 abstract and other modernist art fell into disfavor gradually as being incomprehensible to the masses and, thus, inadequate for propaganda. By 1932 art had suffered the same fate as the other forms of culture. The Association of Artists of Revolutionary Russia had boasted that "content will form its own style," but in fact Stalin dictated both content and style. He especially favored posters and cartoons

"The Unruly Stallions" by V. Vysotsky

On the edge of the abyss,
On the very edge
I'm driving my stallions
I'm whipping them
I'm short of breath,
I'm drinking the wind,
I'm swallowing fog,
I can smell it with agonizing delight:
I'm dying, I'm dying.

Refrain
Slow down, my stallions
Slow down, please
Don't mind the tight whip.
But the stallions I have got are so unruly,
I won't last to the end,
I won't have time to sing to the end.
I will give my stallions a drink
I will sing this verse of the song
If I have a moment, I will stand on the edge.
I'll perish
I'll be swept off the palm as a snowflake by the hurricane
I'll be dragged behind the sleigh sometime early winter morning
Please give me some time before my way to the last resort.

II
We are on time,
Nobody's late on one's appointment to God
Why do the angels then sing in such vicious voices?
Maybe this is just my bell's sobbing
Or maybe it's my voice yelling to the stallions not to drag my sleigh
so fast.

Refrain

because their propaganda messages were clear and direct.

Socialist Realism was particularly devastating on the graphic arts because its effect was even more retrograde than in other fields. The best artists (painters Marc Chagall and Wassily Kandinsky, sculptors Anton Pevsner, Alexander Arpichenko, and Naum Gabo) emigrated. Those who remained active in their homeland produced propagandistic and predictable work that made them the laughingstock of the art world.

After 1953 art benefitted intermittently from de-Stalinization. Occasional unofficial shows of underground art were permitted. However, Khrushchev detested abstract art, characterizing it in unprintable language. Under Brezhnev some relaxation occurred, including the opening of an unofficial art gallery in 1978, but art stagnated with the rest of society.

Art offers some freedom for Soviets, but as the Leningrad rock group Televizor shows, the state is never very far away.

> *OK, so they let us break-dance,*
> *OK, so we can be happy sometimes.*
> *But still standing behind the column*
> *Is the man in the thin tie*
> *With cement in his eyes.*

Translated by Paul Easton

Gorbachev has stopped the vicious attacks on nonconformity and relaxed controls somewhat without, however, discarding Socialist Realism. Official art must still serve the old purposes, but unorthodoxy is permitted and even encouraged in unofficial art shows and markets, especially under new policies permitting individual enterprise and cooperatives. Special exhibitions, new training schools, etc., for young artists are intended to bring forth a new, more creative generation. Early-twentieth-century avant-garde works are on display again in museums.

Unfortunately, *glasnost's* effects have been limited. Even official exhibitions display some individualism and novelty, and unofficial artists are undertaking much experimentation. However, no important new movements or exciting artists have emerged so far.

Museums   The Soviet Union has more than two thousand state museums and some twelve thousand run by public organizations on a volunteer basis. More than 186 million people visit them annually. Virtually all are overcrowded, being able to exhibit only about 10 percent of their holdings.

Leningrad's Hermitage has 2.5 million works of art, one of the world's finest collections, especially in Impressionism. Other noted art museums are the Tretyakov Gallery and the Pushkin Museum in Moscow. Historical museums emphasize revolutions, but some are the former residences of great historical figures such as Tchaikovsky, Pushkin, Chekhov, Dostoyevski, and Tolstoy. Moscow has major science and technology museums, and all parts of the country have museums on specific topics.

Science

Marx believed that his socialism was superior to all other economic systems because it was scientific. The Soviet Union is based on that ideology and calls itself "the only socioeconomic formation that took root and developed on the basis of an established [scientific] theory—Marxism-Leninism." Not surprisingly, then, it gives top priority to science and has a very large number of scientists and engineers, 1.5 million (U.S. 1.7 million). Yet its scientific achievements are spotty and generally unimpressive.

Science

After the October Revolution, science became the concern of the state. From its inception, the socialist state, the sole owner of the country's land and all its productive forces, organized its economy on a scientific basis. As early as 1918, Lenin insisted that scientists help draft and apply the plans for the country's economic development.

This approach required that scientific development itself be planned. And so the Academy of Science gradually became the headquarters responsible for organizing, controlling, and planning the country's scientific development.

This requires that internal and external factors be taken into account. The internal is the logic of the development of science itself and the external is the needs and requirements of the society. The point where these factors intersect determines the basic line of scientific development.

Adapted from *Soviet Life*, September 1974

In part the explanation for that paradox is historical. The Russian empire's legacy was less brilliant in science than in the arts and culture. Russian science was staffed mostly by Westerners until the nineteenth century. By 1900 great progress had been made, and a number of Russian scientists were well known internationally. However, in depth, comprehensiveness, and overall development, Russia lagged far behind.

However, that paradox also results from Marxism-Leninism's mystical faith in science. That belief is evident in Lenin's proclamation that "Science has actually entered into our flesh and blood, being fully and genuinely transformed into a component element of our daily life."

Viewing science more practically, he said, "Communism is Soviet power plus the electrification of the whole country."

More recently, former Soviet prime minister Alexei Kosygin declared that "On the degree of scientific development and utilization of the results of scientific research in production depends to a considerable extent the course of the economic competition of the two world systems." Furthermore, Brezhnev emphasized his attachment to science by designating his historical phase as that of "building the scientific-technological foundations for communism."

The Soviet system gives effect to that rhetoric by making scientists part of its privileged class. Their salaries are double the average. The members of the Academy of Sciences are part of the official elite, with special living quarters, government cars and chauffeurs, unusual traveling rights, and access to special shops.

Scientific work was thoroughly disrupted by the Civil War, but had largely recovered by the middle 1920's and functioned fairly normally under the careful scrutiny of the state. Then Marxist-Leninists created a science, called "pedology," that was "a unified, independent science built on the foundation of dialectical materialism" for the "development of the new socialist individual."

By the early 1930's Stalin applied to science the same principles he used on the arts, except that he related them directly to dialectical materialism rather than calling them Socialist Realism. He abolished pedology and imposed democratic centralism by giving the Academy of Sciences general authority over all scientific endeavor. The Academy members were elected by qualified scientists in the various disciplines. However, Stalin manipulated the elections and intimidated the members to ensure that his will prevailed.

Stalin redefined the Academy's task as being "to assist in developing a unitary scientific method based on the materialist worldview, consistently orienting the entire system of scientific knowledge toward the satisfaction of the needs of socialist reconstruction of the country and the further development of socialist society." In 1936 the Academy accepted that role by promising to "resolve all problems that arise before us with the only scientific method, the method of Marx, Engels, Lenin, and Stalin."

In practice, ideological conformity has been imposed less stringently in most of the natural sciences than in the arts. Notable exceptions have been the longtime rejections of Einstein's theory of relativity and of cybernetics on doctrinal grounds. On the other hand, nuclear physicists secured an ideological free rein after they informed Stalin, in effect, that if he required a dialectical-materialist atom bomb he would have no bomb at all.

Lysenko's Ideology in Place of Science   The most notorious case of ideological interference in scientific research was Lysenkoist genetics. In the mid-1930's agrobiologist Trofim Lysenko propounded a theory of the inheritability of acquired characteristics that Stalin called more compatible with dialectical materialism than were conventional Mendelian genetics. Furthermore, Lysenko's theories promised agricultural miracles: "Pears would grow on apple trees and ears of wheat on the stems of couch grass."

In 1948 the CPSU Central Committee endorsed Lysenkoism and banned other genetics. Biologists who deviated from orthodoxy were dismissed, and some were imprisoned. Khrushchev supported Lysenko for the same reasons. Not until the mid-1960's was Lysenkoism rejected and Soviet genetics restored as a legitimate scientific discipline. Meanwhile, an entire branch of Soviet science had been virtually dead for nearly a generation. Moreover, the example of genetics had a chilling effect in other sciences, encouraging the making of scientific decisions on political and ideological bases.

Stalin also stunted Soviet science by isolating it internationally. Researchers could not travel to scientific conferences abroad nor foreign-

T. D. Lysenko, charlatan geneticist who dominated Soviet biology under Stalin and Khrushchev, holds aloft evidence of the validity of his theories of the inheritability of acquired characteristics. Library of Congress

ers enter the Soviet Union. Foreign scholarly journals were banned, and research reports could not be published abroad. An official translation service provided Russian versions of foreign articles, but was notoriously slow and unreliable. By forbidding normal international contacts, Stalin deprived Soviet science of its lifeblood.

Since Stalin the isolation has eased gradually, but Soviet science continues to be plagued by Marxism-Leninism's quantitative measures of productivity, by rigid bureaucracy, and by grossly inadequate resources. The Soviet Union spends only about $3.2 billion annually on basic research (U.S. $15 billion), and computers are not yet readily available.

Alongside the Academy of Sciences and its subordinate affiliates in the union republics are two other major scientific structures: the higher-education system and industrial-research institutes. Under Stalin the academies had overall responsibility for basic and applied research but performed very little basic research itself. After Stalin, they shifted heavily to basic research. At the other extreme, most research by the institutes is related very closely to the economic activities of the enterprises to which they are attached and has little theoretical value. All university faculty members are expected to engage in research, which usually falls in the middle ground between the academies and the institutes. In 1965 the State Committee for Science and Technology was created at the U.S.S.R. ministerial level to coordinate applied research. It has become increasingly important and rivals the Academy for control of science. The Committee's position seems to have been strengthened in 1986 when its chairman, Guri Marchuk, who is not a leading scientist, was elected Academy president.

The High Point of Soviet Science   Despite their serious ideological and organizational handicaps, Soviet scientists have achieved impressive results in some areas. The most obvious successes have been in nuclear physics and space exploration. The Soviets deto-

nated the world's first hydrogen bomb in 1953, began operating the first nuclear power plant in 1954, and launched the first space satellite in 1957. More recently, they have achieved impressive results in interplanetary exploration, theoretical physics and mathematics, computer technology, lasers, and genetic engineering.

Soviet scientists have won or shared only five Nobel Prizes in physics, one in chemistry, and none in physiology or medicine since 1917 (Comparative figures for the U.S.: 33, 21, and 35). Physicists Lev Landau, Andrei Sakharov (who was also a courageous crusader for human rights), Igor Tamm, and Peter Kapitsa rank among the very best of this century. So do physiologist-psychologist Ivan Pavlov and chemist Nikolai Semenov. However, that is a rather meager record for such a massive scientific establishment—another indication of the damage inflicted by ideology on Soviet life. In recognition of that, Gorbachev decreed in 1990 that the Academy of Sciences should be given "total autonomy in leadership and decision" with respect to basic research and training scientists—apparently releasing it, finally, from the iron grip of Marxism-Leninism.

Cosmonauts Leonid Kizim and Vladimir Solovyov conducting a press conference at the mission control center of the Mir orbital space station.   Novosti

Conclusion

Russian history is remarkable for its continuity. Even the Bolshevik Revolution of 1917 was less a sharp break with the past than a changing of the guard. This makes the great enterprise of Mikhail Gorbachev especially astonishing, for he seems to be undertaking a colossal effort to reverse the course of those centuries of history.

Three fundamental aspects of that history are the special objects of Gorbachev's reform efforts. One of them is Russia's unbroken record of autocratic rule. The Russian people have never experienced authentic democracy, at least at the national level. Nor have the other peoples of the Soviet Union, with the possible partial exception of the Baltic states between 1920 and 1940. Political and governmental power has always been monopolized by autocrats and their close associates. In 1917 commissars replaced tsars, but the autocracy continued. Even worse, both before and after 1917, counterfeit versions of democracy were practiced, concealing from the people the true meaning and value of popular rule.

Not only have the peoples of Russia and the Soviet Union lacked effective control over their governments, but both tsars and commissars imposed harsh controls over the people. The Russian and Soviet states have rested on sanctified, privileged organizations that were, in turn, based on scripture—first the Russian Orthodox Church and the Bible, then the Communist Party of the Soviet Union and Marxism-Leninism. This raised the systems above earthly criticism or attack and justified strict regulation of the lives of the people, not only to maintain order but to ensure maximum conformity to the ideals they espouse. The main difference between tsarism and communism has been one of degree. The tyranny of the Soviet state was more efficient than that of its predecessor, with more devastating effects on cultural, artistic, and scientific life.

Other persistent aspects of that history lie in the economy. The state has always dominated the economy, not simply as regulator but as owner and operator as well. Neither tsars nor Bolsheviks permitted supply and demand and private enterprise to run freely. Nor have either been willing to trust indirect controls. The Bolshevik Revolution simply marked the passage from state capitalism to state socialism. However, neither form of state domination engendered prosperity. Both before and after 1917, the real standard of living of the average person remained appallingly low.

A third striking continuity in Russian-Soviet history has been the almost inexorable extension of Russian rule geographically. For a thousand years, almost without a break, the ancient principality of Muscovy grew gradually from a few hundred square miles, until by the end of Stalin's life it had become much the largest empire in the world, stretching from the Bering Strait to the center of Europe. The Russians ruled more than one hundred nations within the Soviet Union and another dozen or so in satellite states.

Gorbachev's leadership is so extraordinary—indeed, is unique—precisely because he is attempting to undo a thousand years of history in all three of those areas. No previous ruler—in Russia or, perhaps, anywhere else—has attempted so Herculean a task. If he succeeds, his revolution will be far more sweeping than Lenin's.

Politically and governmentally, Gorbachev's *glasnost* and *perestroika* have unleashed a veritable avalanche of reform measures. Democratization, liberalization, and constitutionalization have developed at astonishing speed. Hardly a week passes without some new proposal being brought forward, adopted, or implemented. The Soviet Union has some distance to travel yet before becoming a fully democratic, liberal, constitutional state in the Western tradition, but the progress so far has been dramatic.

Ironically, that democratization has been accomplished mainly by a dictator using largely autocratic methods. How firmly rooted it is in its essential popular base remains unclear. A great, unanswered question is whether the Soviet people can overcome a thousand years of obedience and assume, effectively, the responsibilities of self-rule.

Economically, Gorbachev's reform efforts have been no less impressive. He has introduced a dazzling succession of measures to take the state out of the economy by decentralizing and privatizing. He has shown great flexibility and pragmatism in recognizing failures and trying alternative approaches. Even more than in the political realm, past economic habits have resisted change tenaciously. Moreover, here Gorbachev himself has shown the limitations of his ideology. He seems willing to go almost any lengths to avoid saying "private property," "free enterprise," or "capitalism"—even though he seems to recognize their inevitability.

So far, Soviet economic problems have seemed intractable. None of Gorbachev's economic reform campaigns has improved the operation of the economy or the living standards of the average person. Indeed, the situation has been deteriorating, and no responsible official or observer forecasts an early reversal of that decline. The Russian people are noted for their patience in the face of severe adversity, but it cannot be inexhaustible. Every serious student of Soviet affairs must wonder how much longer they will tolerate Gorbachev's economic failures.

However dramatic may be Gorbachev's efforts in the political and economic spheres, they pale beside the decolonization process he has launched. By renouncing the Brezhnev Doctrine, he became perhaps the first leader in Russia's history to accept voluntarily the loss of control over territory that had become part of its empire. As soon as the implications of that announcement were grasped, every former Soviet satellite in Eastern Europe set about to abandon communism as rapidly as possible.

The reverberations of decolonization did not stop at the Soviet borders. Soviet non-Russians have joined enthusiastically in the exodus process. Because of the intermixing of peoples, especially the presence of millions of Russians in non-Russian republics, the decolonization process is much more complex and difficult within the Soviet Union than in Eastern Europe. Moreover, *glasnost* seems to have unleashed ethnic rivalries and hatreds whose expression had been repressed through the long decades of Bolshevik tyranny.

The disintegration of the Soviet Union through decolonization is seen widely as portending destruction for Russia. It need not be. Decolonization did not destroy France or Great Britain. Nor are the conflicts between Azerbaijanis and Armenians, for instance, likely to be bloodier than those between Hindus and Moslems in decolonizing India. The process has been an agony so far and may well worsen, especially as the Soviet empire consists of adjacent territories rather than scattered overseas possessions like those of the Western colonial powers.

At least models of decolonization exist. The Soviets can learn from the lessons of their Western predecessors who traveled that difficult road. This is true, also, in the political realm. Autocracies have been dismantled before. This happened in Spain, Portugal, and Greece in the

1970's and Brazil, Argentina, and Chile in 1980's. Eastern Europe is now going through the same process. In none of those examples, however, was the dictatorship so total or deeply entrenched.

Models for decommunizing an economy are less available. Before Gorbachev, only Yugoslavia and Hungary had made very limited progress in that respect. The other Eastern European countries are now stumbling along the same path. None of them can provide much guidance.

Until recently, the way to communism had been regarded widely as a one-way street. This belief owed much to a book, *Road to Serfdom*, by economist Friedrich von Hayek, which argued that socialism inevitably destroys freedom. He implied that public ownership of productive property was a steep, slippery slope leading irreversibly to tyranny.

The most monumental of Gorbachev's many tasks is to struggle back up that incline dragging the enormous, dilapidated economic apparatus of the Soviet Union with him. En route, he is battling long-entrenched economic interests and the skepticism of even disinterested compatriots, doubts reinforced by generations of State propaganda. Moreover, he is still weighed down with the remnants of the Marxism-Leninism that he rode to the pinnacle of Soviet power. Despite his basic pragmatism, he still has not faced up to the wrenching chore of chucking out the ideological baggage that has plagued his country so long.

None of those great tasks, however, is more pioneering than the general effort to break the inexorable continuity of Russian history. When its difficulties are added to the others, the risks facing Gorbachev become clear. How they affect his prospects for success is much less evident. Indeed, therein lie the great imponderables of the next few years in the Soviet Union. *Glasnost* may have gone far to unwrap the riddles, mysteries, and enigmas of the Soviet past and present, but Churchill's famous phrase continues to fit well the Soviet future.

Glossary

Administrative divisions in the Soviet Union are supposed to reflect regions inhabited by distinct ethnic groups, though in practice Russians have moved into many regions and other groups have been moved from their homelands. A.S.S.R.—autonomous soviet socialist republic, a type of territorial unit in the U.S.S.R. next in constitutional status below the union republic (or S.S.R.). A.S.S.R. are areas containing significant non-Russian populations; they are also known as Autonomous Republics (A.R.'s). Autonomous Oblast (A.O.)—*oblast* means "area" or "province," another type of territorial unit in the U.S.S.R., ranking just below the A.S.S.R. Ethnic minorities have certain legal rights based on their own customs and beliefs within Autonomous Oblasts. Smaller minorities form National Regions within the larger units listed above.
Bolshevik—the Russian word for "majority," assumed in 1903 by Lenin as the name for the faction that he led in the Russian Social Democratic Workers Party.
command economy—a form of system for the production, distribution, and consumption of goods and services in a society in which the government makes most major decisions and imposes them on individuals and enterprises.
federalism—a form of governmental system in which the national and regional levels are coordinate in constitutional authority; in contrast to unitary systems, where the regional level is subordinate to the national level, and confederal systems, where the national level is subordinate to the regional level.

free market economy—a form of system for the production, distribution, and consumption of goods and services in a society that is regulated by the laws of supply and demand without interference from the government.

ideology—a system of philosophical principles intended to serve as a guide for social, economic, political, and governmental action, a term commonly applied to Marxism and Marxism-Leninism.

Menshevik—the Russian word for "minority," applied from 1903 to the faction led by L. Martov in the Russian Social Democratic Workers Party.

Narodnik—the Russian word for "of the people," used to designate a nineteenth-century slavophile social and political movement that advocated radical reform by arousing and organizing forces rooted deeply in Russian traditions, especially in the peasantry.

oligarchy—a word of Greek origin referring to a governmental system in which a small group rules; used also to refer to such a group.

Prussian—a resident of Prussia, a small Germanic state on the Baltic Sea; used also to refer to personal characteristics believed to be common among Prussians, especially a highly developed sense of self-discipline, hard-work ethic, authoritarian attitudes, militarism, social-class snobbishness.

rehabilitation—the act of restoring to good standing a disgraced person or group; may be posthumous.

slavophile—one who advocates seeking solutions to Russian problems in Russian traditions, as opposed to a "westernizer."

Soviet of Workers' Deputies—*soviet* is the Russian word for "council," one of the irregular, revolutionary institutions that emerged more or less spontaneously and briefly early in the twentieth century.

westernizer—one who advocates seeking solutions to Russian problems in emulation of Western Europe, especially through acquiring its technology and adopting similar social, economic, and political institutions.

Suggestions for Further Reading and Study

Bibliography

Books on current developments in the Soviet Union are pouring from the printing presses in such a torrent that only the last one published can be considered up-to-date. The most recent at this writing will be superseded by several others by the time this list appears in print. Therefore, these suggestions will include only items of more enduring value.

The most useful single source in English on current affairs in the Soviet Union is the weekly *Current Digest of the Soviet Press*, which publishes in translation articles from many Soviet newspapers and periodicals and may be found in most research libraries. Another excellent such source that is aimed at a more general audience and expresses a Gorbachevian viewpoint is the weekly *Moscow News*, published in Moscow and distributed in the United States through several agencies, including Victor Kamkin, 12224 Parklawn Drive, Rockville, Md. The monthly magazine *Soviet Life*, also published in Moscow in English, is less oriented toward news and more toward features on culture, tourism, and youth. A useful recent book on those topics is James Cracraft, ed., *The Soviet Union Today: An Interpretive Guide* (Chicago: University of Chicago Press, 2nd ed. 1988), a collection of essays by experts on history, politics, the armed forces, the physical context, the economy, science and technology, culture, and society.

Several reference works are also rich general sources. Much the most important is the thirty-two-volume English edition of *The Great Soviet*

Encyclopedia (New York: Macmillan, 1973–82), but of course it gives only the official, pre-Gorbachev interpretation. A useful but dated single-volume encyclopedia is Michael T. Florinsky, ed., *Encyclopedia of Russia and the Soviet Union* (New York: McGraw-Hill, 1961), 624 pp. A more recent one-volume encyclopedia with fewer, longer articles is Archie Brown et al, gen. eds., *The Cambridge Encyclopedia of Russia and the Soviet Union* (Cambridge, England: Cambridge University Press, 1982), 492 pp. A handy annual statistical reference is Alan P. Pollard, *USSR Facts and Figures Annual* (Gulf Breeze, Fla.: Academic International Press).

Two standard surveys of the physical context of the Soviet Union are John C. Dewdney, *A Geography of the Soviet Union* (New York: Pergamon, 2nd ed. 1971), 169 pp., and Paul E. Lydolph, *The Geography of the U.S.S.R.: A Topical Analysis* (Elkhart Lake, Wisc.: Misty Valley Publishers, 1979), 522 pp.

Russian and Soviet history is a well-worked field, with many substantial books providing divergent approaches and interpretations. A classic survey, mainly on the pre-Soviet period, is George Vernadsky, *A History of Russia* (New Haven: Yale University Press, 3rd ed. 1951), 533 pp. An excellent history textbook is Nicholas V. Riasanovsky, *A History of Russia* (New York: Oxford University Press, 4th ed. 1984).

A text most useful for those who might like college-level interpretations and comprehensive references to primary and secondary sources is David MacKenzie and Michael W. Curran, *A History of Russia and the Soviet Union* (Homewood, Ill.: Dorsey Press, 3rd ed. 1987).

Conflicting interpretations of Soviet history are provided in Stephen F. Cohen, *Rethinking the Soviet Experience: Politics and History since 1917* (New York: Oxford University Press, 1985), and Mikhail Heller and Aleksander Nekrich, *Utopia in Power: The History of the Soviet Union from 1917 to the Present* (New York: Summit Books, 1986).

Some biographies and memoirs also give valuable insight into aspects of Russian and Soviet leaders and history.

Robert Massie, *Peter the Great: His Life and World* (New York: Alfred A. Knopf, 1980), is a most comprehensive study. Another important biography of Peter is Marc Raeff, ed., *Peter the Great Changes Russia* (Lexington, Mass.: D.C. Heath, 1982).

Catherine the Great has also been the subject of numerous literary studies, including John T. Alexander, *Catherine the Great: Life and Legend* (London: Oxford University Press, 1989), which is notable for its coverage of the many legends about this leader. Zoe Oldenbourg, *Catherine the Great* (New York: Pantheon, 1965), is easy to read.

Biographies of at least two other pre-Soviet era leaders bear noting, including Marc Raeff, *Michael Speransky: Statesman of Imperial Russia, 1722 to 1839* (The Hague, Netherlands: Martinus Nijhoff Press, 1957), and M. Malia, *Alexander Herzen and the Birth of Russian Socialism* (Cambridge, Mass.: Harvard University Press, 1961).

The most interesting memoir is the two-volume tape-recorded reflections of Nikita S. Khrushchev, *Khrushchev Remembers,* with an introduction, commentary, and notes by Edward Crankshaw (New York: Bantam, 1971), and *Khrushchev Remembers: The Last Testament,* translated and edited by Strobe Talbot with a foreword by Edward Crankshaw and an introduction by Jerrold L. Schechter (Boston: Little, Brown, 1974). A third volume appeared in 1990. Important biographies include Adam Ulam, *The Bolsheviks* (New York: Macmillan, 1965), which, despite its title, is mainly a biography of Lenin, and Robert Payne, *The Rise and Fall of Stalin* (New York: Simon & Schuster, 1966). For Gorbachev's early views on his policy plans, see his *Perestroika: New Thinking for Our Country and the World* (New York: Harper & Row, 1987), and for a study of the background factors in his reform program see Jerry Hough, *Russia and the West: Gorbachev and the Politics of Reform* (New York: Simon & Schuster, 1988).

The classic study of Soviet politics and government is Merle Fainsod and Jerry Hough, *How the Soviet Union Is Governed* (Cambridge: Harvard University Press, 1979). A shorter, more recent textbook on that topic is D. Richard Little, *Governing the Soviet Union* (New York: Longman, 1989). For a Soviet reformer-historian's perceptions of Stalin, see Roy A. Medvedev, *Let History Judge: The Origins and Consequences of Stalinism* (New York: Vintage, 1973). The standard survey of Soviet foreign policy is Adam Ulam, *Expansion and Coexistence: The History of Soviet Foreign Policy, 1917–1973* (New York: Praeger, 1974). For the more recent period, see his *Dangerous Relations: The Soviet Union in World Politics, 1970–1982* (New York: Oxford University Press, 1983). On the economy, the standard works are two books by Alec Nove, *An Economic History of the U.S.S.R.* (London: Penguin, rev. ed. 1982), and *The Soviet Economic System* (London: Allen & Unwin, 3rd ed. 1986).

On religion in the U.S.S.R., see Trevor Beeson, *Discretion and Valor: Religious Conditions in Russia and Eastern Europe* (Philadelphia: Fortress Press, rev. ed. 1982), and Pedro Ramet, ed., *Religion and Nationalism in Soviet and Eastern European Politics* (Durham, N.C.: Duke University Press, 1984). Jane Ellis, *The Russian Orthodox Church Today: A Contemporary History* (Bloomington, Ind.: Indiana University Press, 1986), is the standard work on the largest Soviet religious group. A useful reference work on Soviet nationalities is Ronald Wixman, *The Peoples of the U.S.S.R.: An Ethnographic Handbook* (Armonk, N.Y.: M. E. Sharpe, 1984), and a scholarly study of that topic is Viktor Kozlov, *The Peoples of the Soviet Union* (Bloomington, Ind.: Indiana University Press, 1988).

Several good books on daily life in the Soviet Union have been published by journalists in recent years. Perhaps the best and most substantial view of the typical Soviet citizen is by Hedrick Smith, former *New York Times* correspondent in Moscow: *The Russians* (New York: Times Books, 1976). His successor, David Shipler, wrote a similar account: *Russia: Broken Idols, Solemn Dreams* (New York: Times Books, 1983). Their *Times* of London colleague Michael Binyon placed the same topic in historical context in *Life in Russia* (New

York: Pantheon, 1983). More specific views are provided by William Taubman and Jane Taubman, *Moscow Spring: January to June 1988* (New York: Summit Books, 1989), and Jerrold Schechter et al., *Back in the U.S.S.R.* (New York: Charles Scribner's Sons, 1989), by an American journalist and his family returning to the Soviet Union after twenty years. For special attention to the daily life of Soviet youth, see Jim Riordan, ed., *Soviet Youth Culture* (Bloomington, Ind.: Indiana University Press, 1989). *A Day in the Life of the Soviet Union* (New York: Harper & Row, 1987) is a richly illustrated view of Soviet life at one moment.

A clear guide to how—through books, newspapers, and films—the people of the Soviet Union and the United States learn about one another is Robert D. English and Jonathan Halperin, *The Other Side: How Soviets and Americans Perceive Each Other* (Washington, D.C.: Commission for National Security, 1987).

An interesting new source on current Soviet intellectual and cultural life is *The Literary Gazette International*, a monthly English edition of the leading Soviet periodical in that field, printed in El Paso, Tex., and distributed by Sun Mailing Co., 900 Magoffin, El Paso, Tex. 79901-9957. Authoritative studies of various aspects of Soviet culture include Katerina Clark, *The Soviet Novel: History as Ritual* (Chicago: University of Chicago Press, 1981); Harold B. Segel, *Twentieth-Century Russian Drama from Gorky to the Present* (New York: Columbia University Press, 1979); Boris Schwarz, *Music and Musical Life in Soviet Russia* (Bloomington, Ind.: Indiana University Press, 1983); Jay Leyda, *Kino: A History of the Russian and Soviet Film*.(Princeton: Princeton University Press, 1983); James Riordan, *Sport in Soviet Society* (Cambridge, England: Cambridge University Press, 1980); and Ellen Propper Michiewicz, *Media and the Russian Public* (New York: Praeger, 1981). A recent standard view of Soviet science is Peter Kneen, *Soviet Scientists and the State* (Albany, N.Y.: State University of New York Press, 1984).

Discography

Western classical music, played by Soviet musicians and composed by Russian and later Soviet composers, is widely available in the United States. Soviet rock music, however, has only very recently become available to American music fans.

As of 1990, cassettes from popular groups like these can be found in many major record stores:

Gorky Park: Park Gorkova (Mercury)
Kino: Grupakrovy (Blood Group) (Gold Castle)
(Boris) Grebenshikov: B.G. (Columbia)
Vlady Vysotski: Vlady Vysotski (Melodia)
Kuriokhin: Kuriokhin (Ryko)

Filmography

Only a very few years ago, few Soviet-made films (documentaries, videotapes, or feature length) were available in the United States. In 1990 hundreds are available through a bevy of suppliers. The following brief, annotated listing is an introduction to the kind and type of films that will give readers a new glimpse of Soviet life:

Burglar (1987); directed by Valeri Ogorodnikov; feature length. Available from International Film Exchange Ltd. *Glasnost* meets punk rock. Kostya, a young rocker, begins to hang out with an alienated and alienating group of friends—with disastrous results. English subtitles.

Come and See (1985); directed by Elem Klimov; feature length. Available from International Film Exchange Ltd. War drama about a young boy from Byelorussia who, in 1943, leaves home to fight the Nazis. English subtitles.

Is It Easy to Be Young? (1987); directed by Yuri Podniek; feature length. Available from International Film Exchange Ltd. Youths of the Soviet Union are just as alienated as their counterparts are in the United States, as this documentary reveals in its portraits of teens at a rock concert, a dropout seeking his soul in a Hare Krishna cult, and a young veteran who feels "unclean" after experiencing the horrors of war.

Private Life (1983); directed by Yuli Raizman; feature length. Available from International Film Exchange Ltd. A recently dismissed factory executive is forced to reexamine relationships with friends and family. Nominated for Academy Award, Best Foreign Language Film of 1983. English subtitles.

Repentance (1987); directed by Tenghiz Abuladze; feature length. Presented by the Cannon Group, Inc., in association with Sovexportfilm. English subtitles. In a small Russian town, a woman is put on trial for repeatedly digging up the body of the town's recently deceased ruler. As the trial progresses, the nature of the leader's reign—vicious and despotic—comes to light. 1987 Cannes Film Festival Special Jury Prize Winner.

Scarecrow (1985); directed by Rolan Bykov; feature length. As seen through the eyes of one ostracized sixth grader, the incredible cruelty young people are capable of inflicting upon one another is quite clear. Most popular film in the Soviet Union in its year of release. Based on the book of the same title by Vladimir Zheleznikov (New York: Harper & Row, 1990)

International Film Exchange (201 West 52nd Street, New York, N.Y. 10019; 212 582–4318) has extensive additional listings of new and old Russian- and Soviet-made films, including *Little Vera*, *Moscow Does Not Believe in Tears*, and many others, including a reconstruction of Eisenstein's *Que Viva Mexico.* Most are available in a variety of formats.

Older, classic films such as *Ten Days That Shook the World* and *Battleship Potemkin* are widely available, through your local video store.

Two well-known outside views of Russia and the Soviet Union are David Lean's *Doctor Zhivago* and Warren Beatty's *Reds*, both of which can be found at your local video store.

Acknowledgments

"Uncovering Novgorod" on page 46 is based on and taken from "The Archaeology of Novgorod," by Valentine L. Yanin, which appeared in *Scientific American* (February 1990, page 87).

Excerpts on pages 193 and 222 are from *The Russians* by Hedrick Smith. Copyright © 1976 by Hedrick Smith. Reprinted by permission of Times Books, a division of Random House, Inc.

Excerpts on pages 260–261 are from *One Day in the Life of Ivan Denisovich* by Alexander Solzhenitsyn, translated by Max Hayward and Ronald Hingley. Copyright © 1963 by Frederick A. Praeger, Inc., Publishers. Reprinted by permission of Henry Holt and Company, Inc.

Excerpts on pages 212–13 are from *Growing Up in Moscow* by Catherine Young. Copyright © 1989 by Cathy Young. Reprinted by permission of Ticknor & Fields, a Houghton Mifflin Company.

Excerpt on page 99 is from *Ten Days That Shook the World* by John Reed. Copyright © 1960 by Random House, Inc.

Excerpt on page 133 is from *Khrushchev Remembers,* translated and edited by Strobe Talbott. Copyright © 1970 by Little, Brown and Co. (Inc.).

Index

Abba (rock band), 269
Abkhazians, 175
Abramov, Feodor, 258
Abuladze, Tengis, 265
Academy of Arts, 256
Academy of Sciences, 62, 274–76, 278–79
Achishko, 27
Afanaseyev, Yuri N., 145–46
Afghanistan, 127, 138, 148, 176, 178–79
AIDS, 239
Alai Mountains, 18
Alans, 44, 180
Alaska, 65, 76, 182
Albania, 121
Alcoholics Anonymous, 242
Aleuts, 182
Alexander I, tsar, 67–68, 70–71
Alexander II, tsar, 41, 74–77, 81, 84
Alexander III, tsar, 41, 78, 84
Alexander the Great, 40
Alexandra, tsarina, 94
Alexei Michailovich, tsar, 62
Alexius, tsarevich, 94
All-Russian Congress of Soviets, 97, 99, 106, 111
All-Union Council of Evangelical Christians and Baptists, 194
All-Union Society of Stamp Collectors, 251
Alma-Ata, 153, 178, 220
Altai, 18–19, 181
Amu Darya, 21–22, 34–35

Amur River, 20, 73, 77
And Quiet Flows the Don (Sholokhov), 259
Andropov, Yuri, 127, 136, 139–40
Angola, 138
Anna, Princess, 48
Anne, tsarina, 65
Antes, 45
Antis (rock band), 167
Anti-Party Group, 126, 129
Aquarium (rock band), 269
Arabia, peoples of, 45, 172, 175, 177
Arabic, 187
Aral Sea, 22–24
Arctic Ocean, 14, 21
Ardagan, 102
Argentina, 284
Armenia, 34, 104, 152, 163, 172, 174–75, 229; peoples of, 44, 164, 173, 195, 283
Armens, 174
Arpichenko, Alexander, 272
Aryan, 176
Asian nomads, 44
Association of Artists of Revolutionary Russia, 270
Assyrians, 44
Atlantic Ocean, 19
August 1914 (Solzhenitsyn), 259
Austria, 92, 171
Austria-Hungary, 70, 73–74, 90

Avars, 44
Avdeyenko, Alexander, 115
Azerbaijan, 67, 104, 163, 172–75, 195, 200, 283
Azov Sea, 171

Bactria, peoples of, 180
Baikal, Lake, 22–24, 154, 181, 251
Balanchine, George, 265–66
Balkans, 20, 77–78, 87, 179, 184
Balkars, 158, 175
Balkash, 22, 24
Baltic Sea, 14, 20, 57, 64, 152
Baltic States, 30, 104, 120, 181, 280; peoples of, 159, 166, 221, 223
Baptist church, 194
Barazikhin, Mikhail, 218
Barents Sea, 20
Baryshnikov, Mikhail, 266
Bashkir A.S.S.R., 179
Batum, 102
Begelman, P., 246
Beria, Lavrentia, 125–26, 128
Bering Sea, 61
Berlin, 121, 126–27, 134
Bessarabia, 45, 67, 74, 102, 104, 170
Black Sea, 18–20, 24, 44, 64–65, 73–74, 166, 171, 251
Black Power (opera), 168
Bloody Sunday (1905), 86
Bolshevik(s), 40–41, 82–83, 90, 94–95, 97–104, 106, 108, 110–11, 127, 173, 175, 183, 255, 262–66, 270, 281; Revolution, 86, 98–99, 216, 218, 221, 262, 265, 274, 280–81
Borodin, Alexander, 254
Bosporus Straits, 20, 73
Brandes, Georg, 31
Brazil, 284
Breshko-Breshkovskaya, Ekaterina Konstantinova, 81
Brest-Litovsk Treaty, 102–3, 104

Brezhnev doctrine, 137–38, 148, 186, 257, 258, 283
Brezhnev, Leonid, 124, 126–27, 135–40, 178, 260, 272, 275
Britain, 70, 74, 87
Brodsky, Joseph, 262
Buddhism, 179, 195
Bukhara, 177
Bukharin, Nikolai I., 110, 113, 117
Bulgaria, 121; peoples of, 171
Bulgars, 44, 171, 179, 223
Bunin, Ivan, 261
Buryats, 181, 195
Butashevich-Petrashevsky, M. V., 81
Butyrsky Market, 198
Byelorussia, 29–30, 35, 48, 151, 163–64, 166, 171, 183
Byzantium, peoples of, 44–45, 48–49, 55, 172

California, 65
Canada, 182
Cancer Ward, The (Solzhenitsyn), 259
Carpathia, peoples of, 17, 34–35, 45, 163
Caspian Sea, 18, 20, 22–23, 24, 32, 153
Catherine I, tsarina, 65
Catherine II (the Great), tsarina, 41, 65, 171
Caucasus, 16, 18, 26–27, 42, 57, 121, 172, 175, 179, 195, 210, 251; peoples of the, 172, 221
Central Asia, 29, 34, 40, 42, 73, 76, 78, 104–5, 122, 158, 172–73, 176, 178–79, 184, 191–92, 195, 210, 219, 221, 223
Chagall, Marc, 272
Chechens, 158
Cheka (secret police), 83
Chekhov, Anton, 254, 273
Chernenko, Konstantin Ustinovich, 127, 139–41
Chernobyl, 37

Kurds, 158, 175, 180
Kurile Islands, 65
Kutuzov, General Mikhail, 68

Ladoga, Lake, 22, 24
Land and Liberty Party, 84
Landau, Levi, 279
Latvia, 102, 163, 239; peoples of, 167, 194
Law on Religious Association, 186
Leesment, J., 169
Lena River, 20, 22
Lenin, Vladimir Ilyich (Ulyanov), 3, 8–10, 82–83, 88–89, 90, 95, 97, 100, 103, 107–11, 113, 116–19, 123, 125, 129, 137, 141, 164, 184–85, 186, 194, 203, 200, 222, 255, 262, 264, 274, 276; "21 Points," 108
Leningrad, 13, 64, 121, 135, 141
Leninism, 114, 181
Liberation of Labor Party, 82, 83, 84
Lifar, Sergei, 265
Lithuania, 102, 127, 171; peoples of, 44, 166, 168, 194
London, Jack, 262
Louis XIV, 119
Luzhniki Stadium, 146
Lvov, Prince George, 95
Lysenko, Trofim, 276–77
Lyubimov, Yuri, 263

Magadan Province, 155–56
Magyars, 47
Makarova, Natalya, 266
Malenkov, Georgy Maksimilianovich, 125, 128
Malevich, Kazimir, 254
Maly Hills, 152
Man from Outside, The (Dvoretsky), 256
Mandelstam, Osip, 116
Marchuk, 278
Mari, 181

Marmara, Sea of, 20
Martov, Julius, 88, 90
Marx, Karl, 2, 6–8, 134, 185, 194, 203, 255, 273, 276
Marxism, 6–8, 79, 84, 88–89, 100, 107, 218, 226
Marxism-Leninism, x, 3, 10, 36, 108, 114, 118, 133–34, 142, 159, 163, 178, 185, 194, 196, 203, 205, 208, 210–11, 214, 216–17, 223, 232, 243–44, 248, 255, 273–75, 278–80, 284
Maslyennitsa, 48
Mattiisen, Alo, 169
McDonald's, 143, 209, 235
Mecca, 195
Mekhs, 172–73
Memorial (political group), 117
Mennonites, 194
Mensheviks, 90, 95, 97, 100
Meshalkin, Yevgeny N., 146
Meskhs, 158
Methodius (monk), 49
Mikoyan, Anastas, 135
Military-Revolutionary Committee, 98
Milstein, Nathan, 268
Mingrelians, 172
Moldava, 73–74, 139, 158, 170, 171, 183, 188, 219; Moldavian S.S.R., 171, 179
Molotov, Vyacheslav Mikhailovich (Scriabin), 125–26
Molotov-Ribbentrop treaty, 103, 120
Mongolia, 178, 181; peoples of, 44, 172, 175, 178, 180–81
Mongolian People's Republic, 180
moral renewal, 142
Mordovians, 181
Moscow, xiv, 13, 64, 67, 107, 121, 123, 128, 130, 141, 152, 244
Moscow News, x
Moslems, 105, 189, 191–92, 195, 219, 234
Mount Elbrus, 18

Murmansk, 20
Muscovy, state of, 40, 52, 281
Music Conservatory, 268
Mussorgsky, Modest, 254

Nabokov, Vladimir, 261
Nagorno-Karabakh Autonomous Oblast, 175
Napoleon Bonaparte, 66–67, 70–71
Narodniks, 81–82, 84, 88
Naryshkina, Natalie, 62
Neanderthal-type human, 42
Nenarokov, Albert, 95
Neolithic settlements, 42
Neva River, 94
Nevsky, Alexander, 40
New Economic Policy (NEP), 103, 107–8, 114, 257
Nicaragua, 138
Nicholas I, tsar, 70–74, 81, 92
Nicholas II, tsar, 41, 83–85, 87–88, 93–95, 103
Nijinsky, Vaclav, 254, 265
1935 and Other Years (Rybakov), 262
Nogai, 175
Novaya Zemlya, 16
Novgorod, 46–47, 57
Novo-Shuiski, 154
Nuclear Test Ban Treaty, 126, 134
Nureyev, Rudolf, 266

Ob River, 20, 22–23
October 1916 (Solzhenitsyn), 259
Oistrakh, David, 268
Okhotsk, 61, 154
Old Believers, 59, 194
Old Bolsheviks, 126
Olympic Games, 253
Onega, Lake, 22, 24
Orwell, George, 150
Ossetians, 180
Ottoman empire, 77

Pacific Ocean, 14, 19–20, 64
Paleo-Asiatic peoples, 181–82
Pamir Mountains, 18–19, 195
Pan-Slavs, 77
Panov, Valery and Galina, 266
Pasternak, Boris, 259
Paul I, tsar, 66
Pauls, Raimonds, 268
Pavlov, Ivan, 279
Pavlova, Anna, 254, 265
peaceful coexistence, 134
Pel'she, Arvid, 140
Pentecostal church, 194
People's Mountain, 16
Pepsi-Cola, 143
perestroika, 142–43, 147, 149–50, 156, 205, 207, 210, 217, 231, 263, 282
Persia, 87, 184; peoples of, 44, 172, 174–75, 177. *See also* Iran.
Peter and Paul Fortress, 98
Peter I (the Great), tsar, 41, 61, 64–65
Peter II, tsar, 65
Peter III, tsar, 65
Petrashevsky Circle, 82
Petrograd, 92, 95, 107
Petropavlovsk, 156
Pevsner, Anton, 272
Piatigorsky, Grigory, 268
Plehve, Vyacheslav Konstantinovich, 84
Plekhanov, Georgy, 82, 84
Pobedonostev, Constantine, 78
Podgorny, Nikolai Viktovich, 135
Podolia, 31
Poland, 65, 102, 104, 120–21, 126, 134, 138, 166, 171, 183–84; peoples of, 59, 73, 75, 96, 158, 167, 171, 194
Popov, (deputy), 146
Popular Front, 168
Portugal, 283
Pravda (newspaper), 111, 113, 123
Prokofiev, Sergei, 267
Protestantism, 189, 191, 194
Provisional Committee, 95
Provisional Government, 95–98, 101

Prussia, 78, 152, 171
Pskov, 250
Pugachev, Emelian, 41, 65
Pushkin, Alexander, 64, 254, 262, 273
Pushkin museum, 273

Quadruple Alliance, 70

Rachmaninoff, Sergei, 254, 267
Rasputin, Grigory Yefimovich (Novykh),
    83–84, 92–94
Rasputin, Valentin, 158
Razin, Stenka, 41
Red Army, 103–4, 121, 148, 175,
    184
Red Guard, 98
Red Square, 109
Red Wheel, The (Solzhenitsyn), 259
Reed, John, 99
Repentance (film), 265
Repin, Ilya, 58
Revolution of 1905, 85, 90, 100
Riga, 167
Rimsky-Korsakov, Nikolai, 254
Road to Serfdom (von Hayek), 284
Roman Catholic Church, 194
Romania, 120–21, 171; peoples of, 170
Romanov, Grigory, 139
Romanov, Grand Duke Mikhail, 94
Romanov, Mikhail, tsar, 41, 57
Romanovs, 80
Romans, 44, 172, 174
Romeo and Juliet (ballet), 266
Rostropovich, Mstislav, 268
Rubenstein, Anton, 254
Rukhs-As, 45
Russia, 42, 45, 48, 66, 70, 102, 125, 166,
    171, 173, 175, 183; peoples of,
    156, 163–64, 167–68, 170, 174,
    177–78, 181, 193, 195, 214, 223,
    263, 280, 283; origins, 46–47
Russian empire, 159, 185, 215, 274

Russian Orthodox Church, 40, 59–60, 66,
    121, 185–86, 191–95, 281
Russian Peasantry, The (Stepniak), 60, 73,
    76–77
Russian Platform, 16
Russian Social Democratic Workers Party,
    82, 88–90, 113
Russian Soviet Federated Socialist
    Republic, 162
Russians, The (Smith), 193
Russo-Japanese War, 82, 84, 87
Rybakov, Anatoly, 261
Rykov, Alexei I., 110, 113

Saamis, 181
St. Basil Cathedral, 127
St. Petersburg, 41, 64, 83, 95, 100, 135
Saint-Simon, Claude-Henri, count, 81
Sajudis, 166
Sakhalin Island, 19, 73, 77, 182
Sakharov, Andrei, 279
Samoyedic, 181
Sarmatians, 44
Sayan, 19
Schnittke, Alfred, 267
Scriabin, Alexander, 126, 254
Scythians, 40, 44–45
Serbia, 90
Seventh-Day Adventists, 194
Shchedrin, Rodion, 267
Shi'ites, 195
Shmelyov, Nikolia, 203
Sholokhov, Mikhail, 259
Shostakovich, Dmitri, 267
Siberia, 19–20, 26, 29, 31, 34–35, 42,
    56–57, 61, 64–65, 89, 104, 122,
    132, 139, 154–55, 157–58, 163,
    172, 180–82, 235
Siberian Platform, 16
Sikhote-Alin, 19
Simbirsk, 82, 89, 95
Slavonic peoples, 163
Slavophiles, 66

Slavs, 45, 92, 163–64, 171, 194, 221, 230
Smith, Hedrick, 193, 222
socialism in one country, 119
Socialist Realism, 255, 257–59, 262–67, 270, 272, 275
Socialist Revolutionary Party, 81–82, 84, 88, 95–97, 101
Soghdian peoples, 180
Solovyov, Victor, 51
Solzhenitsyn, Alexander, 259–61
Sophia, regent, 41
South Africa, 148
Soviet Asia, 18, 36, 158
Soviet Constitution, 103, 106, 118, 127, 137, 188, 210, 214
Soviet Germans, 158, 171–72, 194
Soviet of Nationalities, 118
Soviet of the Union, 118
Soviet of Workers' Deputies (1905), 86, 100–11
Soviet of Workers', Farmhands', and Peasants' Deputies, 95
Soviet of Workers' and Soldiers' Deputies, 83, 95–98
Spain, 283
Speransky, Michael, 67
Sredinny Khrebet Mountains, 18
Stalin, Joseph Vissarionovich (Dzhugashvili), 2, 82, 90, 100, 103, 110–11, 113–26, 128–29, 132, 134–37, 142, 148, 152–53, 158, 162, 164, 166, 168, 171–73, 175, 179, 181, 183, 186, 191, 194–95, 242, 255, 257–58, 262, 265, 270, 275–76, 278, 281
Stalin Canal, 115
Stalingrad, 130
Stalinism, 115, 120, 142, 217
Stalino, 130
Stanislavsky, Konstantin, 254
Stanovoi, 19
State Committee for Science and Technology, 278
State Planning Commission, 206

Stavropol, 126, 139–40
Stern, Isaac, 268
Stolypin, P. A., 83, 87
Stravinsky, Igor F., 267
Sumgait, 174
Sunni Moslems, 195
Supreme Economic Council, 104
Supreme Soviet, 118, 127, 135, 140, 143, 145–46, 187
Suslov, Mikhail A., 136, 139
Svans, 172
Sweden, peoples of, 46, 59, 64, 167–68
Syr Darya, 21
Syrov, S., 49

Tadzhikistan, 158, 239; Tadzhik S.S.R., 179; peoples of, 178–80
Taganka theater, 263, 270
Talyshi, 180
Tamm, Igor, 279
Tatars, 40, 52–53, 55, 57, 59, 153, 158, 179
Tatlin, Vladimir, 270
Tats, 180
Tbilisi, 173
Tchaikovsky, Peter I., 273
Televizor (rock band), 272
Teutonic knights, 167–68
Third World, 134
Tiflis Theological Seminary, 111
Tikhonov, Nikolai, 136
Time of Troubles, 41, 57
Tofa, 181
Tolstoy, Leo, 68, 254, 273
Tomsky, Mikhail P., 110, 113
Trans-Siberian railroad, 78, 85
Transcaucasian Federation, 172, 175
Treaty of Union, 184
Tretyakov Gallery, 273
Trotsky, Leon (Lev Davidovich Bronstein), 3, 98, 100, 103, 110–11, 113
Trudoviki (Labor) Party, 88
Tungus-Manchurian peoples, 181–82